Lecture Notes in Computer Science 11563

Commenced Publication in 1973
Founding and Former Series Editors:
Gerhard Goos, Juris Hartmanis, and Jan van Leeuwen

More information about this series at http://www.springer.com/series/7407

José Luiz Fiadeiro · Ionuț Țuțu (Eds.)

Recent Trends in Algebraic Development Techniques

24th IFIP WG 1.3 International Workshop, WADT 2018
Egham, UK, July 2–5, 2018
Revised Selected Papers

 Springer

Editors
José Luiz Fiadeiro
Royal Holloway University
of London
Egham, UK

Ionuț Țuțu
Simion Stoilow Institute
of Mathematics of the Romanian
Academy
Bucharest, Romania

Royal Holloway University
of London
Egham, UK

ISSN 0302-9743   ISSN 1611-3349   (electronic)
Lecture Notes in Computer Science
ISBN 978-3-030-23219-1   ISBN 978-3-030-23220-7   (eBook)
https://doi.org/10.1007/978-3-030-23220-7

LNCS Sublibrary: SL1 – Theoretical Computer Science and General Issues

This Springer imprint is published by the registered company Springer Nature Switzerland AG
The registered company address is: Gewerbestrasse 11, 6330 Cham, Switzerland

Preface

The 24th International Workshop on Algebraic Development Techniques (WADT 2018) was held in Egham, UK, during July 2–5, 2018. The workshop took place under the auspices of IFIP WG 1.3 and was organized by the Department of Computer Science at Royal Holloway, University of London.

The workshop provided an opportunity to present recent and ongoing work, to meet colleagues, and to discuss new ideas and future trends. Its scientific program consisted of four invited talks by Rolf Hennicker (Ludwig Maximilian University of Munich, Germany), Artur d'Avila Garcez (City, University of London, UK), Kai-Uwe Kühnberger (University of Osnabrück, Germany), and Fernando Orejas (Technical University of Catalonia, Spain).

Fig. 1. Participants of WADT 2018 at Royal Holloway

In addition, 17 contributed presentations covered a range of topics: specification and modelling languages such as CASL, Event-B, Maude, MMT, and SRML; foundations of system specification such as graph transformation, categorical semantics, fuzzy and temporal logics, institutions, module systems and parameterization, refinement, static analysis, and substitutions; and applications including categorical programming, communicating finite state machines, neural-symbolic integration, relational databases, and service-oriented computing.

Participants of this edition of the Workshop on Algebraic Development Techniques travelled from Argentina, Belgium, Brazil, Canada, Germany, Ireland, Italy, The Netherlands, Norway, Portugal, Romania, Spain, and the UK.

As for previous ADT events, the authors were invited after the workshop to submit full papers, which underwent a thorough peer-review process. Each paper was reviewed by at least two referees – and most papers were examined by three referees. This volume contains those papers that were accepted by the Program Committee. We wish to thank all authors, the members of the Program Committee for their diligent work in the selection process, and the external reviewers for their support in evaluating the papers.

The algebraic approach to system specification encompasses many aspects of the formal design of software systems. Originally born as a method for reasoning about abstract data types, it now covers new specification frameworks and programming paradigms (logic programming, higher-order functional programming, and object-oriented, aspect-oriented, and agent-oriented paradigms, to name only a few) as well as a wide range of application areas (including information systems and concurrent, distributed, and mobile systems).

The ADT workshop has a proud history of previous editions. The first workshop took place in 1982 in Sorpesee, followed by Passau (1983), Bremen (1984), Braunschweig (1986), Gullane (1987), Berlin (1988), Wusterhausen (1990), Dourdan (1991), Caldes de Malavella (1992), S. Margherita (1994), Oslo (1995), Tarquinia (1997), Lisbon (1998), Chateau de Bonas (1999), Genoa (2001), Frauenchiemsee (2002), Barcelona (2004), La Roche en Ardenne (2006), Pisa (2008), Etelsen (2010), Salamanca (2012), Sinaia (2014), and Gregynog (2016).

We would like to thank Claudia Chiriţă for her contribution to the organisation of the workshop, including the design of the posters and the website. We are also grateful to Royal Holloway, University of London, for hosting WADT 2018, to the Leverhulme Trust, who supported the organization of the co-located School on Graph Transformation Techniques and the invited talk by Fernando Orejas, and to EasyChair and Springer for supporting the management of the workshop and the publication of this volume.

April 2019

José Luiz Fiadeiro
Ionuţ Ţuţu

Organization

Steering Committee

Andrea Corradini	University of Pisa, Italy
José Luiz Fiadeiro	Royal Holloway University of London, UK
Rolf Hennicker	Ludwig Maximilian University of Munich, Germany
Hans-Jörg Kreowski	University of Bremen, Germany
Till Mossakowski	Otto von Guericke University Magdeburg, Germany
Fernando Orejas	Technical University of Catalonia, Spain
Markus Roggenbach	Swansea University, UK
Grigore Roşu	University of Illinois at Urbana-Champaign, USA

Organizing Committee

Claudia-Elena Chiriţă	Royal Holloway University of London, UK
José Luiz Fiadeiro	Royal Holloway University of London, UK
Ionuţ Ţuţu	Royal Holloway University of London, UK

Program Committee

Paolo Baldan	University of Padua, Italy
Andrea Corradini	University of Pisa, Italy
José Luiz Fiadeiro (Co-chair)	Royal Holloway University of London, UK
Fabio Gadducci	University of Pisa, Italy
Reiko Heckel	University of Leicester, UK
Rolf Hennicker	Ludwig Maximilian University of Munich, Germany
Alexander Knapp	University of Augsburg, Germany
Barbara König	University of Duisburg-Essen, Germany
Antónia Lopes	University of Lisbon, Portugal
Narciso Marti-Oliet	Complutense University of Madrid, Spain
Till Mossakowski	Otto von Guericke University Magdeburg, Germany
Fernando Orejas	Technical University of Catalonia, Spain
Markus Roggenbach	Swansea University, UK
Pierre-Yves Schobbens	University of Namur, Belgium
Lutz Schröder	University of Erlangen–Nuremberg, Germany
Pawel Sobocinski	University of Southampton, UK
Ionuţ Ţuţu (Co-chair)	Institute of Mathematics of the Romanian Academy and Royal Holloway University of London, UK
Martin Wirsing	Ludwig Maximilian University of Munich, Germany

Additional Reviewers

Mihai Codescu
Harsh Beohar
Christina Mika-Michalski

Contents

Invited Talk

Role-Based Development of Dynamically Evolving Esembles

Rolf Hennicker$^{(\boxtimes)}$

Ludwig-Maximilians-Universität München, München, Germany
hennicker@ifi.lmu.de

Abstract. An ensemble is a set of computing entities that collaborate to perform a certain task. Typically an ensemble changes dynamically its constitution such that new members can join and other members can leave an ensemble during its execution. The members of an ensemble interact through message exchange. They are modelled as instances of certain role types which can be adopted by components of an underlying component system. We propose a dynamic logic to describe the evolution of ensembles from a global perspective. Using the power of dynamic logic with diamond and box modalities over regular expressions of actions (involving role instance creation, message exchange and component access) we can specify safety and liveness properties as well as desired and forbidden interaction scenarios. Thus our approach is suitable to write formal requirements specifications for ensemble behaviours. For ensemble design and implementation we propose ensemble realisations. An ensemble realisation takes a local view by giving a constructive specification for each single role type in terms of a process algebraic expression. Correctness of an ensemble realisation is defined semantically: its generated ensemble transition system must be a model of the requirements specification. We consider bisimulation of ensemble transition systems and show that our approach enjoys the Hennessy-Milner property.

Keywords: Ensemble · Distributed system · Component · Role · Dynamic logic · Interaction scenario · Bisimulation equivalence

1 Introduction

Autonomic computing and global interconnectedness of nodes allow the dynamic formation of collective systems which pose new challenges to software engineers. Typically autonomic nodes have the ability to perceive their environment and adapt their behaviour accordingly. They interact with other nodes in the system to collaborate in teams for some global goal. Such teams are called ensembles in the EU project ASCENS [15,16]. We claim that well-known techniques, like component-based software engineering, are not sufficient for modelling ensembles but must be augmented with other features to deal with the particular characteristics of ensembles. As a framework for rigorous ensemble development we have

© IFIP International Federation for Information Processing 2019
Published by Springer Nature Switzerland AG 2019
J. L. Fiadeiro and I. Țuțu (Eds.): WADT 2018, LNCS 11563, pp. 3–24, 2019.
https://doi.org/10.1007/978-3-030-23220-7_1

proposed the two-layer approach HELENA [7,12] whose design is motivated by the following considerations. While a component model describes the architecture of a target system, ensembles are dynamically formed on demand as specific, goal-oriented communication groups running on top of a target system. In particular, different ensembles may run concurrently on the same target system (dealing with different tasks). In HELENA the target platform is component-based, but it is crucial to recognise that the same component instance may take part in different ensembles under particular, ensemble-specific *roles*. Thus a role is an abstraction of the part that an individual component plays in a specific collaboration. Focusing on roles allows us to put different views on a component and to concentrate on those capabilities needed for the execution of a particular ensemble. Ensemble modelling it is then the task to identify which roles are needed in an ensemble, which components could play the roles, and how role instances communicate when pursuing a common goal.

HELENA introduces roles as first-class artefacts in ensemble models and implementations. Components form the basic layer. Component instances are passive objects (of long term nature) storing data and providing operations which implement certain functionalities, mostly related to the components' data. Components have a simple life-cycle; their operations can be called at any time. Ensembles, however, evolve dynamically which may involve ensemble extensions when components join an ensemble under some role. Role instances are active entities (i.e. processes), often of short term nature, having role-specific communication abilities (in the form of input and output messages) and running concurrently on top of their owning components. Role instances can access the operations of their owning component by operation calls. Components do not talk to each other; any kind of collaboration is performed by message exchange between the active role instances played by components. Thus, by separating roles and components, we get a two-layered approach which decouples communication (performed between roles) and computation (performed by components). Moreover, designing a behaviour for each role of a component (which is implemented by a single thread per role) is much simpler then designing a complex life-cycle for a component which then must integrate all the different tasks a component might be involved. A prototypical, two-layered implementation framework for HELENA models is described in [13,14]. The two-layered approach supports also adaptation of components by switching between roles as discussed in [11].

Constructive descriptions of ensemble-based systems are supported by the high-level programming language SCEL [3] for autonomic systems, by the component-based DEECo framework [1] and by HELENA where process-algebraic expressions are provided for describing role behaviours. A more abstract level is considered in [9] where, similarly to "classical" top down methodologies, the development of an ensemble-based system starts with a property-oriented specification and only later a concrete realisation is constructed, which can then be checked for correctness. The approach in [9] deals, however, only with ensembles of processes and does not take into account components and the roles they play.

The goal of the current paper is to provide an appropriate extension which can be used for a top down development of ensembles in accordance with the component and role layers of HELENA. Therefore, in contrast to [9], this paper incorporates the two-layer approach which requires significant syntactic and semantic extensions of [9]. On the syntactic side we integrate component system signatures, their connection to ensemble signatures (in terms of the "canPlay" relations) and we have new actions in the logic for component access as well as actions with "wild cards". The latter allow us, in particular, to express safety and liveness properties. The semantic notions and results of [9] are extended accordingly. In particular, we define semantic component models on top of which semantic structures for ensembles are constructed.

In our approach specifications describe *global* properties of collaborations performed by an ensemble. They are written in a dynamic logic style [4]. This allows us to focus, in contrast to temporal logics, on explicit interactions and complex interaction scenarios which are typical for a certain ensemble. The logic uses diamond and box modalities equipped with regular expressions of actions, like sequential composition and iteration. Atomic actions are either interactions - in the form of message exchange between two role instances - or the creation of a new role instance on top of a component (i.e. the specified component instance joins an ensemble under a particular role), or component access performed by a role instance. Additionally we allow quantification over role instances. Using the power of dynamic logic we can thus specify desired and forbidden interaction scenarios. Hence, our approach is suitable to write formal requirements specifications for global, complex interaction behaviours.

Semantic structures of our logic are ensemble transition systems. They have two layers: a transition system for the underlying component system and a transition system describing the execution of an ensemble on top of it, in particular involving all the role instances played by component instances. The semantics of an ensemble specification is given by the class of its models, i.e. by all ensemble transition systems which satisfy the axioms of the specification. Thus we support loose specification and underspecification. A refinement relation between ensemble specifications is defined by model class inclusion. We define a bisimulation relation between ensemble transition systems and show that the validity of ensemble sentences is preserved by ensemble bisimulation. Hence, the semantics of an ensemble specification is closed under bisimulation equivalence. Moreover, for image-finite ensemble transition systems the validity of the same sentences implies bisimulation; thus the Hennessy-Milner property holds.

In the last part of this work, we consider ensemble realisations and a formal correctness notion. An ensemble realisation takes a *local* view and specifies, as in a HELENA design model, a behaviour for each single role type in terms of a process algebraic expression. All instances of the type must respect the prescribed behaviour. We show how a (global) ensemble transition system can be generated from the local behaviours of role instances. An ensemble realisation is correct, if its generated ensemble transition system satisfies the (logical) sentences of the specification. In particular, two (bisimulation) equivalent ensemble realisations implement the same specifications.

The paper is organised as follows: Sect. 2 defines the syntactic notions of ensemble specifications based on ensemble signatures and sentences. In Sect. 3 we consider ensemble transition systems used for the semantics of ensemble specifications and we show the invariance of sentences under ensemble bisimulation and the Hennessy-Milner property. Then, in Sect. 4, we study correct ensemble realisations. Concluding remarks are given in Sect. 5.

2   Ensemble Specifications

Our approach relies on a strict separation of syntax and semantics, in particular between types and their instances. In this section we consider component types, role types, ensembles signatures, ensemble formulas and specifications. To get an intuition we will sometimes also refer to component and role instances to be introduced later, in Sect. 3. In the following we assume given a not further specified set of data types.

Component Types. Components form the basic layer of our approach. To classify components we use component types. A *component type* $ct = (ctnm, attrs, opns)$ has a name $ctnm$ and declares a set of attributes $attrs$ to store information and a set of operations $opns$ which can be exploited by the roles of components. We write opns$[ct]$ for the operations of ct. An *attribute* $t\ a$ has a name a and a type t. An attribute type is either a data type or a component type such that an attribute value can point to a component instance. In this case the attribute is called *reference attribute*. An *operation* is of the form $opnm(fparams)$ or $t\ opnm(fparams)$, the former being a *pure operation* and the latter an *operation with result*. $opnm$ is the name of the operation, $fparams = t_1\ p_1, \ldots, t_n\ p_n$ is a list of typed formal parameters and t a result type. The types $t, t_1, \ldots, t_n$ of an operation are data types not further specified here.

Component System Signature. A *component system signature* $C\Sigma$ is a set of component types whose reference attributes use only component types in $C\Sigma$. We write opns$[C\Sigma]$ for the set of all operations used in the component types of $C\Sigma$. A component system signature $C\Sigma$ is *finite* if it has finitely many component types each with finitely many attributes and operations.

Role Types. For performing certain tasks, components team up in ensembles. Each participant in the ensemble contributes specific functionalities to the collaboration; we say, the participant plays a certain *role* in the ensemble. To classify roles we use role types. A *role type* $rt = (rtnm, mts_{in}, mts_{out})$ has a name $rtnm$ and sets mts_{in} and mts_{out} of input and output message types respectively, which model the interaction capabilities provided by each instance of a role type. We write mts$_{in}[rt]$ for mts_{in}, mts$_{out}[rt]$ for mts_{out}, and mts$[rt]$ for $mts_{in} \cup mts_{out}$. A *message type* is of the form $mtnm(fparams)$ where $mtnm$ is a message type name and $fparams = t_1\ p_1, \ldots, t_n\ p_n$ is a list of typed formal parameters. Here the parameter types $t_1, \ldots, t_n$ are either role types or data types.

Ensemble Signature. Let $C\Sigma$ be a component system signature. An *ensemble signature* $E\Sigma = (rtypes, canPlay)$ *over* $C\Sigma$ consists of a set *rtypes* of role types and a surjective relation $canPlay \subseteq C\Sigma \times rtypes$. This relation indicates that, whenever $(ct, rt) \in canPlay$, then any component instance of type ct can potentially play the role rt (being represented later on by a role instance of type rt). We write $\mathsf{rtypes}[E\Sigma]$ for *rtypes*, $\mathsf{canPlay}[E\Sigma]$ for *canPlay* and $\mathsf{mts}[E\Sigma]$ for the set $\bigcup_{rt \in \mathsf{rtypes}[E\Sigma]} \mathsf{mts}[rt]$ of all message types used in the role types of $E\Sigma$.

We assume that these message types use in their parameter lists, besides data types, only role types in *rtypes*. In this work we consider only closed systems where $\bigcup_{rt \in \mathsf{rtypes}[E\Sigma]} \mathsf{mts}_{in}[rt] = \bigcup_{rt \in \mathsf{rtypes}[E\Sigma]} \mathsf{mts}_{out}[rt]$. An ensemble signature $E\Sigma$ is *finite* if it has finitely many role types each with finitely many message types.

Example 1. Throughout this paper we consider a (simplified version of a) file transfer ensemble which runs on a peer-2-peer network supporting the distributed storage of files that can be retrieved upon request. Several peer components work together to request and transfer a file: One peer plays the role of a $\mathsf{Requester}$ of the file, other peers act as $\mathsf{Routers}$ and the peer storing the requested file adopts the role of a $\mathsf{Provider}$. The component type Peer models peers. Each peer stores a file in the corresponding attribute and it has a neighbour whose identity is stored in the corresponding reference attribute. Peers provide operations to get files and to store files. Each kind of role is modelled by a role type whose instances can be created and run on the peer components. The idea of the collaboration is that a requester issues a request for the address of a provider of a certain file identified by a string (message type $\mathsf{reqAddr(Requester}$ $\mathsf{r, \ String \ s)}$). This address request is forwarded by routers through the network until a provider is found. Then the provider address is sent from the last active router to the requester ($\mathsf{sndAddr(Provider \ p)}$). Finally, the requester asks the provider for the file ($\mathsf{reqFile(Requester \ r, \ String \ s)}$) which is then sent to the requester ($\mathsf{sndFile(File \ f)}$). It may also happen that no appropriate provider is found. In this case a router sends a notification to the requester ($\mathsf{notFound()}$). The ensemble signature of the file transfer ensemble is graphically presented in Fig. 1. The directions of the message type arrows indicate for which role types a message type is input or output or both. Note that for Router the $\mathsf{reqAddr}$ message type is input *and* output since routers may forward address requests to other routers. □

An ensemble specification describes static and dynamic properties of a system of collaborating entities. The static aspects are represented by an ensemble signature. For the dynamic properties a specification takes a global view of an ensemble focusing on the desired (and not desired) interactions between the participants of an ensemble, on the creation of new ensemble members and on component access. To specify collaborations we use atomic actions and composed (structured) actions formed by sequential composition (;), union (+) and iteration (*) borrowed from dynamic logic [4].

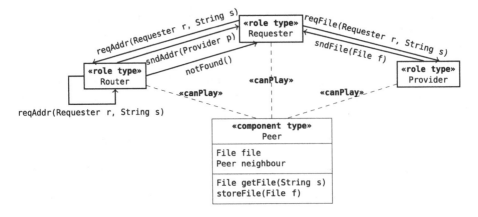

Fig. 1. Ensemble signature for the file transfer ensemble

In the following let $E\Sigma$ be a finite ensemble signature over a finite component system signature $C\Sigma$. We assume given countably infinite sets $RVar$ of role instance variables and $DVar$ of data variables.

Actions. Four kinds of *atomic actions* are distinguished where p, r are variables in $RVar$ and $d \in DVar$ is a data variable.

(a) A create action $p := r.\mathbf{create}(rt, ce)$ describes when a role instance denoted by r creates a new role instance of role type rt played by a component instance denoted by the component expression ce. The new role instance is assigned to variable p. The component expression can either be $r.\mathbf{playedBy}$ or $r.\mathbf{playedBy}.a$ where a is a reference attribute. Let us remark that we do not introduce an explicit action for deleting a role instance. A component simply gives up a role if its role instance becomes inactive.

(b) A communication action $(r \rightarrow p).mtnm(e_1, \ldots, e_n)$ describes when a role instance denoted by r sends a message with name $mtnm$ to a role instance denoted by p transmitting the values of the actual parameter expressions $e_1, \ldots, e_n$. These expressions are either role instance variables or data type expressions not further detailed here.

(c) A component access action $r.\mathbf{playedBy}.opnm(e_1, \ldots, e_n)$ describes when a role instance denoted by r accesses its owning component instance calling an operation with name $opnm$ and handing over the values of the actual parameter expressions $e_1, \ldots, e_n$. These expressions are data type expressions. Component access actions can also have the form $t\ d := r.\mathbf{playedBy}.opnm(e_1, \ldots, e_n)$ if the operation delivers a result which is then bound to variable d of data type t.

(d) A variable assignment $r := p$ assigns the role instance denoted by p to variable r.

We also allow generalisations of the atomic actions of type (a) - (c) where the variables p, r, d and expressions $ce, e_1, \ldots, e_n$ are partly or fully replaced by a "wild card" represented by the special name **any**. Generalised create actions are, for instance, **any** := r.**create**(rt, ce), p := **any**.**create**(rt, **any**), or **any** := **any**.**create**(rt, **any**). The idea is that when **any** is used the particular instance involved in the action at the position of **any** is not relevant. An atomic action is called *fully generalised* if it has **any** at all possible positions.

The set $Act(E\Sigma, C\Sigma)$ of (structured) *actions over $E\Sigma$ and $C\Sigma$* is defined by the grammar

$$\alpha ::= a \mid \alpha; \alpha \mid \alpha + \alpha \mid \alpha^*$$

where a is a, possibly generalised, atomic action[1]. The sets $FV(\alpha)$ of free variables and $BV(\alpha)$ of bound variables of an action α are defined as expected where binding of a variable p to a role type rt can only happen via a create action p := r.**create**(rt, ce) and binding of a data variable d to a data type t can only happen via a component access action $t\,d$:= $ce.opnm(...)$.

Shorthand Notations. For a set $a_1, \ldots, a_n$ of fully generalised atomic actions we write $\{a_1, \ldots, a_n\}$ to denote the composed action $a_1 + \ldots + a_n$. We write $-\{a_1, \ldots, a_n\}$ to denote the composed action obtained from the union of all generalised atomic actions apart from those in $\{a_1, \ldots, a_n\}$. Note that this union is finite since there are only finitely many generalised atomic actions. This is due to the finiteness assumption for the underlying ensemble and component signatures. We write **allAct** for the composed action obtained by the union of all generalised atomic actions. It captures all actions that are semantically possible in an ensemble transition system; see below.

Ensemble Formulas and Sentences. Besides the usual propositional logic constructs ensemble formulas can compare the identity of role instances, they can be a modal formula with (composed) action α or they can be existentially quantified. The set $Fm(E\Sigma, C\Sigma)$ of *formulas over $E\Sigma$ and $C\Sigma$* is defined by the following grammar

$$\varphi ::= \mathbf{tt} \mid r = p \mid \neg\varphi \mid \varphi \vee \varphi \mid \langle\alpha\rangle\varphi \mid \exists r{:}rt.\varphi$$

where $\alpha \in Act(E\Sigma, C\Sigma)$ and $r, p \in RVar$. The set $FV(\varphi)$ of free variables of a formula φ is defined as expected where binding of variables can happen by $FV(\langle\alpha\rangle\varphi) = FV(\alpha) \cup (FV(\varphi) \backslash BV(\alpha))$ and $FV(\exists r{:}rt.\varphi) = FV(\varphi) \backslash \{r\}$.

A *sentence over $E\Sigma$ and $C\Sigma$* is a formula φ without free variables, i.e. $FV(\varphi) = \emptyset$. The set of sentences over $E\Sigma$ and $C\Sigma$ is denoted by $Sen(E\Sigma, C\Sigma)$. An *initialisation sentence* is a sentence φ, that does not contain any modality $\langle\alpha\rangle$. The set of initialisation sentences is denoted by $ISen(E\Sigma, C\Sigma)$. We use the usual abbreviations: $\mathbf{ff} = \neg\mathbf{tt}, r \neq p = \neg(r = p), \varphi \wedge \psi = \neg(\neg\varphi \vee \neg\psi), [\alpha]\varphi = \neg\langle\alpha\rangle\neg\varphi, \forall r{:}rt.\varphi = \neg\exists r{:}rt.\neg\varphi$.

Let us note that by using generalised atomic actions and, in particular, the **allAct** notation, we can specify safety and liveness properties. Safety properties are expressed by sentences of the form $[\mathbf{allAct}^*]\varphi$. In particular, deadlock freeness is expressed by $[\mathbf{allAct}^*]\langle\mathbf{allAct}\rangle\mathbf{tt}$. Liveness properties, like "whenever an

---

[1] We could also add tests, as in dynamic logic, but we omit them for simplification.

action a has happened, an action b can eventually occur", can be expressed by $[\mathbf{allAct}^*; a]\langle \mathbf{allAct}^*; b\rangle \mathbf{tt}$.

Definition 1 (Ensemble specification). *Let $C\Sigma$ be a component system signature. An* ensemble specification *over $C\Sigma$ is a triple $EnsSpec = (E\Sigma, \Phi, \phi_0)$ where $E\Sigma$ is an ensemble signature over $C\Sigma$, $\Phi \subseteq \mathrm{Sen}(E\Sigma, C\Sigma)$ is a set of sentences, called* axioms *of EnsSpec, and $\phi_0 \in \mathrm{ISen}(E\Sigma, C\Sigma)$ is an* initialisation axiom.

Example 2. We formulate an ensemble specification for the file transfer ensemble introduced in Example 1. Concerning the starting condition of an ensemble the specification requires that in the initial ensemble state there is one role instance of type `Requester` and no role instances for any other type. The initialisation axiom ϕ_0 is

$(\exists \mathrm{req}{:}\mathrm{Requester}.\forall \mathrm{req'}{:}\mathrm{Requester}.\mathrm{req'} = \mathrm{req}) \wedge$
$\neg \exists \mathrm{rout}{:}\mathrm{Router}.\mathbf{tt} \wedge \neg \exists \mathrm{prov}{:}\mathrm{Provider}.\mathbf{tt}$

For ensemble execution we first require two abstract properties: (a) "whenever a file has been requested, it can eventually be sent" and (b) "a file cannot be sent if it hasn't been requested before". Using generalised atomic actions properties (a) and (b) can be expressed by the following two sentences φ_1 and φ_2 respectively:

$\varphi_1 = [\mathbf{allAct}^*; \mathrm{reqFile}]\langle \mathbf{allAct}^*; \mathrm{sndFile}\rangle \mathbf{tt}$
$\varphi_2 = [(-\mathrm{reqFile})^*; \mathrm{sndFile}]\mathbf{ff}$

where reqFile stands for $(\mathbf{any} \rightarrow \mathbf{any}).\mathrm{reqFile}(\mathbf{any}, \mathbf{any})$ and sndFile stands for $(\mathbf{any} \rightarrow \mathbf{any}).\mathrm{sndFile}(\mathbf{any})$.

At next, we are interested in the feasibility of a primary scenario that describes a successful execution of a file request. A requester `req` starts the collaboration by creating a router role (on its connected peer) and asks the router for the address of a provider (see α below). Arbitrarily, but finitely many routers forward the request by creating a next router on their neighbour component (see β^* below). The last router (whose owning component has the file) creates a provider role on its component and sends the address of the provider to the requester (see γ below). Then the requester asks the provider for the file, the provider gets the file by accessing its peer component, sends the file to the requester and, finally, the requester stores the file on its peer component (see δ below). The primary scenario is specified by the sentence

$\varphi_3 = \forall \mathrm{req}{:}\mathrm{Requester}.\langle \alpha; \beta^*; \gamma; \delta; \rangle \mathbf{tt}$

where

$\alpha =$
```
rout:=req.create(Router,req.playedBy.neighbour);
(req→rout).reqAddr(req,"song")
```

$\beta =$

```
rout':=rout.create(Router,rout.playedBy.neighbour);
(rout→rout').reqAddr(req,"song");
rout:=rout'
```

$\gamma =$

```
prov:=rout.create(Provider,rout.playedBy);
(rout→req).sndAddr(prov)
```

$\delta =$

```
(req→prov).reqFile(req,"song");
song:=prov.playedBy.getFile("song");
(prov→req).sndFile(song);
req.playedBy.storeFile(song)
```

φ_3 allows iterations of arbitrary (but finite) length for forwarding the request to newly created router roles until a provider is found. Actually, the formula is still of abstract nature and does not really determine when a router component stores the requested file and therefore will adapt the role of a provider. This could, however, be easily done if we would extend our logic by tests. Moreover, let us remark that we have assumed a fixed name of the requested file. This could be avoided if we would go to open systems where the requester first would expect an input of an arbitrary file name from the environment captured by a formal parameter of the input message.

An alternative (secondary) scenario showing the possibility of a non successful delivery is specified by the sentence

$$\varphi_4 = \forall \text{req:Requester}.[\alpha; \beta^*](\langle \gamma; \delta \rangle \mathbf{tt} \wedge \langle \mu \rangle \mathbf{tt})$$

where $\mu = (\text{rout} \rightarrow \text{req}).\text{notFound}()$

The sentence φ_4 requires that during a routing phase a successful delivery of the file is possible and it is also possible that a requester is informed by the current router that no provider is found.   □

3   Semantics of Ensemble Specifications and Bisimulation

For the semantic interpretation of ensemble specifications we use ensemble transition systems. Analogously to the two syntactic levels of components and ensembles, also the semantics is based on two levels.

We start by considering semantic models for a component system signature $C\Sigma$. A *component system state* over $C\Sigma$ is a pair $c\sigma = (cinsts, cdata)$ where $cinsts = \bigcup_{ct \in C\Sigma} cinsts_{ct}$ is the disjoint union of finite sets $cinsts_{ct}$ of (identifiers for) currently existing component instances of component type ct - similarly to a heap in object-oriented systems - and $cdata$ is a function assigning to each component instance $ci \in cinsts_{ct}$ a valuation of the attributes declared in ct. We do not further detail attribute valuations here, but we assume that whenever $a : ct'$ is a reference attribute of ct then $cdata(ci)(a) \in cinsts_{ct'}$ for each $ci \in cinsts_{ct}$. If $c\sigma = (cinsts, cdata)$ we write $\texttt{cinsts}[c\sigma]$ for $cinsts$. The set of component system states over $C\Sigma$ is denoted by $States(C\Sigma)$.

Component system models over $C\Sigma$, called $C\Sigma$-models, are labelled transition systems whose transitions express state changes caused by the execution of component operations. Thus the labels are *component access labels* of the form $ci.opnm(v_1, \ldots, v_n)$ expressing that the operation with name $opnm$ is called on the component instance ci with data values $v_1, \ldots, v_n$. If the operation delivers a result value v, this will also be recorded on the transition by the notation $v = ci.opnm(v_1, \ldots, v_n)$. The set of labels over $C\Sigma$ is denoted by $Lab(C\Sigma)$.

$C\Sigma$-models constrain the use of labels on transitions by appropriate pre- and postconditions like "a component access on a component instance ci can only be executed if ci exists in the source state of the transition".

Definition 2 ($C\Sigma$-models). *Let $C\Sigma$ be a component system signature. A $C\Sigma$-model is a labelled transition system $M = (States(C\Sigma), c\sigma_0, Lab(C\Sigma), \rightarrow_M)$ such that*

- $c\sigma_0 \in States(C\Sigma)$ *is the initial component system state,*
- $\rightarrow_M \subseteq States(C\Sigma) \times Lab(C\Sigma) \times States(C\Sigma)$ *is a deterministic[2] transition relation such that for all $c\sigma \xrightarrow{ci.opnm(v_1,\ldots,v_n)}_M c\sigma'$ ($c\sigma \xrightarrow{v=ci.opnm(v_1,\ldots,v_n)}_M$ $c\sigma'$ resp.) the following well-formedness conditions are satisfied:*
  (pre) there exists $ct \in C\Sigma$ such that $opnm(t_1 \, p_1, \ldots t_n \, p_n) \in \mathsf{opns}[ct]$ ($t \, opnm(t_1 \, p_1, \ldots t_n \, p_n) \in \mathsf{opns}[ct]$ resp.), $ci \in \mathsf{cinsts}[c\sigma]_{ct}$ and $v_1, \ldots, v_n$ are valid parameter values, i.e. fit to the data type parameters.
  (post) if the operation has a result type t then v is a value of data type t.

General Assumption: From now on, we assume given, whenever we consider a component system signature $C\Sigma$, a fixed $C\Sigma$-model M. We do this, since we are not interested in this paper in the specification of component systems but rather on the specification of ensembles built over a given component system semantically represented by M.

Ensemble States. Let $E\Sigma = (rtypes, canPlay)$ be an ensemble signature over a component system signature $C\Sigma$ with $canPlay \subseteq C\Sigma \times rtypes$. An *ensemble state* over a component system state $c\sigma = (cinsts, cdata)$ is a triple

$$e\sigma = (rinsts, playedBy, ctrl), \text{ where}$$

$rinsts = \bigcup_{rt \in rtypes} rinsts_{rt}$ is the disjoint union of finite sets $rinsts_{rt}$ of (identifiers for) currently existing role instances of type rt, $playedBy : rinsts \rightarrow cinsts$ is a function assigning to each role instance $ri \in rinsts_{rt}$ a component instance $ci \in cinsts_{ct}$ with $(ct, rt) \in canPlay$, and $ctrl$ is a global control state recording the current execution state of an ensemble.

---

[2] It is not important here whether the transition relation is deterministic or not, but if we think on standard implementations of operations, like in object-oriented languages, the execution of an operation is deterministic.

We write $\texttt{rinsts}[e\sigma]$ for $rinsts$, $\texttt{playedBy}[e\sigma]$ for $playedBy$ and $\texttt{ctrl}[e\sigma]$ for $ctrl$. Moreover, we write $\texttt{playedBy}[e\sigma][rj \mapsto cj]$ for the updated function with $\texttt{playedBy}[e\sigma][rj \mapsto cj](rj) = cj$ and $\texttt{playedBy}[e\sigma][rj \mapsto cj](ri) = \texttt{playedBy}[e\sigma](ri)$ for $ri \neq rj$. The set of pairs $(e\sigma, c\sigma)$ where $e\sigma$ is an ensemble state over component state $c\sigma$ is denoted by $States(E\Sigma, C\Sigma)$.

Labels. Three kinds of labels are used on transitions which interpret the syntactic actions (a)–(c) defined in Sect. 2.

(a) A create label $rj = ri.\textbf{create}(rt, cj)$ expresses that role instance ri creates a role instance rj of type rt which is then played by component instance cj.
(b) A communication label $(ri \rightarrow rj).mtnm(v_1, \ldots, v_n)$ expresses that role instance ri sends a message with name $mtnm$ to role instance rj transmitting the values $v_1, \ldots, v_n$ which are (identifiers of) role instances or data values.
(c) A component access label $ci.opnm(v_1, \ldots, v_n)$ or $v = ci.opnm(v_1, \ldots, v_n)$ is defined as before for labels of $C\Sigma$-models.

The set of labels over $E\Sigma$ and $C\Sigma$ is denoted by $Lab(E\Sigma, C\Sigma)$.

Ensemble transition systems constrain the use of labels on transitions by appropriate pre- and postconditions, like "a role instance rj of type rt can only be created on top of a component instance cj of type ct if the ensemble signature allows that roles of type rt can be played by components of type ct".

Definition 3 (Ensemble transition system). *Let $C\Sigma$ be a component system signature with model $M = (States(C\Sigma), c\sigma_0, Lab(C\Sigma), \rightarrow_M)$. Let $E\Sigma$ be an ensemble signature over $C\Sigma$. An ensemble transition system (shortly ETS) for $E\Sigma$ and $C\Sigma$ is a tuple $T = (States(E\Sigma, C\Sigma), (e\sigma_0, c\sigma_0), Lab(E\Sigma, C\Sigma), \rightarrow)$ such that*

- *$(e\sigma_0, c\sigma_0) \in States(E\Sigma, C\Sigma)$ is the initial ensemble state $e\sigma_0$ over $c\sigma_0$,*
- *$\rightarrow \subseteq States(E\Sigma, C\Sigma) \times Lab(E\Sigma, C\Sigma) \times States(E\Sigma, C\Sigma)$ is a transition relation such that for all $(e\sigma, c\sigma) \xrightarrow{l} (e\sigma', c\sigma')$ the following well-formedness conditions are satisfied:*
  (a) if l is of the form $rj = ri.\textbf{create}(rt, cj)$ then
       (pre) $ri \in rinsts[e\sigma], rj \notin rinsts[e\sigma]$, and there exists $ct \in C\Sigma$ such that $cj \in cinsts[c\sigma]_{ct}$ and $(ct, rt) \in canPlay[E\Sigma]$,
       (post) $rinsts[e\sigma'] = rinsts[e\sigma] \cup \{rj\}, rj \in rinsts[e\sigma']_{rt}$,
       $\texttt{playedBy}[e\sigma'] = \texttt{playedBy}[e\sigma][rj \mapsto cj]$, and $c\sigma' = c\sigma$.
  (b) if l is of the form $(ri \rightarrow rj).mtnm(v_1, \ldots, v_n)$ then
       (pre) there exist $rt, rt' \in rtypes[E\Sigma]$ such that $mtnm(t_1\, p_1, \ldots t_n\, p_n) \in mts_{out}[rt] \cap mts_{in}[rt'], ri \in rinsts[e\sigma]_{rt}, rj \in rinsts[e\sigma]_{rt'}$ and $v_1, \ldots, v_n$ are valid parameter values; in particular, if a parameter type t_k is a role type then $v_k \in rinsts[e\sigma]_{t_k}$,
       (post) $rinsts[e\sigma'] = rinsts[e\sigma], \texttt{playedBy}[e\sigma'] = \texttt{playedBy}[e\sigma]$, and $c\sigma' = c\sigma$.

(c) if l is of the form $ci.opnm(v_1, \ldots, v_n)$ $(v = ci.opnm(v_1, \ldots, v_n)$ resp.) then

$$co \xrightarrow{\;ci.opnm(v_1,\ldots,v_n)\;}_M co' \quad (co \xrightarrow{\;v=ci.opnm(v_1,\ldots,v_n)\;}_M co' \text{ resp.}) \text{ and,}$$

$\mathtt{rinsts}[eo'] = \mathtt{rinsts}[eo], \mathtt{playedBy}[eo'] = \mathtt{playedBy}[eo'].$

Note that in all transitions the control state of an ensemble may change in accordance with the execution progress of the ensemble. The class of all ensemble transition systems for $E\Sigma$ and $C\Sigma$ is denoted by $Trans(E\Sigma, C\Sigma)$.

At next we define the satisfaction relation between ensemble transition systems and ensemble formulas. For this purpose, we have to consider environments ρ which map variables to values, more precisely, role instance variables to role instance identifiers and data variables to data values. The set of all environments over $E\Sigma$ is denoted by $Env(E\Sigma)$. Updating an environment ρ with a value v for a variable var is denoted by $\rho[var \mapsto v]$. We assume given an interpretation function $I_{\sigma,\rho}$ which maps, depending on a state $\sigma \in States(E\Sigma, C\Sigma)$ and an environment $\rho \in Env(E\Sigma)$, expressions to values. We do not detail the interpretation function but assume that it is inductively defined as usual along the structure of expressions. In particular, we assume that $I_{\sigma,\rho}(r.\mathbf{playedBy}) = \mathtt{playedBy}[eo](\rho(r))$ for any $\sigma = (eo, co) \in States(E\Sigma, C\Sigma), \rho \in Env(E\Sigma)$ and $r \in RVar$.

To define the satisfaction relation for formulas of the form $\langle \alpha \rangle \varphi$ with $\alpha \in Act(E\Sigma, C\Sigma)$ we lift the semantic transition relation $\to$ of an ETS T to environments and use the syntactic actions in $Act(E\Sigma, C\Sigma)$ on the transitions. Each ensemble transition system $T = (States(E\Sigma, C\Sigma), (eo_0, co_0), Lab(E\Sigma, C\Sigma), \to)$ gives rise to a transition relation

$$\twoheadrightarrow \subseteq (States(E\Sigma, C\Sigma) \times Env(E\Sigma)) \times Act(E\Sigma, C\Sigma) \times$$
$$(States(E\Sigma, C\Sigma) \times Env(E\Sigma))$$

which is constructed according to the rules in Fig. 2.

The first four rules have transitions of T (denoted by $\to$) in their premises. The fourth rule considers component access for pure operations. The case of operations with result types is analogous but needs two rules similarly to the two create rules. The other rules deal with composed, structured actions and have transitions of the form $\twoheadrightarrow$ in their premises.

Then, for any state $\sigma \in States(E\Sigma, C\Sigma)$ and environment $\rho \in Env(E\Sigma, C\Sigma)$, the satisfaction of ensemble formulas by T is inductively defined as follows:

- $T, \sigma, \rho \models \mathbf{tt}$,
- $T, \sigma, \rho \models r = p$ if $\rho(r) = \rho(p)$,
- $T, \sigma, \rho \models \neg\varphi$ if not $T, \sigma, \rho \models \varphi$,
- $T, \sigma, \rho \models \varphi \vee \psi$ if $T, \sigma, \rho \models \varphi$ or $T, \sigma, \rho \models \psi$,
- $T, \sigma, \rho \models \langle \alpha \rangle \varphi$ if there exist $(\sigma', \rho') \in States(E\Sigma, C\Sigma) \times Env(E\Sigma, C\Sigma)$ such that $(\sigma, \rho) \xrightarrow{\alpha} (\sigma', \rho')$ and $T, \sigma', \rho' \models \varphi$,
- $T, \sigma, \rho \models \exists r{:}rt.\varphi$ if there exists $ri \in \mathtt{rinsts}[\sigma]_{rt}$ such that $T, \sigma, \rho[r \mapsto ri] \models \varphi$.

(create1)

$$\frac{\sigma \xrightarrow{rj=ri.\mathbf{create}(cj)} \sigma'}{(\sigma,\rho) \xrightarrow{p:=r.\mathbf{create}(rt,ce)} (\sigma',\rho[p \mapsto rj])}$$

whenever $p \neq \mathbf{any}$ and $(r = \mathbf{any}$ or $\rho(r) = ri)$ and
$(ce = \mathbf{any}$ or $I_{\sigma,\rho}(ce) = cj)$

(create2)

$$\frac{\sigma \xrightarrow{rj=ri.\mathbf{create}(cj)} \sigma'}{(\sigma,\rho) \xrightarrow{\mathbf{any}:=r.\mathbf{create}(rt,ce)} (\sigma',\rho)}$$

whenever $(r = \mathbf{any}$ or $\rho(r) = ri)$ and
$(ce = \mathbf{any}$ or $I_{\sigma,\rho}(ce) = cj)$

(comm)

$$\frac{\sigma \xrightarrow{(ri \to rj).mtnm(v_1,\ldots,v_n)} \sigma'}{(\sigma,\rho) \xrightarrow{(r \to p).mtnm(e_1,\ldots,e_n)} (\sigma',\rho)}$$

whenever $(r = \mathbf{any}$ or $\rho(r) = ri)$ and
$(p = \mathbf{any}$ or $\rho(r) = rj)$ and, for $i = 1,\ldots,n$,
$(e_i = \mathbf{any}$ or $I_{\sigma,\rho}(e_i) = v_i)$

(comp access)

$$\frac{\sigma \xrightarrow{ci.opnm(v_1,\ldots,v_n)} \sigma'}{(\sigma,\rho) \xrightarrow{r.\mathbf{playedBy}.opnm(e_1,\ldots,e_n)} (\sigma',\rho)}$$

whenever $(r = \mathbf{any}$ or $I_{\sigma,\rho}(r.\mathbf{playedBy}) = ci)$ and,
for $i = 1,\ldots,n$, $(e_i = \mathbf{any}$ or $I_{\sigma,\rho}(e_i) = v_i)$

(assignment)

$$(\sigma,\rho) \xrightarrow{r:=p} (\sigma,\rho[r \mapsto \rho(p)])$$
for all $(\sigma,\rho) \in States(E\Sigma, C\Sigma) \times Env(E\Sigma)$

(seq. composition)

$$\frac{(\sigma,\rho) \xrightarrow{\alpha} (\hat{\sigma},\hat{\rho}), (\hat{\sigma},\hat{\rho}) \xrightarrow{\beta} (\sigma',\rho')}{(\sigma,\rho) \xrightarrow{\alpha;\beta} (\sigma',\rho')}$$

(union)

$$\frac{(\sigma,\rho) \xrightarrow{\alpha} (\sigma',\rho')}{(\sigma,\rho) \xrightarrow{\alpha+\beta} (\sigma',\rho')} \qquad \frac{(\sigma,\rho) \xrightarrow{\beta} (\sigma',\rho')}{(\sigma,\rho) \xrightarrow{\alpha+\beta} (\sigma',\rho')}$$

(iteration refl.)

$$(\sigma,\rho) \xrightarrow{\alpha^*} (\sigma,\rho)$$
for all $(\sigma,\rho) \in States(E\Sigma, C\Sigma) \times Env(E\Sigma)$

(iteration trans.)

$$\frac{(\sigma,\rho) \xrightarrow{\alpha^*} (\hat{\sigma},\hat{\rho}), (\hat{\sigma},\hat{\rho}) \xrightarrow{\alpha} (\sigma',\rho')}{(\sigma,\rho) \xrightarrow{\alpha^*} (\sigma',\rho')}$$

Fig. 2. Lifting from semantic labels to syntactic actions and environments

If φ is a sentence the environment ρ is irrelevant. T *satisfies* a sentence $\varphi \in$ Sen$(E\Sigma, C\Sigma)$, denoted by $T \models \varphi$, if $T, \sigma_0 \models \varphi$ with $\sigma_0 = (e\sigma_0, c\sigma_0)$.

Definition 4 (Semantics of ensemble specifications and refinement).
Let $C\Sigma$ be a component system signature and $EnsSpec = (E\Sigma, \Phi, \phi_0)$ be an ensemble specification over $C\Sigma$. A model *of $EnsSpec$ is an ETS which satisfies Φ and ϕ_0. The semantics of $EnsSpec$ is given by its model class, i.e. by the class*

$$Mod(EnsSpec) = \{T \in Trans(E\Sigma, C\Sigma) \mid T \models \varphi \text{ for all } \varphi \in \Phi \cup \{\phi_0\}\}.$$

An ensemble specification $EnsSpec' = (E\Sigma, \Phi', \phi_0')$ is a refinement *of $EnsSpec$ if $\emptyset \neq Mod(EnsSpec') \subseteq Mod(EnsSpec)$.*

As an equivalence relation for ETSs we use ensemble bisimulation. In contrast to the usual bisimulation relation between processes, special care must be taken about the treatment of role instances. We abstract from the particular names of role instances by using, for related ensemble states $e\sigma_1 = (rinsts_1, playedBy_1, c_1)$ and $e\sigma_2 = (rinsts_2, playedBy_2, c_2)$, a *role instance mapping* between $rinsts_1$ and $rinsts_2$. A role instance mapping is a bijective function $\kappa : rinsts_1 \rightarrow rinsts_2$ which (a) preserves role types and (b) is compatible with the "playedBy" functions. This means that (a) $\kappa((rinsts_1)_{rt}) = (rinsts_2)_{rt}$ for all role types rt of the ensemble signature, and (b) $playedBy_1(ri) = playedBy_2(\kappa(ri))$ for each $ri \in rinsts_1$. Note, however, that there may be many role instances in $rinsts_1$ and $rinsts_2$ which are played by the same component instance, since the "playedBy" functions are usually neither injective nor surjective. We assume above that $e\sigma_1$ and $e\sigma_2$ are ensemble states over the same component system state $c\sigma$. As a consequence of this discussion, our bisimulation relation is ternary and relates states in accordance with a bijective mapping between role instances.

Remark 1. One may wonder whether role instance mappings κ must really be bijective functions or whether the use of relations would be sufficient. A first observation shows that satisfaction of sentences involving equations $r = p$ (with role instance variables r and p) would, in general, not be preserved and reflected by ensemble bisimulation if κ is not a bijective function. So, let us consider for a moment a sub-logic without equations. In order to preserve and reflect satisfaction of sentences of the form $\exists r{:}rt.\varphi$, κ must at least be a relation which is surjective in both directions. We suggest that then satisfaction of sentences would be invariant under ensemble bisimulation. On the other hand, we claim that - besides very simple examples - an ensemble bisimulation can anyway only be established in terms of a bijective function between role instances.

Definition 5 (Ensemble bisimulation). *Let $C\Sigma$ be a component system signature and $E\Sigma$ be an ensemble signature over $C\Sigma$. Let*

$T_1 = (States(E\Sigma, C\Sigma), (e\sigma_{1,0}, c\sigma_0), Lab(E\Sigma, C\Sigma), \rightarrow_1)$ *and*
$T_2 = (States(E\Sigma, C\Sigma), (e\sigma_{2,0}, c\sigma_0), Lab(E\Sigma, C\Sigma), \rightarrow_2)$
be two ensemble transition systems for $E\Sigma$ and $C\Sigma$.

Let $\Delta = \{(\sigma_1, \sigma_2, \kappa) \mid \sigma_1 = (e\sigma_1, c\sigma), \sigma_2 = (e\sigma_2, c\sigma) \in States(E\Sigma, C\Sigma), \kappa :$ $rinsts[e\sigma_1] \rightarrow rinsts[e\sigma_2]$ is a role instance mapping$\}$.

A bisimulation relation between T_1 and T_2 is a relation $R \subseteq \Delta$, such that for all $(\sigma_1, \sigma_2, \kappa) \in R$ the following holds:

(1.1) If $\sigma_1 \xrightarrow{\ rj_1 = ri_1.\textbf{create}(rt, cj)\ }_1 \sigma_1'$ then there exist σ_2' and

$\sigma_2 \xrightarrow{\ rj_2 = \kappa(ri_1).\textbf{create}(rt, cj)\ }_2 \sigma_2'$ such that $(\sigma_1', \sigma_2', \kappa[rj_1 \mapsto rj_2]) \in R$.

(1.2) If $\sigma_1 \xrightarrow{\ (ri_1 \rightarrow rj_1).mtnm(v_1, \ldots, v_n)\ }_1 \sigma_1'$ then there exist σ_2' and

$\sigma_2 \xrightarrow{\ (\kappa(ri_1) \rightarrow \kappa(rj_1)).mtnm(\overrightarrow{\kappa}(v_1, \ldots, v_n))\ }_2 \sigma_2'$ such that $(\sigma_1', \sigma_2', \kappa) \in R$.

$\overrightarrow{\kappa}(v_1, \ldots, v_n)$ denotes the pointwise application of κ to those values which are role instances.

(1.3) If $\sigma_1 \xrightarrow{\ v = ci.opnm(v_1, \ldots, v_n)\ }_1 \sigma_1'$ then there exist σ_2' and

$\sigma_2 \xrightarrow{\ v = ci.opnm(v_1, \ldots, v_n)\ }_2 \sigma_2'$ such that $(\sigma_1', \sigma_2', \kappa) \in R$.

(2.1) If $\sigma_2 \xrightarrow{\ rj_2 = ri_2.\textbf{create}(rt, cj)\ }_2 \sigma_2'$ then there exist σ_1' and

$\sigma_1 \xrightarrow{\ rj_1 = \kappa^{-1}(ri_2).\textbf{create}(rt, cj)\ }_1 \sigma_1'$ such that $(\sigma_1', \sigma_2', \kappa[rj_1 \mapsto rj_2]) \in R$.

(2.2) If $\sigma_2 \xrightarrow{\ (ri_2 \rightarrow rj_2).mtnm(v_1, \ldots, v_n)\ }_2 \sigma_2'$ then there exist σ_1' and

$\sigma_1 \xrightarrow{\ (\kappa^{-1}(ri_2) \rightarrow \kappa^{-1}(rj_2)).mtnm(\overrightarrow{\kappa^{-1}}(v_1, \ldots, v_n))\ }_1 \sigma_1'$ such that $(\sigma_1', \sigma_2', \kappa) \in R$.

(2.3) If $\sigma_2 \xrightarrow{\ v = ci.opnm(v_1, \ldots, v_n)\ }_2 \sigma_2'$ then there exist σ_1' and

$\sigma_1 \xrightarrow{\ v = ci.opnm(v_1, \ldots, v_n)\ }_2 \sigma_2'$ such that $(\sigma_1', \sigma_2', \kappa) \in R$.

The rules (1.3) and (2.3) consider component access for operations with results. The case of pure operations is analogously and omitted here.

T_1 and T_2 are bisimulation equivalent, denoted by $T_1 \sim_e T_2$, if there exists a bisimulation relation $R \subseteq \Delta$ between T_1 and T_2 and $\kappa_0 : rinsts[e\sigma_{1,0}] \rightarrow rinsts[e\sigma_{2,0}]$ such that $((e\sigma_{1,0}, c\sigma_0), (e\sigma_{2,0}, c\sigma_0), \kappa_0) \in R$.

The following theorem, part (1), shows that the satisfaction of sentences is invariant (i.e. preserved and reflected) under ensemble bisimulation. The proof relies on the fact that any bisimulation relation between two ETSs T_1 and T_2 can be lifted from semantic labels to syntactic labels, i.e. actions in $Act(E\Sigma, C\Sigma)$. Part (2) of the theorem shows, that, if the two ETSs are image-finite[3] then also the converse holds. Thus the modal logic for ensembles satisfies the Hennessy-Milner property. Theorem 1 extends an analogous theorem in [9] by taking into account components and component access.

Theorem 1. Let T_1 and T_2 be two ETSs for an ensemble signature $E\Sigma$ and component system signature $C\Sigma$.

(1) If $T_1 \sim_e T_2$ then, for any sentence $\varphi \in Sen(E\Sigma, C\Sigma)$, $T_1 \models \varphi$ iff $T_2 \models \varphi$.

---

[3] This means that in any state there are at most finitely many outgoing transitions labelled with the same action. In particular, for any create action (see Definition 3(a)), the instance rj should be chosen from a finite set of instance identifiers.

(2) *If T_1 and T_2 are image-finite then the converse of* (1) *holds, i.e. if for any* $\varphi \in \text{Sen}(E\Sigma, C\Sigma)$, $T_1 \models \varphi$ *iff* $T_2 \models \varphi$, *then* $T_1 \sim_e T_2$.

As a consequence of (1), the model class *Mod(EnsSpec)* of an ensemble specification *EnsSpec* is closed under bisimulation equivalence.

4   Ensemble Realisations

Ensemble specifications describe properties of collaborating ensemble participants from a gobal perspective. In this section we consider ensemble realisations which define, for each role type rt of an ensemble signature, a local behaviour to be respected by all instances of rt. Behaviours are described in a constructive way by process expressions. Given a component signature $C\Sigma$ and an ensemble signature $E\Sigma = (rtypes, canPlay)$ over $C\Sigma$, process expressions and (local) role actions are defined by the following grammar:[4]

$P ::= \textbf{nil} \mid aP \mid P_1 + P_2 \mid rt$
$a ::= p := \textbf{create}(rt, \textbf{playedBy}) \mid p := \textbf{create}(rt, \textbf{playedBy}.att) \mid$
$\qquad ?mtnm(t_1\,p_1, \ldots, t_n\,p_n) \mid !p.mtnm(e_1, \ldots, e_n) \mid$
$\qquad [t\,d :=]\textbf{playedBy}.opnm(e_1, \ldots, e_n)$

In this grammar rt ranges over the role types in *rtypes*, p is a process instance variable, *att* is a reference attribute, *mtnm* ranges over the names of message types in $\mathtt{mts}[E\Sigma]$, $t_1\,p_1, \ldots, t_n\,p_n$ are formal parameters, $e_1, \ldots, e_n$ are expressions, *opnm* ranges over the names of operations in $\mathsf{opns}[C\Sigma]$, and d is a variable of type t (if t is the result type of *opnm*). We assume that there is a predefined variable **self** which can be used as an actual role type parameter in messages in order to transmit the identity of a role instance for possible callbacks.

The set of process expressions over $E\Sigma$ and $C\Sigma$ is denoted by $PExp(E\Sigma, C\Sigma)$. **nil** denotes the null process, aP action prefix, $P_1 + P_2$ nondeterministic choice and rt process invocation. In contrast to communication actions in $Act(E\Sigma, C\Sigma)$, process expressions contain distinguished receive and send actions seen from the perspective of a single role instance. A receive action $?mtnm(t_1\,p_1, \ldots t_n\,p_n)$ expresses that the current role instance is enabled to receive a message with values $v_1, \ldots, v_n$ of types $t_1, \ldots, t_n$ which will be stored in local variables $p_1, \ldots, p_n$ of the instance. A send action $!p.mtnm(e_1, \ldots, e_n)$ expresses that the current role instance is enabled to send a message to the role instance, denoted by the local variable p, transmitting the values of the expressions $e_1, \ldots, e_n$. A create action $p := \textbf{create}(rt, \textbf{playedBy})$ expresses that the current role instance is enabled to create a role instance of type rt on its owning component instance or, if the parameter is **playedBy**.*att*, on the component instance accessed by the reference attribute *att*. The new role instance is stored in the local variable p. A component access action **playedBy**.$opnm(e_1, \ldots, e_n)$ expresses that the current role instance is enabled to call the operation *opnm* on its owning

---

[4] A more expressive syntax allowing, e.g., conditional expressions with Boolean guards can be found in [12].

component instance handing over the values of the expressions $e_1, \ldots, e_n$. If the operation delivers a result then the result is stored in the local variable d of the role instance.

Definition 6 (Ensemble realisation). *Let $C\Sigma$ be a component system signature with model M. An ensemble realisation over $C\Sigma$ is a triple $EnsReal = (E\Sigma, Reals, (rinsts_0, playedBy_0))$ where $E\Sigma = (rtypes, canPlay)$ is an ensemble signature over $C\Sigma$, $Reals = \{rt = P_{rt} \mid rt \in rtypes\}$ is a set of role type realisations with $P_{rt} \in PExp(E\Sigma, C\Sigma)$, $rinsts_0$ is a non-empty set of initially existing role instances and $playedBy_0 : rinsts_0 \rightarrow \texttt{cinsts}[c\sigma_0]$ assigns to each $ri \in rinsts_0$ a component instance of the initial state $c\sigma_0$ of M.*

The semantics of an ensemble realisation is given in terms of an ensemble transition system. In this case the global control state $\texttt{ctrl}$ of an ensemble state $e\sigma = (rinsts, playedBy, ctrl)$ has a particular form: it is a function $ctrl : rinsts \rightarrow LStates(E\Sigma)$ assigning to each currently existing role instance $ri \in rinsts$ a local state. A *local state* is a pair $l = (\eta, P)$ where η is valuation of the local variables of role instance ri and P is a process expression recording the current computation state of ri. We write $\texttt{val}[l]$ for η and $\texttt{proc}[l]$ for P. The set of all local states over $E\Sigma$ is denoted by $LStates(E\Sigma)$. The set of all local variable valuations is denoted by $Val(E\Sigma)$. Updating a valuation η with a value v for a variable var is denoted by $\eta[var \mapsto v]$. The valuation of an empty set of local variables is denoted by $\emptyset$. Similarly to Sect. 3 we assume given an interpretation function $I_{\sigma,\eta}$ which maps, depending on a state $\sigma \in States(E\Sigma, C\Sigma)$ and a local variable valuation $\eta \in Val(E\Sigma)$, expressions to values.

An ensemble realisation $EnsReal = (E\Sigma, Reals, (rinsts_0, playedBy_0))$ determines the set $rinsts_0$ of role instances when the ensemble starts its execution. This set determines also a starting control state $ctrl_0$ of the ensemble which maps, for all role types rt of $E\Sigma$, each $ri \in (rinsts_0)_{rt}$ to the local state $(\emptyset[\texttt{self} \mapsto ri], P_{rt})$ where $rt = P_{rt}$ is the realisation of rt in $Reals$. In summary we obtain the *initial ensemble realisation state* $e\sigma_0 = (rinsts_0, playedBy_0, ctrl_0)$.

In contrast to the loose semantics of ensemble specifications, an ensemble realisation determines, up to identifiers of newly created role instances, a unique ensemble transition system. Structural operational semantics (SOS) rules define the allowed transitions. We pursue an incremental approach, similar to the Fork Calculus in [5], by splitting the semantics into two different layers. The first layer describes how a process expression evolves according to the given constructs for process expressions. The second layer builds on the first one by defining the evolution of ensemble realisation states $e\sigma$ over component system states $c\sigma$.

Evolution of Process Expressions: Figure 3 provides the SOS rules for the progress of process expressions. The rule for process invocation relies on the role type realisations $Reals$ given in an ensemble realisation. We use the symbol $\hookrightarrow$ for transitions on the process level.

Evolution of Ensembles: On the next level we consider ensemble realisation states and their transitions denoted by $\rightarrow$ in Fig. 4. The transitions in Fig. 4 are derived

(action prefix)	$a.P \overset{a}{\hookrightarrow} P$
(choice-left)	$\dfrac{P_1 \overset{a}{\hookrightarrow} P_1'}{P_1 + P_2 \overset{a}{\hookrightarrow} P_1'}$
(choice-right)	$\dfrac{P_2 \overset{a}{\hookrightarrow} P_2'}{P_1 + P_2 \overset{a}{\hookrightarrow} P_2'}$
(process type invocation)	$\dfrac{rt = P_{rt} \in Reals,\ P_{rt} \overset{a}{\hookrightarrow} P'}{rt \overset{a}{\hookrightarrow} P'}$

Fig. 3. SOS rules for process expressions

as follows: create actions $p := \mathbf{create}(rt, \mathbf{playedBy})$ on the process type level cause the creation of a new role instance in a given ensemble state $e\sigma$ which is now played by the component instance being the owner of the creating role instance. We use the notation $fresh(e\sigma, rt)$ to refer to the choice of a unique role instance of type rt, which does not belong to $\mathsf{rinsts}[e\sigma]_{rt}$. We have omitted in Fig. 4 the rule for create actions of the form $p := \mathbf{create}(rt, \mathbf{playedBy}.att)$ which is analogous, but now the created role is played by the component instance obtained by evaluation of the reference attribute att. Let us now consider communication inside an ensemble by message exchange. In the semantics presented here we use synchronous, binary communication - rule (comm) - where message output and message input are performed simultaneously when role instances are able to communicate.

Definition 7 (Semantics of an ensemble realisation). *Let $C\Sigma$ be a component system signature with model M and EnsReal be an ensemble realisation with signature $E\Sigma$ over $C\Sigma$. The semantics of EnsReal is the ensemble transition system*

$$[\![EnsReal]\!] = (States(E\Sigma, C\Sigma), (e\sigma_0, c\sigma_0), Lab(E\Sigma, C\Sigma), \rightarrow)$$

where $e\sigma_0$ is the initial ensemble realisation state (derived from EnsReal as explained above), $c\sigma_0$ is the initial component system state of M and $\rightarrow$ is the transition relation generated from $(e\sigma_0, c\sigma_0)$ by applying the rules in Figs. 3 and 4.

Note that the rules in Fig. 4 guarantee the constraints for an ensemble transition system formulated in Definition 3. Our semantic concepts lead to an obvious correctness notion for ensemble specifications and their realisations:

Definition 8 (Correct ensemble realisation). *Let EnsSpec be an ensemble specification and EnsReal be an ensemble realisation over the same signature. EnsReal is a correct realisation of EnsSpec if $[\![EnsReal]\!] \in Mod(EnsSpec)$.*

(create)

$$\dfrac{P_i \xrightarrow{\;p:=\textbf{create}(rt,\textbf{playedBy})\;} P_i'}{(e\sigma, c\sigma) \xrightarrow{\;fresh(e\sigma,rt)=ri.\textbf{create}(rt,ci)\;} (e\sigma', c\sigma)}$$

whenever $ri \in \mathsf{rinsts}[e\sigma], \mathsf{proc}[\mathsf{ctrl}[e\sigma](ri)] = P_i$, and,
there exists $ct \in C\Sigma$ such that :
$\mathsf{playedBy}[e\sigma](ri) = ci \in \mathsf{cinsts}[c\sigma]_{ct}, (ct, rt) \in \mathsf{canPlay}[E\Sigma]$,
$\mathsf{rinsts}[e\sigma'] = \mathsf{rinsts}[e\sigma] \cup \{fresh(e\sigma, rt)\}$,
$\mathsf{playedBy}[e\sigma'] = \mathsf{playedBy}[e\sigma][fresh(e\sigma, rt) \mapsto ci]$,
and, for $\eta = \mathsf{val}[\mathsf{ctrl}[e\sigma](ri)]$,
$\mathsf{ctrl}[e\sigma'] = \mathsf{ctrl}[e\sigma][ri \mapsto (\eta[p \mapsto fresh(e\sigma, rt)], P_i')]$
$\qquad\qquad\qquad [fresh(e\sigma, rt) \mapsto (\emptyset[\mathbf{self} \mapsto fresh(e\sigma, rt)], P_{rt})]$
$\qquad\qquad$ where $rt = P_{rt} \in Reals$.

(comm)

$$\dfrac{P_i \xrightarrow{\;!p.mtnm(e_1,...,e_n)\;} P_i',\; P_j \xrightarrow{\;?mtnm(t_1\,p_1,...,t_n\,p_n)\;} P_j'}{(e\sigma, c\sigma) \xrightarrow{\;(ri \to rj).mtnm(v_1,...,v_n)\;} (e\sigma', c\sigma)}$$

whenever there exist $rt, rt' \in \mathsf{rtypes}[E\Sigma]$ such that :
$mtnm(t_1\,p_1, \ldots, t_n\,p_n) \in \mathsf{mts}_{out}[rt] \cap \mathsf{mts}_{in}[rt']$,
$ri \in \mathsf{rinsts}[e\sigma]_{rt}, \mathsf{proc}[\mathsf{ctrl}[e\sigma](ri)] = P_i$,
$rj \in \mathsf{rinsts}[e\sigma]_{rt'}, \mathsf{proc}[\mathsf{ctrl}[e\sigma](rj)] = P_j, rj \neq ri$,
and, for $\eta_i = \mathsf{val}[\mathsf{ctrl}[e\sigma](ri)]$, we have $\eta_i(p) = rj$,
$I_{\sigma, \eta_i}(e_k) = v_k$ are valid parameter values for $k = 1, \ldots, n$,
$\mathsf{rinsts}[e\sigma'] = \mathsf{rinsts}[e\sigma], \mathsf{playedBy}[e\sigma'] = \mathsf{playedBy}[e\sigma]$, and
$\mathsf{ctrl}[e\sigma'] = \mathsf{ctrl}[e\sigma][ri \mapsto (\eta_i, P_i')][rj \mapsto (\eta_j[p_1 \mapsto v_1] \ldots [p_n \mapsto v_n], P_j')]$
where $\eta_j = \mathsf{val}[\mathsf{ctrl}[e\sigma](rj)]$.

(comp)

$$\dfrac{P_i \xrightarrow{\;t\,d:=\textbf{playedBy}.opnm(e_1,...,e_n)\;} P_i',}{(e\sigma, c\sigma) \xrightarrow{\;v=\textbf{playedBy}[e\sigma](ri).opnm(v_1,...,v_n)\;} (e\sigma', c\sigma')}$$

whenever $ri \in \mathsf{rinsts}[e\sigma], \mathsf{proc}[\mathsf{ctrl}[e\sigma](ri)] = P_i$,
$\mathsf{rinsts}[e\sigma'] = \mathsf{rinsts}[e\sigma], \mathsf{playedBy}[e\sigma'] = \mathsf{playedBy}[e\sigma]$,
and, for $\eta = \mathsf{val}[\mathsf{ctrl}[e\sigma](ri)]$,
$\mathsf{ctrl}[e\sigma'] = \mathsf{ctrl}[e\sigma][ri \mapsto (\eta[d \mapsto v], P_i')]$, and
$c\sigma \xrightarrow{\;v=\textbf{playedBy}[e\sigma](ri).opnm(v_1,...,v_n)\;}_M c\sigma'$.

Fig. 4. SOS rules for ensembles

Example 3. We provide a realisation of the file transfer ensemble which satisfies the specification in Example 2. The behaviour of each of the three role types is defined in Fig. 5. For the initial state of the component system model we assume that there exists a fixed number of component instances of type `Peer` organised in a ring structure. For the initial ensemble state we require that there exists exactly one role instance which is of type `Requester` and played by the first peer. Let us remark that the role behaviour specified for a router is non-deterministic (with internal choice) for what concerns the creation of a new router or a new provider role instance. It does not take into account when the owning component of a router stores the requested file and therefore will adapt the role of a provider. This could, however, be easily done if we would use the full HELENA language [12] which includes guarded choice. Moreover, as already discussed earlier, the name of the requested file is fixed which could be avoided if we would use open systems where the requester first would expect an input of a file name from the environment.   □

```
roleBehaviour Requester =
   router :=
      create(Router,playedBy.neighbour) .
   !router.reqAddr(self,''song'') .
   (( ?sndAddr(Provider prov) .
      !prov.reqFile(self,''song'') .
      ?sndFile(File f) . nil)
    +
    ( ?notFound() . nil))

roleBehaviour Provider =
   ?reqFile(Requester req, String s) .
   File song = playedBy.getFile(''song'').
   !req.sndFile(song) . nil
```

```
roleBehaviour Router =
   ?reqAddr(Requester req, String s) .
   ( router :=
        create(Router,playedBy.neighbour).
      !router.reqAddr(req,''song'') . nil)
    +
    ( prov := create(Provider,playedBy) .
      !req.sndAddr(prov) . nil)
    +
    ( !req.notFound() . nil)
```

Fig. 5. Realisation of the file transfer ensemble

As an immediate consequence of Theorem 1(1) we obtain:

Theorem 2 (Equivalent correct ensemble realisations). *Let EnsSpec be an ensemble specification and $EnsReal_1$ and $EnsReal_2$ be two equivalent ensemble realisations, i.e., $[\![EnsReal_1]\!] \sim_e [\![EnsReal_2]\!]$. Then $EnsReal_1$ is a correct realisation of EnsSpec if and only if $EnsReal_2$ is a correct realisation of EnsSpec.*

It remains the question how to prove that two ensemble realisations $EnsReal_1$ and $EnsReal_2$ are equivalent? The idea is to look to the role type realisations $rt = P_{1,rt}$ and $rt = P_{2,rt}$ of $EnsReal_1$ and $EnsReal_2$ and to show that, for each role type rt, the process expressions $P_{1,rt}$ and $P_{2,rt}$ are bisimulation equivalent in the usual sense of process algebra. We claim that this implies global bisimulation equivalence of their generated ensemble transition systems. A formal proof of this fact in the absence of component types has been given in [9].

5   Conclusion

In this work we have extended the (constructive) HELENA approach for modelling ensemble-based systems by a logic for specifying properties of ensembles. The logic should be useful for any kind of distributed system where cooperation is a central requirement. It is also useful for specifying allowed and forbidden scenarios which underlie use case driven approaches to software development. Our logic complements temporal logics, as used, e.g., in [8] for the verification of HELENA models, since it focuses on interactions and scenarios. Of course, more case studies are still needed to validate the expressiveness of our logic.

Our approach relies on a rigorous discrimination between syntax and semantics which allows us to study ensemble bisimulation and a correctness notion for ensemble realisations. Currently this correctness notion relies on synchronous message passing in (the semantics of) ensemble realisations. In future work this should be extended to support also asynchronous communication styles, like in [8,12] or in asynchronous multiparty session types [10]. In contrast to our approach, the framework of multiparty session types is strongly influenced by the π-calculus. It is not aimed at a logic but at process algebraic descriptions of global interaction protocols from which realisations (in the form of sets of local types) can be extracted by projection. An approach to specifying multiparty sessions carrying a logical flavour is given by the global types in [2]. Such global types use also compound actions, like sequential composition and iteration, and, moreover, are able to specify unconstrained composition of parallel activities which would also be an issue for extension of our logic. But they rely on a fixed number of ensemble participants and do not support modalities and negation. Moreover, to the best of our knowledge, the session type formalisms do not distinguish between components and roles which is a crucial aspect of our approach.

Further aspects for future research are investigating methods for proving correctness of ensemble realisations and studying open ensembles and their composition by extending [6] to components. Currently an ensemble specification describes the behaviour of one kind of ensemble but we are also interested to incorporate possibilities for talking about different kinds of ensembles in the logic and in realisations.

Acknowledgement. I am grateful for the scientific cooperation with Martin Wirsing on ensemble-based systems and his support for the current study.

References

1. Bures, T., Gerostathopoulos, I., Hnetynka, P., Keznikl, J., Kit, M., Plasil, F.: DEECO: an ensemble-based component system. In: Proceedings of the 16th ACM SIGSOFT Symposium on Component Based Software Engineering (CBSE 2013), pp. 81–90. ACM (2013)
2. Castagna, G., Dezani-Ciancaglini, M., Padovani, L.: On global types and multiparty sessions. Log. Methods Comput. Sci. **8**(1) (2012). https://doi.org/10.2168/LMCS-8(1:24)2012

3. De Nicola, R., Loreti, M., Pugliese, R., Tiezzi, F.: A formal approach to autonomic systems programming: the SCEL language. ACM Trans. Auton. Adapt. Syst. (TAAS) **9**(2), 1–29 (2014)
4. Harel, D., Kozen, D., Tiuryn, J. (eds.): Dynamic Logic. MIT Press, Cambridge (2000)
5. Havelund, K., Larsen, K.G.: The fork calculus. In: Lingas, A., Karlsson, R., Carlsson, S. (eds.) ICALP 1993. LNCS, vol. 700, pp. 544–557. Springer, Heidelberg (1993). https://doi.org/10.1007/3-540-56939-1_101
6. Hennicker, R.: A calculus for open ensembles and their composition. In: Margaria, T., Steffen, B. (eds.) ISoLA 2016. LNCS, vol. 9952, pp. 570–588. Springer, Cham (2016). https://doi.org/10.1007/978-3-319-47166-2_40
7. Hennicker, R., Klarl, A.: Foundations for ensemble modeling – the HELENA approach. In: Iida, S., Meseguer, J., Ogata, K. (eds.) Specification, Algebra, and Software. LNCS, vol. 8373, pp. 359–381. Springer, Heidelberg (2014). https://doi.org/10.1007/978-3-642-54624-2_18
8. Hennicker, R., Klarl, A., Wirsing, M.: Model-checking HELENA ensembles with spin. In: Martí-Oliet, N., Ölveczky, P.C., Talcott, C. (eds.) Logic, Rewriting, and Concurrency. LNCS, vol. 9200, pp. 331–360. Springer, Cham (2015). https://doi.org/10.1007/978-3-319-23165-5_16
9. Hennicker, R., Wirsing, M.: Dynamic logic for ensembles. In: Margaria, T., Steffen, B. (eds.) ISoLA 2018. LNCS, vol. 11246, pp. 32–47. Springer, Cham (2018). https://doi.org/10.1007/978-3-030-03424-5_3
10. Honda, K., Yoshida, N., Carbone, M.: Multiparty asynchronous session types. In: Proceedings of the 35th Annual ACM SIGPLAN-SIGACT Symposium on Principles of Programming Languages (POPL 2008), pp. 273–284. ACM (2008)
11. Klarl, A.: Engineering self-adaptive systems with the role-based architecture of HELENA. In: Proceedings of 24th IEEE International Conference on Enabling Technologies: Infrastructure for Collaborative Enterprises, WETICE 2015, pp. 3–8. IEEE Computer Society (2015)
12. Klarl, A.: HELENA: Handling massively distributed systems with ELaborate ENsemble Architectures. Ph.D. thesis, LMU Munich, Germany (2016)
13. Klarl, A., Cichella, L., Hennicker, R.: From HELENA ensemble specifications to executable code. In: Lanese, I., Madelaine, E. (eds.) FACS 2014. LNCS, vol. 8997, pp. 183–190. Springer, Cham (2015). https://doi.org/10.1007/978-3-319-15317-9_11
14. Klarl, A., Hennicker, R.: Design and implementation of dynamically evolving ensembles with the Helena framework. In: Proceedings of the 23rd Australasian Software Engineering Conference, pp. 15–24. IEEE (2014)
15. Wirsing, M., Hölzl, M., Koch, N., Mayer, P. (eds.): Software Engineering for Collective Autonomic Systems - The ASCENS Approach. LNCS, vol. 8998. Springer, Cham (2015). https://doi.org/10.1007/978-3-319-16310-9
16. Wirsing, M., Hölzl, M., Tribastone, M., Zambonelli, F.: ASCENS: engineering autonomic service-component ensembles. In: Beckert, B., Damiani, F., de Boer, F.S., Bonsangue, M.M. (eds.) FMCO 2011. LNCS, vol. 7542, pp. 1–24. Springer, Heidelberg (2013). https://doi.org/10.1007/978-3-642-35887-6_1

Survey Papers

Parameterized Strategies Specification
in Maude

Rubén Rubio$^{(\boxtimes)}$, Narciso Martí-Oliet, Isabel Pita, and Alberto Verdejo

Universidad Complutense de Madrid, Madrid, Spain
{rubenrub,narciso,ipandreu,jalberto}@ucm.es

Abstract. Strategies and parameterization are two convenient tools for building clear and easily configurable specifications of complex computational systems, compositionally. Parameterization is a widely used feature of the Maude rewriting framework, whose strategy language implementation we have recently completed with strategy modules.

This paper describes the Maude strategy language and the associated parameterization techniques. Then, the specification and analysis of some examples of strategy parameterized systems are shown.

Keywords: Rewriting logic · Strategies · Maude ·
Parameterized specification

1 Introduction

Strategies are ubiquitous in Computer Science. As recipes to tackle search problems and bound nondeterminism, they appear in algorithms, automatic deduction, language semantics, artificial intelligence, ... In *rewriting logic* [13], some of these examples are better specified compositionally, abstracting not only data representation and rules but also the way they are applied. This parametric control of the rewriting process is conveniently expressed using strategies that take other strategies as parameters.

Maude [6,7] is a declarative high-level language based on rewriting logic that allows the description, execution and analysis of concurrent and distributed system models at different levels. First, sorts, symbols, equations and membership axioms are expressed in terms of *membership equational logic* [3]. Then, we add rewrite rules to represent transitions of a concurrent system, which need neither be deterministic, nor confluent, nor terminating. Above this, we can control how rules are applied using a strategy language [8,11]. Its implementation, at the Core Maude level in C++, has been recently completed as an extension of Maude 2.7.1 [7].

Research partially supported by MCIU Spanish project *TRACES* (TIN2015-67522-C3-3-R), and by Comunidad de Madrid project N-Greens Software-CM (S2013/ICE-2731).

ⓒ IFIP International Federation for Information Processing 2019
Published by Springer Nature Switzerland AG 2019
J. L. Fiadeiro and I. Țuțu (Eds.): WADT 2018, LNCS 11563, pp. 27–44, 2019.
https://doi.org/10.1007/978-3-030-23220-7_2

The strategy language is based in its authors experience with strategies in Maude and in previous strategy languages like ELAN [2] and Stratego [5]. It has already been exploited in the specification of algorithms, inference systems, and language semantics: Milner's CCS [12], the ambient calculus [12], the semantics of the parallel functional language Eden [9], equational logic completion procedures [16], a proof calculus for membrane systems [1], etc. These examples are likely to be expressed and generalized using control parameterization with strategies, whose implementation was not available at that time. Once expressed in this way, the specified systems can be both executed and tested with different alternative strategies provided as parameters, or analyzed at different levels with specific tools, like a model checker.

The next section introduces Maude, its strategy language, and the rudiments of parameterization. A generic backtracking scheme serves as an introductory example. The following sections describe some other examples of parameterized systems, targeting the simplex algorithm, the λ-calculus, and a functional program interpreter. These and more examples can be downloaded from [15], as well as the current version of Maude with full strategy support.

2   Maude

A Maude program consists of a hierarchy of modules, describing the data representation and behavior of the system specified. There are different module types for different specification levels.

Functional modules define membership equational logic theories, whose signature (K, Σ, S) consists of a set of kinds K, a many-kinded collection of operators $\Sigma = \{\Sigma_{k_1 \cdots k_n, k} : (k_1 \cdots k_n, k) \in K^* \times K\}$, and $S = \{S_k : k \in K\}$ a many-kinded set of partially ordered sorts. Equations and sort membership axioms E are defined on them

$$(\forall X) \quad \begin{matrix} t = t' \\ t : s \end{matrix} \text{ if } \bigwedge_i u_i = u'_i \wedge \bigwedge_j v_j : s_j$$

In addition, operators can be annotated with structural *axioms*, like commutativity (comm), associativity (assoc), and identity (id). For example, the following functional module specifies sets of integer numbers using both equations and axioms.

```
fmod INT-SET is
    protecting INT .   *** INT module importation
    sort IntSet .
    subsort Int < IntSet .
    *** IntSet contructors (ctor)
    op empty : → IntSet [ctor] .
    op __ : IntSet IntSet → IntSet
               [ctor assoc comm id: empty] . *** union
    var X : Int .
    eq X X  = X .
endfm
```

Functional modules are bound to some executability requirements, like conflu-
ence, termination, and sort-decreasingness.

System modules describe rewriting logic theories $\mathcal{R} = (\Sigma, E \cup A, R)$, adding
rewriting rules R on top of the equational theory. Rules do not have to be either
confluent or terminating, so they are likely to express non-deterministic behavior.

$$(\forall X) \qquad t \Rightarrow t' \text{ if } \bigwedge_i u_i = u_i' \wedge \bigwedge_j v_j : s_j \wedge \bigwedge_k w_k \Rightarrow w_k'$$

Anyhow, rules are required to be coherent with equations and axioms
[7, §5.3]. Conditions of the third type are called *rewriting conditions*, and hold
true iff the term w_k can be rewritten to match the term w_k'.

```
mod SUM-SET is
  protecting INT-SET .
  vars X Y : Int .
  rl [sum] : X Y => X + Y . *** matches any two elems
endm
```

The module SUM-SET above introduces a rule sum that takes two integers in the
set and replaces them by their sum.

Strategy modules allow finer control of the rule rewriting process by means
of the strategy language and recursive strategy definitions. They are described
in the next section.

2.1 The Strategy Language

Rules in rewriting logic can be applied in any order, at any position, and with different matches. Maude provides various commands, like rewrite and frewrite,
that execute all available rules against a given term until none can be applied
or an optional step bound is reached. They use some internal fixed criteria to
select the next rule application. In turn, the search command explores all possible rewriting paths to find a target term meeting some conditions. However, the
specifier is sometimes interested in imposing constrains on the allowed execution
paths, like a particular precedence of rules, or to which subterms they must be
applied, etc. This is when strategies get inside the game.

From the point of view of the results, a strategy α is an operation transform-
ing a term t into a set of terms, since the restrictions need not make the process
deterministic. Strategies can be executed with the command srewrite t using
α. The most elementary strategy is rule application

$$\mathsf{top}\,(label\,[x_1 \mathrel{<\text{-}} t_1\,,\,\ldots\,,\,x_n \mathrel{<\text{-}} t_n]\,\{\alpha_1\,,\,\ldots\,,\alpha_m\})\,,$$

that executes any available rules with label *label* on any subterm of the subject
term. Variables in the rule and its condition can be instantiated before application with the substitution that maps x_k to t_k, and if the rule contains any
rewriting condition, it must be controlled with a substrategy α_k. Moreover, the

optional **top** modifier restricts the application of the rule to the top of the subject term. A more powerful tool for selecting where to apply a strategy is the matchrew operator

$$\textbf{matchrew } P(x_1,\ldots,x_n) \textbf{ s.t. } C \textbf{ by } x_1 \textbf{ using } \alpha_1 \text{ , } \ldots \text{ , } x_n \textbf{ using } \alpha_n$$

It matches the pattern P on top of the subject term, and for each match satisfying the condition C, the subterms corresponding to $x_1,\ldots,x_n$ are rewritten using $\alpha_1,\ldots,\alpha_n$, and reassembled again. The operator name can be prefixed by a or x to match anywhere within the term or modulo structural axioms. Similar format follow the tests **match** P **s.t.** C, to check if P matches the subject term and satisfies C. Regular expressions are included in the strategy language by means of the alternation $\alpha \,|\, \beta$, the concatenation $\alpha \,;\, \beta$, the Kleene star α^*, and the constants **idle** and **fail**. A conditional strategy $\alpha\,?\,\beta:\gamma$ is also available. It executes α and then β on its results, but if α does not produce any, it applies γ to the initial term.

The last ingredient of the strategy language are potentially recursive named strategies. These strategies are defined in strategy modules, which have the form **smod** M **is** ... **endsm** and contain:

- Strategy declarations **strat sname : T1 ... Tn @ T**, which state their parameter types T_1 to T_n, and the type T of the subject terms the strategy will be applied to.
- Strategy definitions **sd sname**$(t_1,\ldots,t_n)$ **:=** α. The free variables in the right-hand side strategy expression α must be included in the terms t_1 to t_n. Conditional strategy definitions, introduced by **csd**, are available too, and impose conditions as in regular equations. A named strategy can be given any number of strategy definitions, and all definitions whose left-hand side matches the call term will be executed.

Now, we will illustrate all the different strategy constructors described above with a very simple example. Consider the following system module:

```
mod SIMPLE is
  sort Term .

  ops a b c d : → Term [ctor] .
  op f : Term → Term [ctor] .
  op g : Term Term → Term [ctor] .

  vars X Y : Term .

  rl [ab] : a ⇒ b .        rl [ac] : a ⇒ c .
  rl [bc] : b ⇒ c .        rl [pf] : f(X) ⇒ X .
  rl [ad] : f(a) ⇒ d .
endm
```

The SIMPLE module defines some constants and functions to build terms, and various rules that transform them. For example, we can apply the pf rule to the term f(g(f(a), b)) by means of the srewrite command, whose initial keyword can be abbreviated to srew:

```
Maude> srew f(g(f(a), b)) using pf .

Solution 1
result Term: g(f(a), b)

Solution 2
result Term: f(g(a, b))

No more solutions.
Maude> srew f(g(f(a), b)) using pf[T <- a] .

Solution 1
result Term: f(g(a, b))

No more solutions.
```

Notice that all possible rewrites are returned as different solutions. In the first case, the rule can be applied both to the first and to the second occurrence of f. However, in the second case, the initial substitution restricts its application to the subterm f(a). Using the strategy top(pf) instead, pf is only applied on top and only g(f(a), b) is obtained. Finer precision on where to apply a strategy can be achieved by the subterm rewriting operator. For example, matchrew g(X, Y) by X using pf restricts the application to the first argument of g. Then g(f(b), f(c)) rewrites only to g(b, f(c)). Moreover, multiple subterms can be rewritten in parallel by strategies like

amatchrew g(X, Y) by X using pf, Y using bc,

which transforms the initial term f(g(f(a), b)) in f(g(a, c)).

Once we are able to apply strategies to particular subterms, we need regular expressions to compose rewriting sequences. If we rewrite g(a, b) by the concatenation ab ; bc, we obtain g(c, b) and g(b, c), since the rule bc has been applied after ab, at the same or at a different position. Instead, when executing the alternation ab | bc, only one of these is applied, and we get g(b, b) and g(a, c) as solutions. Finally, the iteration pf* applies pf zero or more times consecutively, so it rewrites f(f(a)) to f(f(a)), f(a), and a.

Other useful resources are the tests like match g(X, Y) s.t. X ≠ Y. It does not produce any solution for g(a, a), but for g(a, b), the solution is the term itself. Tests easily combine with conditionals. For example, the strategy match f(X) ? ab : bc applies ab if the subject term top symbol is an f, and otherwise executes bc. Then, f(a) rewrites to f(b), b to c, and no solution is produced for a. However, conditionals can be used with any strategy as condition, as we will see soon and throughout the paper.

Finally, to define named and recursive strategies, we need to write strategy modules like the following:

```
smod SIMPLE-STRAT is
    protecting SIMPLE .    *** controls SIMPLE

    strat rewrite @ Term .
    sd rewrite := all ? rewrite : idle .
endsm
```

where `all` is a built-in constant that executes any available rule. In this case, it can be seen as equivalent to `ab | ac | bc | pf | ad`. Hence, the strategy `rewrite` applies any rule until no more rules can be applied, as the usual `rewrite` command does. Running this strategy for the term `g(f(a), f(b))` we obtain:

```
Maude> srew g(f(a), f(b)) using rewrite .

Solution 1
result Term: g(d, c)

Solution 2
result Term: g(c, c)

No more solutions.
```

In Fig. 1, the strategy language semantics is described in brief. Apart from the initial term, the semantic function $[\![\alpha]\!] : (X \to T_{\Sigma/E}) \times T_{\Sigma/E} \to \mathcal{P}(T_{\Sigma/E})$ receives a substitution by way of variable environment, because function calls and `matchrews` bind variables. The semantics of the strategy definitions δ is calculated as a fixed point of a continuous operator, and here $\Delta(sl, t_1 \cdots t_n)$ refers to the set of strategy definitions for sl whose left-hand side matches $t_1, \ldots, t_n$, along with the corresponding substitution σ.

2.2 Parameterization

Parameterization is achieved using three basic building blocks: theories, views, and parameterized modules [6,7]. A parameterized module is a usual module taking a set of formal parameters, bound to some theories.

mod NAME{X1 :: TH1, ..., XN :: THN} is ... endm.

A theory declares the interface, the syntactic and semantic requirements, the actual parameter must respect. Each module type (functional, system, strategy) has its theory counterpart. They are structurally identical, but theories are not required to fulfill the executability properties of a module. Module parameters can only be bound to theories of their type or simpler types. Finally, a view is the way to express how a module honors a theory, mapping each sort, operator, and strategy declared in the theory to the actual value in the module. Then, views are used to instantiate parameterized modules.

As an example, the most basic predefined theory is `TRIV`, which declares a single sort.

$$[\![\mathbf{idle}]\!](\theta, t) = \{t\} \qquad\qquad\qquad [\![\mathbf{fail}]\!](\theta, t) = \emptyset$$

$$[\![\alpha \mathbin{;} \beta]\!](\theta, t) = \bigcup_{t' \in [\![\alpha]\!](\theta, t)} [\![\beta]\!](\theta, t') \qquad\qquad [\![\alpha \mid \beta]\!](\theta, t) = [\![\alpha]\!](\theta, t) \cup [\![\beta]\!](\theta, t)$$

$$[\![\alpha *]\!](\theta, t) = \bigcup_{n \geq 0} [\![\alpha]\!]^n(\theta, t)$$

$$[\![\alpha \mathbin{?} \beta : \gamma]\!](t) = \begin{cases} [\![\alpha \mathbin{;} \beta]\!](\theta, t) & \text{if } [\![\alpha]\!](\theta, t) \neq \emptyset \\ [\![\gamma]\!](\theta, t) & \text{if } [\![\alpha]\!](\theta, t) = \emptyset \end{cases}$$

$$[\![\mathbf{match}\ P\ \mathbf{s.t.}\ C\ ]\!](\theta, t) = \begin{cases} \{t\} & \text{if } \mathrm{match}(P, t, C, \theta_{-\mathrm{occur}(P)}) \neq \emptyset \\ \emptyset & \text{otherwise} \end{cases}$$

$$[\![\mathbf{matchrew}\ P\ \mathbf{s.t.}\ C\ \mathbf{by}\ x_1\ \mathbf{using}\ \alpha_1\ ,\ldots,\ x_n\ \mathbf{using}\ \alpha_n]\!](\theta, t) =$$

$$\bigcup_{\sigma \in \mathrm{match}(P, t, C, \theta_{-\mathrm{occur}(P)})} \ \bigcup_{t_1 \in [\![\alpha_1]\!](\sigma \circ \theta, \sigma(x_1))} \cdots \bigcup_{t_n \in [\![\alpha_n]\!](\sigma \circ \theta, \sigma(x_n))} P[x_1/t_1, \ldots, x_n/t_n]$$

$$[\![sl(t_1, \ldots, t_n)]\!](\theta, t) = \bigcup_{(\delta, \sigma) \in \Delta(sl, \theta(t_1) \cdots \theta(t_n))} [\![\delta]\!](\sigma, t)$$

Fig. 1. Strategic set-theoretic semantics definitions

```
fth TRIV is
  sort Elt .
endfth
```

The module NAT can be viewed as a TRIV:

```
view Nat from TRIV to NAT is
  sort Elt to Nat .
endv
```

Then, the view Nat can be used to instantiate modules like lists LIST{Nat}, sets SET{Nat}, ... Module instantiation is based on the pushout along a view:

$$
\begin{array}{ccc}
\text{TRIV} & \xrightarrow{\ \text{Nat}\ } & \text{NAT} \\
\downarrow & & \downarrow \\
\text{LIST\{X :: TRIV\}} & \longrightarrow & \text{LIST\{Nat\}}
\end{array}
$$

A simplified version of the LIST module is the following:

```
fmod LIST{X :: TRIV} is
  sort List .
  subsort X$Elt < List .
  op nil : → List [ctor] .
  op __ : List List → List [ctor assoc id: nil] .
endfm
```

Inside parameterized modules, sorts coming from theories are accessed by prefixing their names by their parameter name followed by a $ sign. Operators and strategies retain their names as in the parameter theory. The Maude standard prelude includes some general theories like TRIV, TOTAL-PREORDER, STRICT-WEAK-ORDER, ..., and many views from the standard data types to those theories [6,7].

3   An Introductory Example

A simple example of parameterized control is the generic backtracking scheme.

The abstract backtracking problem is specified in two nested theories, the first proclaims the functional requirements, and the second extends it with the strategic ones. They require a State sort for states, and a strategy expand to rewrite a state to any of its direct successors, non-deterministically. We admit that the generated successors may not be valid, so we require a predicate isOk to test them, and also a predicate isSolution to determine whether a given state is already a solution.

```
fth BT-ELEMS-BASE is
  protecting BOOL .
  sort State .
  op isOk : State → Bool .
  op isSolution : State → Bool .
endfth
```

```
sth BT-ELEMS is
  including BT-ELEMS-BASE .
  strat expand @ State .
endsth
```

Then, a parameterized module BT-STRAT, given the specification of the problem following BT-ELEMS, defines a strategy solve for executing the backtracking algorithm. This is the following module, where parameters are highlighted in italics.

```
smod BT-STRAT{X :: BT-ELEMS} is
  strat solve @ X$State .
  var S : X$State .
  sd solve := (match S s.t. isSolution(S)) ? idle
        : (expand ; match S s.t. isOk(S) ; solve) .
endsm
```

The `solve` strategy is recursive. It concludes successfully when it finds a solution. Otherwise, it applies the strategy `expand` to obtain a successor, tests whether it is valid, and iterates the process by a recursive call. Rewriting paths are discarded either when a successor not satisfying `isOk` is reached or when the `expand` strategy does not provide any successor. Indeed, each result of the `expand` strategy opens a new branch of the execution tree.

Although we call it *backtracking*, the strategy is abstract enough to be interpreted or executed otherwise, depending on the order in which the branches are explored. For backtracking, we understand a depth-first exploration, going backwards to try another branch when the current one has been exhausted without finding a solution. However, the default strategy rewriting implementation obeys a fair scheduling, which combines depth and breadth-first search. Here, the fair execution policy will usually require more time and memory usage than a real backtracking.

The generic algorithm is useless without actual instances. They can be specified in separate modules or files, but finally they have to fit in the frame of an abstract backtracking problem by means of a view from `BT-ELEMS`. The following module specifies the search for a Hamiltonian cycle in a graph, i.e. a cycle visiting every vertex of the graph only once.

```
mod HAMILTONIAN is
  protecting LIST{Nat} .
  sorts Edge Adjacency Graph .
  subsort Edge < Adjacency .
  op e : Nat Nat → Edge [ctor comm] .
  op nil : → Adjacency [ctor] .
  op __ : Adjacency Adjacency → Adjacency
                          [ctor assoc comm id: nil] .

  op noCross : List{Nat} → Bool .
  vars K L N V : Nat .
  vars P Q R : List{Nat} .
  var As : Adjacency .
  eq noCross(P K Q K R) = false .
  eq noCross(P) = true [owise] .
  op graph : Nat Adjacency List{Nat} → Graph [ctor] .
  op isOk : Graph → Bool .
  op isSolution : Graph → Bool .
  eq isSolution(graph(N,As,V P V)) = N == size(V P) .
  eq isSolution(G:Graph) = false [owise] .
  eq isOk(graph(N, As, V P V)) = noCross(V P) .
  eq isOk(graph(N, As, P)) = noCross(P) [owise] .
  rl [next] : graph(N, e(V, K) As, P V)
                 ⇒ graph(N, As, P V K) .
endm
```

The module defines `Graph`, including both the graph and the current path, which can be extended up to a Hamiltonian cycle using the rule **next** whenever possible. Finally, as we said, the problem has to be presented as a backtracking instance using a view. Identity mappings do not need to be written, but we have included them to illustrate the syntax.

```
view HamiltonianBT from BT-ELEMS to HAMILTONIAN is
  sort State to Graph .
  op isOk to isOk .
  op isSolution to isSolution .
  strat expand to-expr next .
endv
```

This instance is specially simple, the **expand** strategy has been defined inline as the **next** rule. In general, more elaborated strategies can be defined in a strategy module. In that case, the strategy module must be the *to* part of the view and the strategy is mapped by **strat expand to sname**. This can be seen in other examples available in the webpage [15] like the labyrinth escape problem, the n-queens problem, the graph m-coloring problem, etc.

A refinement of backtracking is *branch and bound*. This algorithmic technique was also programmed with parameterized strategies. Its problem specification, its theories, include richer functional and strategic requirements, so we do not describe them here. In this case, we cannot use an **expand** strategy that non-deterministically evolves to a successor, we need to examine them all to decide which to explore first according to the rank function. Hence, we have experimented with multiple approaches using different problem signatures. These can also be downloaded from [15].

4   The Simplex Algorithm

The simplex method [14] is a well-known algorithm for solving linear programming problems, i.e. for finding solutions that maximize (or minimize) a linear functional subject to some linear constraints.

$$\max / \min \ c_1 \ x_1 + \cdots + c_n \ x_n$$
$$a_{11}x_1 + \cdots + a_{1n}x_n \leq b_1$$
$$a_{21}x_1 + \cdots + a_{2n}x_n = b_2$$
$$a_{31}x_1 + \cdots + a_{3n}x_n \geq b_3$$
$$x_1, \ldots, x_n \geq 0$$

Formulated by George Dantzig in the late 1940s, it has had many industrial applications. Here we present an executable linear programming solver written in Maude using this method. The various non-deterministic steps are controlled by strategies, which are configurable through parameterization.

Figure 2 shows all the specification modules. `LINPROG` includes some basic definitions of linear algebra (polynomials, inequalities, ..., and operations on

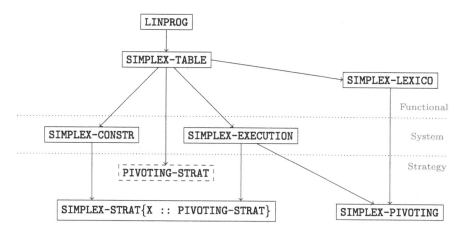

Fig. 2. Module structure for the simplex algorithm specification

them), as well as linear programming problems. Then, SIMPLEX-TABLE defines the simplex tables (the state of the algorithm) and some operations to obtain information and modify them. At the rule level, SIMPLEX-CONSTR defines how to build a table from a linear programming problem, and SIMPLEX-EXECUTION provides the rules for the different actions of the simplex method. The most important is pivot, which changes the algorithm basis

```
crl [pivot] : Table ⇒ pivot(Table, Ve, Vl) if
             Ve, R := enterVars(Table) ∧
             Vl, S := leaveVars(Table, Ve) .
```

This rule is non-deterministic because Ve and Vl can be chosen among different alternatives. Pivoting carelessly may even lead to cycles, so that the algorithm may not terminate. Fortunately, there are different cycle prevention techniques to avoid non-termination. The more common ones are the *Bland rule* and the *lexicographic rule*. These rules (or any other) can be switched by means of parameterization.

The global solving process starts with a linear programming problem. The first stage is the generation of the simplex table, a non-deterministic process which produces equivalent tables up to renaming. So, we will concentrate on the second stage, the simplex method itself.

```
sd solve := makeTable ; simplex .
sd simplex := step ? simplex : idle .
sd step := (unbounded | finish | phase2 | unfeas)
           or−else pivotingStrat .
```

The simplex strategy executes a simplex step until no more can be applied. Each step first applies some rules that transform the table in some specific situations: unbounded detects when the problem is unbounded and transforms the table in a description of the beam of infinite improvement, and finish detects when the problem is already solved and presents the solution in a more readable form. The other rules are related to the *two phases method*, which may be sometimes needed to find an initial feasible solution of the linear system: unfeas signals that the problem is unfeasible; and phase2 transforms the table to a usual table whenever possible. Finally, if none of these (cheaper and concluding) rules can be applied, the pivoting strategy pivotingStrat is applied. This is the parameter of the SIMPLEX-STRAT module, provided by the theory PIVOTING-STRAT, which declares a single strategy without parameters applicable to the simplex table sort. For instance, the Bland rule is specified in SIMPLEX-PIVOTING with the following strategy

```
sd bland := matchrew T s.t.
              Ve := minVar(enterVars(T)) ∧
              Vl := minVar(leaveVars(T, Ve))
              by T using pivot[Ve <- Ve, Vl <- Vl] .
```

where minVar equationally computes the minimum variable within a set (a total order < is defined on them). A view Bland from PIVOTING-STRAT to SIMPLEX-PIVOTING, mapping pivotingStrat to bland, is then used to instantiate SIMPLEX-STRAT.

4.1 Parameterized Analysis

A natural analysis of parameterized systems is the comparison of the behavior of their multiple instances, which can be executed or simulated, looking at the execution time, the number of rewriting steps, or the memory requirements. More essential properties can be inspected by tracing the state of the system while running the simulation. Strategies are a useful tool for that purpose. Apart from this, parameterized modules can be analyzed with specific tools like the Maude model checker.

For the simplex method, we have compared the performance of two pivoting strategies and free rewriting in terms of time and number of rewrites, against a linear programming exercises set. Since these properties depend on the actual Maude implementation, we also consider an intrinsic property of the algorithm: the number of iterations or pivoting steps until a solution is found. To obtain this attribute, we count the number of pivot rule executions with the aid of a parameterized analyzer module that maintains a pair watch(T, N) of a simplex table and a counter, applies the rules to the table using matchrew, and updates the counter accordingly. This can be compared with the unrestricted better case and worst case number of iterations, which can be calculated using strategies too.

We observe that the lexicographic rule reduces the mean number of iterations, but since its decisions require more computations, its performance is similar to Bland's. The free strategy, executing the rules at the discretion of the Maude rewriting engine, performs quite well.

Regarding auxiliary tools, we have applied an experimental prototype of a strategy-aware model checker. Thanks to it, we can check whether the algorithm

	Free	Bland	Lexicographic
Iterations above better case	2.05	2.05	1.47
Number of rewrites	4246	5195	5191
Time (ms)	1.84	2.29	2.2

following a given strategy, for a fixed example, may cycle or not. Predictably, no example cycles with the Bland and lexicographic rules, but some do with free rewriting.

5   The λ-calculus

The λ-calculus can be easily expressed and executed in Maude [10]. β-reduction is the single rule of the rewriting system, so a term can be reduced by simply using the **rewrite** and **search** commands.

```
subsort Var < LambdaTerm .
op \_._ : Var LambdaTerm → LambdaTerm [ctor] .
op __ : LambdaTerm LambdaTerm → LambdaTerm [ctor] .
rl [beta] : (\ x . M) N ⇒ subst(M, x, N) .
```

However, which β-redex is reduced first is an important choice. Some reduction paths may not terminate while others reach an irreducible term, even though this is unique by the Church-Rosser property. The normalization theorem says that reducing the leftmost outermost redex first guarantees finding a normal form in case it exists.

$$(KI)\Omega \begin{array}{c} \longrightarrow (KI)\Omega \circlearrowleft \\ \searrow (\lambda y.I)\Omega \longrightarrow I \end{array} \qquad \begin{array}{l} K = \lambda x.(\lambda y.x) \\ I = \lambda x.x \\ \Omega = (\lambda x.xx)(\lambda x.xx) \end{array}$$

We allow selecting which strategy **step** to use for a single reduction step and, using a parameterized module, we define a strategy that reduces the term to an irreducible form, if any.

```
strat reduce @ LambdaTerm .
sd reduce := step ! .
```

The operator α ! executes α until it cannot be further applied. The different implemented strategies for a single reduction are:

– Applicative order (inner rightmost redex first)

```
sd applicative :=
    matchrew \ x . M by M using applicative
  | matchrew M N by N using applicative
    or−else matchrew M N by M using applicative
    or−else top(beta) .
```

– Normalizing strategy (outer leftmost redex first)

```
sd normal := matchrew \ x . M by M using normal
   | top(beta)
         or−else matchrew M N by M using normal
         or−else matchrew M N by N using normal .
```

– By name (normalizing but no reduction inside abstraction)

```
sd byname := top(beta)
   or−else matchrew M N by M using byname
   or−else matchrew M N by N using byname .
```

– By value (only outermost redex and when argument is value)

```
sd byvalue := (match (\ x . M) z
   | match (\ x . M) (\ y . N)) ; top(beta) .
```

For example, **srew** (K I) Omega **using** applicative does not finish, but **srew** (K I) Omega **using** normal produces \ x . x as a result. Moreover, depending on the reduction strategy, we obtain different canonical forms. From (K z) t we get z using all strategies but byvalue, whose canonical form is the term unchanged.

6   Semantics of Programming Languages

The semantics of programming languages is an interesting field to apply both strategies [4] and parameterization. The Maude implementation of Eden [9], a concurrent language based on Haskell, can be cited as example. The general idea is that strategies control the execution process and can be used to tweak some semantic choices, and see how alternatives perform. Here we describe a simpler example, the *Recursion equations* (REC) language [17, Chapter 9].

A REC program consists of a closed integer expression to evaluate and a set of integer function definitions of the form $f(x_1, \ldots, x_{a_f}) = \langle expr \rangle$. Expressions contain integer constants, sums, products, subtractions, conditionals, and calls to any defined function. Hence, functions can be recursive and mutually recursive. An organized set of modules (see Fig. 3) specifies the representation of REC programs and its basic rules:

```
rl [apply] : Q(Args) ⇒ apply(find(Q, Defs), Args)
                                    [nonexec] .
crl [cond] : if C then E else F ⇒
         if C == 0 then E else F fi if C : Int .
```

The rule **apply** replaces a function call Q(Args) by its definition according to the list of definitions Defs, substituting its variables by the call arguments using the equational function apply. This rule is not directly executable since Defs, absent in the left-hand side, must be provided from the context in the application

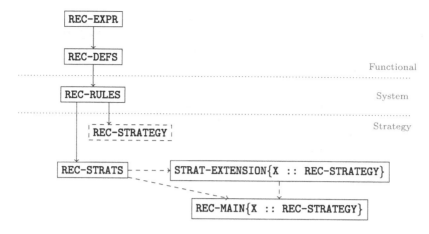

Fig. 3. Module structure for the REC language specification

strategy substitution, as we will see. Rule `cond` resolves a conditional when its condition expression has already been reduced to an integer. In any other case, integer expressions are reduced equationally, since the REC expressions sort `RecExpr` has been defined as an extension of the built-in sort `Int`. REC programs are executed following a `reduce` strategy that receives a list of function definitions as an argument. It is parameterized by a strategy `st` that is intended to expand function calls, and which we will later instantiate with `byvalue` and `byname` alternatives.

```
smod REC-MAIN{X :: REC-STRATEGY} is
  strat reduce : List{FunctionDef} @ RecExpr .
  var FL : List{FunctionDef} .
  sd reduce(FL) := (cond or-else st(FL)) ! .
endsm
```

According to the `reduce` definition, conditionals and calls are reduced as long as possible, but conditionals are reduced first. This is convenient, since function calls may appear anywhere inside the integer expression, and a simple recursive example like the factorial

```
eq factorial = 'f('n) := if 'n then 1
                         else 'n * 'f('n-1) .
```

shows that expanding calls anywhere is problematic. In effect, the precedence of `cond` avoids the non-terminating reduction

```
'f(0) →st if 0 then 1 else 0 * 'f(-1)
     →st if 0 then 1 else 0 * (if -1 then 0 else 'f(-2)) ...
```

Still, this is not enough when evaluating terms like `'f('f(0))`. So, in general, we must ensure not to reduce conditional branches until the condition is solved, no matter if calling by value or by name. To make strategies aware of these

precautions while saving code, we will take advantage of strategy parameterization too: we define an additional parameterized module STRAT-EXTENSION that
extends a strategy facing function calls st to a strategy xst that applies the
reduction step to any program term, but reducing conditions first.

```
smod STRAT-EXTENSION{X :: REC-STRATEGY} is
  strat xst : List{FunctionDef} @ RecExpr .
  vars E F G : RecExpr .
  var  FL    : List{FunctionDef} .

  sd xst(FL) := st(FL)
   | matchrew E + F by E using xst(FL)
       or−else matchrew E + F by F using xst(FL)
   | matchrew E * F by E using xst(FL)
       or−else matchrew E * F by F using xst(FL)
   | (matchrew E - F by E using xst(FL))
       or−else matchrew E - F by F using xst(FL)
   | matchrew if E then F else G by E using xst(FL) .
endsm
```

Now, the strategy extension is a reusable component that can be used to
define the alternative strategies succinctly, avoiding boilerplate code. First, we
instantiate STRAT-EXTENSION with views for byname and byvalue, defined in
REC-STRATS, to obtain the extended strategies. Then, we instantiate REC-MAIN
with new views from REC-STRATEGY to the instantiated modules, mapping st
to the extended strategies. On the contrary, the strategy free applies reduction
carelessly and anywhere, so it instantiates REC-MAIN directly.

```
sd free(FL)    := apply[Defs <- FL] .
sd byname(FL)  := top(apply[Defs <- FL]) .
sd byvalue(FL) := (matchrew E, NeArgs
                     by E using byvalue(FL))
             or−else matchrew E, NeArgs
                     by NeArgs using byvalue(FL)
   | (matchrew Q(Args) by Args using byvalue(FL))
     or−else top(apply[Defs <- FL]) .
```

The FL parameter must be filled with the program function definitions. For
example, with the Ackermann function defined below we execute

```
srew 1 + 'A(2, 3) using reduce(ackermann) .
```

and obtain 10.

```
eq ackermann = 'A('m, 'n) := if 'm then 'n + 1 else
          (if 'n then 'A('m - 1, 1)
                else 'A('m - 1, 'A('m, 'n - 1))) .

eq nameonly = ('f('x) := 'f('x) + 1) ('g('x) := 7) .
```

The differences between call by value and call by name are appreciated with the `nameonly` example, since $g(f(0))$ will be evaluated to 7 by name while it will never finish by value.

7 Conclusions

Rewriting strategies are a useful tool in the description of concurrent and logical systems, in accordance with the *separation of concerns* principle. A stratified specification of rules and its global control allows discharging the functional and rule levels of improper complexity, and makes the specified systems more configurable and adaptable. On the other hand, parameterized modules are a basic feature for building complex systems, reusing abstract specifications, and switching between alternative components. Such specifications can be compared in their multiple instances or analyzed parametrically.

The Maude strategy language implementation is now complete, including parameterized strategy modules. In this paper we have seen some examples of parameterized specification with strategies related to algorithms and programming languages. In the future, the combination of strategies and parameterization can be used as a fundamental approach to specify more complex and interesting systems. Also, more elaborated analyses can be done on these, including model checking, whose strategy-aware implementation is currently under development.

References

1. Andrei, O., Lucanu, D.: Strategy-based proof calculus for membrane systems. In: Roşu, G. (ed.) Proceedings of the Seventh International Workshop on Rewriting Logic and its Applications, WRLA 2008, Budapest, Hungary, 29–30 March 2008. ENTCS, vol. 238, no. 3, pp. 23–43. Elsevier (2009). https://doi.org/10.1016/j.entcs.2009.05.011
2. Borovanský, P., Kirchner, C., Kirchner, H., Ringeissen, C.: Rewriting with strategies in ELAN: a functional semantics. Int. J. Found. Comput. Sci. **12**(1), 69–95 (2001). https://doi.org/10.1142/S0129054101000412
3. Bouhoula, A., Jouannaud, J.P., Meseguer, J.: Specification and proof in membership equational logic. Theor. Comput. Sci. **236**(1), 35–132 (2000). https://doi.org/10.1016/S0304-3975(99)00206-6
4. Braga, C., Verdejo, A.: Modular structural operational semantics with strategies. In: van Glabbeek, R., Mosses, P.D. (eds.) Proceedings of the Third Workshop on Structural Operational Semantics, SOS 2006, Bonn, Germany, 26 August 2006. ENTCS, vol. 175, no. 1, pp. 3–17. Elsevier (2007). https://doi.org/10.1016/j.entcs.2006.10.024
5. Bravenboer, M., Kalleberg, K.T., Vermaas, R., Visser, E.: Stratego/XT 0.17. a language and toolset for program transformation. Sci. Comput. Program. **72**(1–2), 52–70 (2008). https://doi.org/10.1016/j.scico.2007.11.003
6. Clavel, M., et al.: All About Maude - A High-Performance Logical Framework. LNCS, vol. 4350. Springer, Heidelberg (2007). https://doi.org/10.1007/978-3-540-71999-1

7. Clavel, M., Durán, F., Eker, S., Lincoln, P., Martí-Oliet, N., Meseguer, J., Talcott, C.: Maude Manual (v2.7.1), July 2016. http://maude.cs.uiuc.edu/
8. Eker, S., Martí-Oliet, N., Meseguer, J., Verdejo, A.: Deduction, strategies, and rewriting. In: Archer, M., de la Tour, T.B., Muñoz, C. (eds.) Proceedings of the 6th International Workshop on Strategies in Automated Deduction, STRATEGIES 2006, Seattle, WA, USA, 16 August 2006. ENTCS, vol. 174, no. 11, pp. 3–25. Elsevier (2007). https://doi.org/10.1016/j.entcs.2006.03.017
9. Hidalgo-Herrero, M., Verdejo, A., Ortega-Mallén, Y.: Using Maude and its strategies for defining a framework for analyzing Eden semantics. In: Antoy, S. (ed.) Proceedings of the Sixth International Workshop on Reduction Strategies in Rewriting and Programming, WRS 2006, Seattle, WA, USA, 11 August 2006. ENTCS, vol. 174, no. 10, pp. 119–137. Elsevier (2007). https://doi.org/10.1016/j.entcs.2007.02.051
10. Martí-Oliet, N., Meseguer, J.: Rewriting logic as a logical and semantic framework. In: Gabbay, D.M., Guenthner, F. (eds.) Handbook of Philosophical Logic. HALO, vol. 9, pp. 1–87. Springer, Netherlands (2002). https://doi.org/10.1007/978-94-017-0464-9_1
11. Martí-Oliet, N., Meseguer, J., Verdejo, A.: Towards a strategy language for Maude. In: Martí-Oliet, N. (ed.) Proceedings of the Fifth International Workshop on Rewriting Logic and its Applications, WRLA 2004, Barcelona, Spain, 27 March–4 April 2004. ENTCS, vol. 117, pp. 417–441. Elsevier (2004). https://doi.org/10.1016/j.entcs.2004.06.020
12. Martí-Oliet, N., Palomino, M., Verdejo, A.: Strategies and simulations in a semantic framework. J. Algorithms **62**(3), 95–116 (2007). https://doi.org/10.1016/j.jalgor.2007.04.002
13. Meseguer, J.: Conditional rewriting logic as a unified model of concurrency. Theor. Comput. Sci. **96**(1), 73–155 (1992). https://doi.org/10.1016/0304-3975(92)90182-F
14. Murty, K.G.: Linear Programming. Wiley, New York (1983)
15. Rubio, R., Martí-Oliet, N., Pita, I., Verdejo, A.: Strategy language for Maude web page. http://maude.sip.ucm.es/strategies
16. Verdejo, A., Martí-Oliet, N.: Basic completion strategies as another application of the Maude strategy language. In: Escobar, S. (ed.) Proceedings 10th International Workshop on Reduction Strategies in Rewriting and Programming, WRS 2011, Novi Sad, Serbia, 29 May 2011. EPTCS, vol. 82, pp. 17–36 (2011). https://doi.org/10.4204/EPTCS.82.2
17. Winskel, G.: The Formal Semantics of Programming Languages: Foundations of Computing. The MIT Press, Cambridge (1993)

Contributed Papers

An Algebraic Theory for Data Linkage

Liang-Ting Chen, Markus Roggenbach$^{(\boxtimes)}$, and John V. Tucker

Department of Computer Science, Swansea University, Swansea, UK
{liang-ting.chen,m.roggenbach,j.v.tucker}@swansea.ac.uk

Abstract. There are countless sources of data available to governments, companies, and citizens, which can be combined for good or evil. We analyse the concepts of combining data from common sources and linking data from different sources. We model the data and its information content to be found in a single source by an ordered partial monoid, and the transfer of information between sources by different types of morphisms. To capture the linkage between a family of sources, we use a form of Grothendieck construction to create an ordered partial monoid that brings together the global data of the family in a single structure. We apply our approach to database theory and axiomatic structures in approximate reasoning. Thus, ordered partial monoids provide a foundation for the algebraic study for information gathering in its most primitive form.

1 Introduction

There are countless public and private sources of data that can be linked and analysed for all sorts of reasons, and with all sorts of consequences. The extraordinary variety of what may be considered data—i.e., data that is informative in some way—is a challenge to attempts to discover general principles and techniques for understanding linkage. Motivated by movements for data sharing we try to uncover general structures common to disparate situations.

1.1 Motivation: Exploiting Open Datasets

The vast stores of data built up by governments, agencies, institutions and companies in the course of their operations hold information of value in diverse and unexpected situations. Some governments have launched initiatives to encourage bodies to share their data with other organizations and the public. The released open data is intended to improve transparency, allowing accountability and engagement with decision making. A systematic review is [2].

For example, in the UK, there are several national and local registers and a plethora of statistical data that are now widely shared. A simple example of the commercial use of open datasets are web services for selling and letting properties such as Zoopla. In addition to traditional information about a property, official financial data about local house sales and crime statistics are provided.

This research was supported by the EPSRC project *Data Release—Trust, Identity, Privacy and Security (EP/N028139/1 and EP/N027825/1)*.

© IFIP International Federation for Information Processing 2019
Published by Springer Nature Switzerland AG 2019
J. L. Fiadeiro and I. Ţuţu (Eds.): WADT 2018, LNCS 11563, pp. 47–66, 2019.
https://doi.org/10.1007/978-3-030-23220-7_3

The UK's Open Data Initiative demonstrates the ambition to publish internal government data as open datasets. There are many patterns of data sharing, of which three are particularly important: *(i)* making data public—data release into the wild; *(ii)* data sharing by contract with a data analysis organization; and *(iii)* data sharing with delegation to a new data controller for further onward sharing. However, data custodians have a legal duty, and a social duty of care, to ensure that privacy is not breached by the release of open data sets.

The technical question arises: What information is revealed by, or can be inferred from, the data? Naturally, prior to its release, a data set can be filtered and anonymised but *(i)* anonymization is difficult and often flawed; and *(ii)* data from various other sources can be combined with a given data set to reveal much more. There are many data sources to call upon, and many unknown unintended consequences in making data publicly available.

An early example is Sweeney's finding [23] that 97% of voters in Cambridge, Massachusetts, USA, can be uniquely identified by birth dates and postcodes; these can be further linked with a hospital discharge database to discover individuals' medical history—e.g., of the governor of Massachusetts at that time [24].

Lately, Narayanan and Shmatikov [17] devised an algorithm exploiting sparsity to combine datasets. As a case study they analysed the Netflix prize dataset and found '84% of (Netflix) subscribers present in the dataset can be uniquely identified if the adversary knows six out of eight movies outside the top 500' that the subscriber rated. Such source of film ratings may come from social engineering or the Internet Movie Database (IMDb). In response to these privacy concerns, Netflix decided to withdraw the datasets. Unfortunately, they are still available to download using BitTorrent or https://archive.org.

1.2   Algebraic Models of Combination and Linkage

In this paper we take a fresh look at the challenge of combining data sets and linking pieces of data. Our aim is to develop abstract tools to analyse formally the general nature of data sharing, and technical issues of policy specification and compliance. To this end, we seek algebras of data representations, whose operations combine two or more pieces of data from the same source to form data with higher information content. These data representation algebras are to be defined axiomatically. In its simplest form—that presented here—such an algebra is an ordered structure with a partial commutative binary operation $\oplus$ and an identity element 0, namely, an *ordered partial commutative monoid*. The operation $\oplus$ *combines* data from the same source. Morphisms between such monoids model the transfer of data between sources—a process we call *linkage*. We create an ordered partial commutative monoid that brings together all the data from a family of sources using a simplified Grothendieck construction. We show that our monoid theory of linkage applies to databases and approximate reasoning.

A complete set of proofs can be found at arXiv:1810.08096.

2 Algebras for Data Combination

2.1 Information Ordering

Data itself is often hierarchical or due to uncertainty becomes so. In this paper, when we reason about data, we implicitly work on a set with an ordering that measures specificity, knowledge, or informativeness. Ideas of information ordering are nothing new, as they appear to be well-known to different communities working on uncertainty reasoning [11, Section 2.7], multi-valued logic [3], program semantics [20], formal concept analysis [6, Chapter 3], and (implicitly) anonymization techniques [16, 26], to name but a few.

Definition 2.1. *Given a set X, an* information order $\preceq$ *on X is a preorder, i.e. (i) $x \preceq x$ and (ii) $x \preceq y \preceq z$ implies $x \preceq z$. An* information space *is merely a preordered set $(X, \preceq)$.*

To illustrate the use of preordered sets in the context of data release and privacy, we discuss in some detail the use of postcodes to identify locations.

Example 2.2. The taxonomic hierarchy of British postal codes mostly consists of 6 to 8 alphanumeric characters in a format detailed below. Each postcode is divided into the outward code and the inward code by a single space '␣'. Each component is formed of two further parts and each part covers a smaller area. For example, SA2␣8PP is the full postcode of the Singleton Campus of Swansea University and it is understood as follows:

SA	2	8	PP
Postcode Area	Postcode District	Postcode Sector	Postcode Unit
Outward Code		Inward Code	
Postcode			

Let the set of all full postcodes be denoted by $\mathbf{Post}_{\mathrm{UK}}$.

For simplicity, a *partial* postcode refers to a code, where less significant parts might be missing, ordered by prefix order including the empty string 'ϵ' as a special postcode indicating everywhere. For example, SA stands for Swansea and SA2 for a district in Swansea, and we have partial postcodes

$$\epsilon \preceq \text{SA} \preceq \text{SA2} \preceq \text{SA2}␣\text{8} \preceq \text{SA2}␣\text{8PP}$$

note that ???␣8PP is not a partial postcode. Let us denote the set of all partial postcodes by $\mathbf{PPost}_{\mathrm{UK}}$.

Each full postcode is incomparable with another, as each of them stands for a disjoint set of postal addresses. On the contrary, the set of partial postcodes possesses the prefix order $\preceq$ for the hierarchy. Every partial postcode P can be realised as a set of full postcodes by

$$[\![P]\!] := \{\, p \in \mathbf{Post}_{\mathrm{UK}} \mid P \text{ is a prefix of } p \,\}.$$

For instance, an empty string ϵ is realised by $\mathbf{Post}_{\mathrm{UK}}$, as it contains no information apart from being a postcode. Each full postcode P in $\mathbf{Post}_{\mathrm{UK}}$ is realised by the singleton set $\{P\}$. Note that $[\![P]\!]$'s are always non-empty.   □

The reader may find our definition of information space intriguing. For example, why is this only a preordered set instead of a partially ordered set? Indeed, as we can observe from the above example, there are two possible representations of partial knowledge for postcode:

(i) $\mathbb{P}^+(\mathbf{Post}_{UK})$—the non-empty powerset of full postcodes, or
(ii) $\mathbf{PPost}_{UK}$—the set of partial postcodes determined by its format.

The first (i) can be called the *possible world representation* [11, Section 2.1]. It is well-understood in the community of knowledge representation. It is more expressive and general than (ii). Every taxonomic hierarchy of a set of entities can be realised by a possible world interpretation, as each classification level defines a partition of all the entities. The reverse inclusion order '$\supseteq$' reflects the information order of taxonomic hierarchy, i.e. P is of higher hierarchy than Q only if $[\![P]\!] \subseteq [\![Q]\!]$ and '$\supseteq$' is surely a partial order. We return to this general points in Sect. 3.2.

On the other hand, the second kind of representations is often what we have in the first place or what we would like to use in data release. The information order $\preceq$ requires some effort to decide, but generally it is clear from the context. However, we may have two different representations for the very same set of entities. If a weight is attached to the data in question, then the second representation is more manageable than the first:

Example 2.3. Consider a version due to a privacy concern.[1] Both kinds of representations build a frequency distribution, and some probabilities can be calculated based on the information order over postcodes, say, $\Pr[\text{SA2} \preceq X]$.

User ID	Postcode
1	SA2␣8PP
2	SA2␣8PW
3	SA1␣3LP
4	SA2␣8QF

(a) Original dataset

User ID	Postcode
*	SA2␣8
*	SA2␣8
*	SA1␣3
*	SA2␣8

(b) Sanitised dataset

Fig. 1. Datasets containing postal information

In Kolmogorov's probability theory, the first step is to find out a sample space Ω and a σ-algebra Σ, and the typical choice is $\Omega = \mathbf{Post}_{UK}$ and $\Sigma = \mathbb{P}(\mathbf{Post}_{UK})$. The probability measure for the original dataset (Fig. 1a) is clear. But, it is tricky to define faithfully a probability measure for the sanitised dataset (Fig. 1b), since it requires to assign a probability to each full postcode with the prefix SA1␣3. The convention is to apply the principle of indifference—each postcode

---

[1] Some privacy protection models are achieved by generalisation and suppression of cell values, see [24] for example.

of $[\![SA1\sqcup 3]\!]$ has the same probability $1/k$ where k is the possibly *unknown* number of postcodes in $[\![SA1\sqcup 3]\!]$. Even if k is known, the presumed probability $1/k$ is an over-approximation of the given information.

On the other hand, no matter what probability is assigned to subsets of full postcodes, the probability of $\Pr[SA2 \preceq X]$ is always the sum

$$\sum_{SA2 \preceq Q} \Pr[X = Q] = 3/4$$

without knowing any further information. The expressiveness is limited if we confine ourselves to probabilities of partial postcodes only, since partial postcodes are not closed under Boolean connectives contrary to the subset representation. Yet this limitation enables us to represent the *exact* information of data.   □

Another problem of the possible world representation arises if the information order is by nature *not* anti-symmetric. It is intuitive to see that Fig. 1a is more informative than Fig. 1b. There are at least three applicable orderings over subsets P, Q of elements in an information space X, which are

$$P \preceq^{\flat} Q \iff \forall x \in P. \exists y \in Q. x \preceq y$$
$$P \preceq^{\sharp} Q \iff \forall y \in Q. \exists x \in P. x \preceq y$$
$$P \preceq^{\natural} Q \iff P \preceq^{\flat} Q \wedge P \preceq^{\sharp} Q$$

The ordering can model a number of processes or situations. $P \preceq^{\flat} Q$ models that everything in P has a more informative datum in Q. So Q is an enrichment of P. Conversely, $P \preceq^{\sharp} Q$ models that everything in Q has a less informative datum in P, so P is an adulteration of Q.

Each of the orderings plays a role in various contexts, such as non-deterministic computation [9] and relative likelihood [11, Section 2.7]. These orderings are preorders but not anti-symmetric in general.

Example 2.4. Ignoring user ID and repetitions, we have two sets representing the information in Fig. 1:

$$P_1 := \{SA2\sqcup 8PP, SA2\sqcup 8PW, SA1\sqcup 3LP, SA2\sqcup 8QF\}$$
$$P_2 := \{SA2\sqcup 8, SA1\sqcup 3\}$$

The set P_1 is more informative than P_2 with respect to $\preceq^{\flat}$, $\preceq^{\sharp}$, and $\preceq^{\natural}$.   □

Even further, the standard equality '$=$' on the data in X is irrelevant from the information-theoretic perspective, as we only care about the information content of data. For example, any subset P of an information space $(X, \preceq)$ is indistinguishable from but fails to be equal to its *convex hull*[2] $\mathcal{K}(P) := \{a \in X \mid \exists x, y \in P. x \preceq a \preceq y\}$, i.e.

$$P \preceq^{\natural} \mathcal{K}(P) \preceq^{\natural} P \quad \text{but generally} \quad P \neq \mathcal{K}(P).$$

---

[2] See, e.g., [6, p. 63].

So, we introduce:

Definition 2.5. *Given an information order $\preceq$ on a set X, define an equivalence relation by*

$$x \cong y \iff x \preceq y \text{ and } y \preceq x$$

and x is said to be equivalent *to y. Each element in the same equivalence class is of the same* information content.

From a mathematical viewpoint, each element x is a representative of the information class $[x]$. Every representative of the same class embodies the same amount of information with respect to the information order $\preceq$. Computing and deciding the information class could be costly and conceptually gain little, so it is easier to work and present our latter formulations with representatives directly.

Remark 2.6. From this, we can argue further that '$\cong$' is the right notion of equality where the strict equality '$=$' plays no role at all in an ordered setting. Indeed, the convention is to consider the quotient $(X/\cong, \preceq/\cong)$ as the poset of information and $[x] = [y]$ is equivalent to $x \cong y$, but this convention makes notations rather heavy.

So the point is that only the preorder $\preceq$ for information matters and it fails to be a partial order in general.

2.2   Ordered Partial Commutative Monoids

To combine and link data across various domains yields data that is presumably more informative than the separate pieces of information alone. In this section, we introduce an algebraic operation over an information space for combining data. Central to our investigation is the concept of ordered partial commutative monoids. Whilst monoids of many kinds, e.g., ordered commutative monoids [8] and partial commutative monoids [7,27], have been discovered and developed in many application areas, surprisingly we have not found a monoid combining both—ordering and partiality. A possible exception we found is monoids viewed as a degenerated class of partial monoidal categories defined in [5].

Definition 2.7. *An* ordered partial commutative monoid $(M, \preceq, \oplus, 0)$ *consists of* (i) *a preordered set* $(M, \preceq)$, (ii) *a constant* $0 \in M$, *and* (iii) *a partial binary operation* $\oplus: M \times M \rightharpoonup M$, *i.e. $x \oplus y$ may not be defined. For brevity, '$x \perp y$' stands for '$x \oplus y$' is defined. Further, $(M, \preceq, \oplus, 0)$ satisfies the properties below.*

(OPCM1) $0 \oplus x \cong x$.
(OPCM2) $y \perp x$ and $x \oplus y \cong y \oplus x$ if $x \perp y$.
(OPCM3) $x \perp y$, $(x \oplus y) \perp z$, and $x \oplus (y \oplus z) \cong (x \oplus y) \oplus z$ if $y \perp z$ and $x \perp (y \oplus z)$.
(OPCM4) $x_1 \oplus y \preceq x_2 \oplus y$ if $x_i \perp y$ for $i = 1, 2$ and $x_1 \preceq x_2$.

An ordered partial commutative monoid is written as OPCM *for short. An (unordered)* partial commutative monoid $(M, \oplus, 0)$, PCM *for short, is an OPCM with the discrete ordering $x \preceq y \iff x = y$. An ordered commutative monoid is an OPCM with the binary operation $\oplus$ being total.*

The element $x \oplus y$ denotes data that represents a combination of the information of x and y. The constant 0 stands for some vacuous information so that $x \oplus 0$ is always defined and equivalent to x. Partiality enables us to encapsulate consistency or other premises. That is, x may contradict y so that no viable information can be derived; see Example 2.13.

Referring to Remark 2.6, the following fact shows that the use of '$\cong$' is equivalent to the standard equality '$=$' in the partially ordered quotient:

Proposition 2.8. *Let $(M, \preceq, \oplus, 0)$ be an OPCM. Then,*

(i) *the relation defined by $[x] \leq [y] \iff x \preceq y$ on the quotient set $M/\cong$ is a partial order and $[x] = [y] \iff x \cong y$;*

(ii) *$(M/\cong, \leq, [\oplus], [0])$ with $[x]\,[\oplus]\,[y]$ defined as $[x \oplus y]$ is an OPCM.*

The algebraic structure of a PCM also gives rise to a natural ordering between information purely determined by the combination $\oplus$.

Definition 2.9. *The* algebraic ordering *on an OPCM is defined by*

$$x \sqsubseteq y \iff \exists z.\, x \oplus z \cong y.$$

Proposition 2.10. *Every PCM $(M, \oplus, 0)$ with algebraic ordering $\sqsubseteq$ is an*

(i) *OPCM which satisfies*

(ii) *$0 \sqsubseteq x$, and that*

(iii) *if $(x, y) \sqsubseteq (x', y')$, $x' \perp y'$, $x \perp x$, then $x \oplus y \sqsubseteq x' \oplus y'$.*

The algebraic ordering of an OPCM $(M, \preceq, \oplus, 0)$ is compatible with the information ordering if the identity 0 is the $\preceq$-least informative element:

Proposition 2.11. *Let $(M, \preceq, \oplus, 0)$ be an OPCM such that $0 \preceq x$. Then,*

(i) *$x \sqsubseteq y \implies x \preceq y$;*

(ii) *$x, y \preceq x \oplus y$ whenever $x \perp y$.*

Remark 2.12. The implication (i) in Proposition 2.11 along with (ii) in Proposition 2.10 suggests the hypothesis $0 \preceq x$ is decisive, otherwise $\oplus$ may not represent 'combination of information' but something else (cf. the semantics of Belnap's 4-valued logic [1]). However, the property that $0 \preceq x$ for all $x \in M$ is not needed for our technical results.

Example 2.13. Consider the collection of all non-empty subsets of full postcodes $\mathbb{P}^+(\mathbf{Post}_{UK})$ equipped with the reverse inclusion order $P_1 \preceq P_2$ iff $P_2 \subseteq P_1$. The intersection $\cap$ of subsets as a combination operation $\oplus$, is a partial operation, since $P_1 \cap P_2$ might be empty and $\notin \mathbb{P}^+(\mathbf{Post}_{UK})$. Clearly, intersection is monotone with respect to the reverse inclusion order. Similarly, the set of partial postcodes equipped with the prefix ordering $\preceq$ discussed in Example 2.2 has a simple OPCM structure: $x \oplus y$ is defined as $\max\{x, y\}$.

2.3   Homomorphisms

The internal structure of an OPCM models data and information of a single source. So the external interaction between OPCMs models a comparison, combination, interpretation, or linkage between sources. Various kinds of structure preserving maps between OPCMs arise naturally, e.g., order-preserving maps, $\oplus$-preserving maps, or both. We begin with the familiar one.

Definition 2.14. *A homomorphism $M \xrightarrow{f} N$ of OPCMs is a function satisfying*

(HOM1) $x \preceq_M y \implies fx \preceq_N fy$
(HOM2) $f(0_M) \cong 0_N$
(HOM3) $x \perp y \implies f(x \oplus_M y) \cong fx \oplus_N fy$

The collection of OPCMs with their homomorphisms forms a category $\mathbf{PCM}_\preceq$.

An 'interpretation' of information in a different domain of discourse or context, is a typical example of a homomorphism. The *trivial map* $f \colon M \to N$ defined by $f(x) = 0$ is a homomorphism that destroys all the information in M. The set of partial postcodes *per se* is merely a set of strings following a specific format, so it makes little sense to say how rare a postcode P is among other postcodes; it becomes meaningful when it refers to certain geographic area, population, or other associated information.

Example 2.15. Let $\mathbf{Pop}_{UK}$ denote the UK population. Assume that *(i)* everyone (of interest) is registered with exactly one postcode for their main residence, and *(ii)* each postcode is associated with someone. The assumption amounts to a surjective function $f \colon \mathbf{Pop}_{UK} \to \mathbf{Post}_{UK}$.

Consider the possible world representation for $\mathbf{Pop}_{UK}$. Each set S of postcodes then can be interpreted as the set $[\![S]\!] := f^{-1}(S) \subseteq \mathbf{Pop}_{UK}$ of population officially registered in the area specified by P. The mapping $[\![-]\!] \colon \mathbb{P}^+\mathbf{Post}_{UK} \to \mathbb{P}^+\mathbf{Pop}_{UK}$ is clearly homomorphic w.r.t. the OPCM discussed in Example 2.13, since

(i)   it is monotone, as $[\![S_1]\!] \supseteq [\![S_2]\!]$ if $S_1 \supseteq S_2$;
(ii) it preserves the identity, as $f^{-1}(\mathbf{Post}_{UK}) = \mathbf{Pop}_{UK}$;
(iii) and moreover $[\![S_1 \cap S_2]\!] = [\![S_1]\!] \cap [\![S_2]\!]$ as f^{-1} preserves intersection.

$\square$

Besides concrete homomorphisms, one has the following standard notions: *isomorphism, monomorphism, embedding, epimorphism*, and so on, following the doctrine of category theory. Among them, the product of two OPCMs can be understood as pairs of independent sources of information.

Definition 2.16. *The* product monoid $M_1 \times M_2$ *of* $M_i = (M_i, \preceq_i, \oplus_i, 0_i)$ *for* $i = 1, 2$ *is the cartesian product equipped with*

(i) the pointwise ordering $(x_1, x_2) \preceq (y_1, y_2) \iff x_1 \preceq_1 y_1 \wedge x_2 \preceq_2 y_2$,
(ii) $0 := (0_1, 0_2)$, and
(iii) $(x_1, x_2) \oplus (y_1, y_2) := (x_1 \oplus_1 y_1, x_2 \oplus_2 y_2)$ if $x_1 \perp y_1$ and $x_2 \perp y_2$.

The universal property for product shows that $M_1 \times M_2$ consists of pairs of independent pieces of information from M_1 and M_2:

Proposition 2.17. *For any OPCM N and any pair of homomorphisms $f_i \colon N \to M_i$ for $i = 1, 2$, there exists a unique homomorphism $h \colon N \to M_1 \times M_2$ such that $\pi_i \circ h = f_i$, where π_i is the i-th projection homomorphism.*

Other useful notions are embedding and isomorphism.

Definition 2.18. *A homomorphism $e \colon M \rightarrowtail N$ is an* order-embedding *if it not only preserves but also reflects the ordering: $e(x) \preceq e(y) \iff x \preceq y$. An* isomorphism *is a bijective order-embedding.*

3   Further Examples

3.1   Flat Algebras

The most simple OPCM is perhaps a set X equipped with an additional element $\bot$ denoting *unknown* and $x \leq y$ iff $x = \bot$ or $x = y$ with $x \oplus y :=$ (the join of x and y). In spite of its simplicity, it has been elaborated further in relational database theory [4, Chapter 8].

3.2   Possibilities over a Set

We have used a possible world representation discussing postcodes (Sect. 2.2). In this section, we study its general properties. As the reader may have observed from our examples about non-empty subsets of full postcodes, the argument is completely generic and can be applied to any non-empty set X. In short, we have the following generalisation of Example 2.13:

Proposition 3.1. *For any non-empty set X, the non-empty powerset $\mathbb{P}^+ X$ with the reverse inclusion and intersection forms an OPCM $(\mathbb{P}^+ X, \supseteq, \cap, X)$.*

In general, the set X represents some elementary form of atomic information such as *codes*, *labels*, *tags* or *facts* from which is made. The data in the source is a non-empty subset S of X containing a set of possible choices from X.

3.3   Possibilities over an OPCM

It is often the case that only pieces of information shared by a group of people is known instead of each individual's. As each piece of information in our algebraic theory is an element of some OPCM, we proceed with non-empty subsets of an OPCM which is in turn another OPCM.

The starting point is the observation that a mere intersection of two subsets of an OPCM $(M, \preceq, \oplus, 0)$ would exclude combinable but not exactly the same information. Note that we can reformulate intersection in a rather silly way as

$$P \cap Q = \{\, x \mid x \in P, y \in Q, x = y \,\}$$

We can utilise '$\oplus$' and define a combination of two subsets of OPCM by

$$P \oplus Q := \{\, x \oplus y \mid x \in P, y \in Q, x \perp y \,\}$$

consisting of refined information only. How about the information order between subsets? It turns out that only one of the orderings for powersets introduced in Sect. 2.1,

$$P \preceq^\sharp Q \iff \forall y \in Q.\, \exists x \in P.\, x \preceq y$$

is a sensible preorder with respect to the definition of $P \oplus Q$.

Theorem 3.2. *Let $(M, \preceq, \oplus, 0)$ be an OPCM such that M is $\oplus$-downward closed, i.e. if $x \preceq x'$ and $x' \perp y$ then $x \perp y$. For non-empty subsets P and Q,*

$$P \oplus Q := \{\, x \oplus y \mid x \in P, y \in Q, x \perp y \,\}.$$

Then,

(i) $\mathbb{P}^+ M = (\mathbb{P}^+ M, \preceq^\sharp, \oplus, \{0\})$ is also an OPCM;
(ii) $\{0\} \preceq^\sharp P$ for any P if $0 \preceq x$ for any $x \in M$.

4   Data Linkage

A domain of discourse can have a number of data sources so that the same piece of information can be understood in various contexts differently. How do we know that the original information remains intact?

4.1   Change of Domain

A homomorphism $f\colon M \to N$ qualifies as a mapping changing domains from M to N but it can lose data, e.g. the trivial map $f(x) = 0$ destroys all data. One way to avoid this problem is to use homomorphisms with a restriction map $f^*\colon N \to M$ satisfying a 'preservation condition' $x \preceq f^* f(x)$ for $x \in M$.

Definition 4.1. *A homomorphism $f\colon M \to N$ is a change of domain if f is a lower adjoint,[3] i.e. there exists an order-preserving map $f^*\colon N \to M$ such that*

$$f x \preceq_N y \iff x \preceq_M f^* y$$

Our formal definition requires that an extension f with its restriction f^* forms a *Galois connection* [6].

Every Galois connection (f, f^*) gives rise to a *closure operator*—a monotone function $f^* \circ f$ satisfying *(i)* $x \preceq f^* f(x)$ and *(ii)* $f^* f(f^* f x) \preceq f^* f x$. Intuitively, the information represented by $f^* f(x)$ is at least as informative as x.

---

[3] Every adjoint is unique up to order isomorphism—that is, if g is an upper adjoint of f then $f^* y \cong g y$ for any y, so we can say that a homomorphism f is a change of domain without referring to f^*.

The class of changes of domain is closed under composition. It is not hard to see that the composite $k \circ f$ of two lower adjoints is again a lower adjoint, because $k \circ f$ is homomorphic and by definition

$$k(fx) \preceq z \iff fx \preceq k^* z \iff x \preceq f^* k^* z.$$

Trivially, an identity function id is itself a change of domain. Therefore, the class of OPCMs and changes of domain forms a subcategory of $\mathbf{PCM}_{\preceq}$.

Example 4.2. The homomorphism $[\![-]\!]\colon \mathbb{P}^+\mathbf{Post}_{\mathrm{UK}} \to \mathbb{P}^+\mathbf{Pop}_{\mathrm{UK}}$ discussed in Example 2.15 is indeed a change of domain. The restriction from $\mathbb{P}^+\mathbf{Pop}_{\mathrm{UK}}$ to $\mathbb{P}^+\mathbf{Post}_{\mathrm{UK}}$ is given by mapping a set of population to the set of their registered postcodes. The existence of this restriction follows from the assumption that everyone of interest signs a register with a full postcode. Formally, the restriction is the forward-image function of the surjection $f\colon \mathbf{Pop}_{\mathrm{UK}} \to \mathbf{Post}_{\mathrm{UK}}$ given by our assumption, so

$$[\![S]\!] \preceq A \iff f^{-1}(S) \supseteq A \iff S \supseteq f[A] \iff S \preceq f[A]$$

for any non-empty $S \subseteq \mathbf{Post}_{\mathrm{UK}}$ and $A \subseteq \mathbf{Pop}_{\mathrm{UK}}$.

Given a change of domain $f\colon M \to N$, there are two different ways to combine $x \in M$ with $y \in N$. Their relationship can be stated as follows:

Proposition 4.3. *Given a change of domain $f\colon M \to N$, the following*

$$x \oplus f^* y \preceq f^*(fx \oplus y)$$

always holds for any $x \in M$ and $y \in N$.

Armed with these notions, we now formally define 'linkage' as follows.

Definition 4.4. *A linking passage $(f_i, g_i)_{i=1,2}$ of M_1 and M_2 is a commutative diagram of changes of domain up to equivalence:*

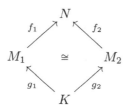

i.e. the equation $f_1 \circ g_1(k) \cong f_2 \circ g_2(k)$ for any $k \in K$. Given a linking passage as above, elements $x_i \in M_i$ can be linked as $\bigoplus_i f_i x_i$ in N.

In the context of information, the OPCM K above is some *common domain* of discourse between M_1 and M_2; N is some domain at least including M_1 and M_2.

Given a linking passage of M_1 and M_2, there are two ways transferring information from M_1 to M_2—one through the larger domain N and the other through their common domain K. The former route intuitively preserves more information than the other, and this intuition can be justified as follows.

Proposition 4.5. *Given a linking passage* $(f_i, g_i)_{i=1,2}$ *and for any* $x \in M_1$, *the inequation* $g_2(g_1^*(x)) \preceq f_2^*(f_1(x))$ *holds. Diagrammatically,*

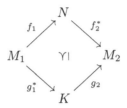

Example 4.6. Assume that $M_1 = \mathbb{P}^+(X \times Y)$ and $M_2 = \mathbb{P}^+(Y \times Z)$. Then,

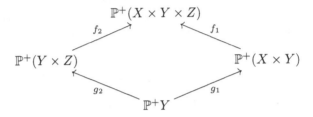

is a linking passage where f_1, f_2, g_1, g_2 are preimage functions of corresponding projections. Moreover, the subset $f_1(U) \cap f_2(V)$ is equal to

$$\{\, (x, y, z) \mid (x, y) \in U \wedge (y, z) \in V \,\}$$

for any non-empty $U \subseteq X \times Y$ and $V \subseteq Y \times Z$, which is the *natural join* in relational database theory. For a plausible example in practice, consider $U \subseteq \textbf{Pop}_{\text{UK}} \times \textbf{Addr}_{\text{UK}}$ a non-empty set of suspects with their hiding places and $V \subseteq \textbf{Addr}_{\text{UK}} \times \textbf{Pop}_{\text{UK}}$ a non-empty set of house addresses and their owners. The combined information $f_1(U) \cap f_2(V)$ may represent triplets of suspects, addresses, and house owners who possibly provide shelters to suspects.

Local Computation Scheme. In practice, each datum x_i about the attribute i is collected from various data sources M_i. To combine all x_i's, we can combine them in a common domain M and then restrict the combined information to a smaller domain N of interest, i.e.

$$g^* \left(\bigoplus_{i=1}^{n} f_i x_i \right)$$

represented symbolically. The computation is usually costly, however. One interesting observation stated as *the combination axiom* from [13] in a similar form is that the above information can be computed locally without the need of extending everything to M if inequalities in Propositions 4.3 and 4.5 are in fact equivalences for the involved changes of domains. This observation would be useful for developing an efficient computation algorithm, however, which is beyond the scope of this paper.

4.2   Possibilities over a Set

A surjective function $X \twoheadrightarrow Y$ gives rise to a change of domain from $\mathbb{P}^+Y$ to $\mathbb{P}^+X$. The surjectivity requirement is essential to ensure that a non-empty subset $S \subseteq Y$ is mapped to a non-empty subset $f^{-1}(S) \subseteq X$.

Proposition 4.7. *For any surjective function $f\colon X \twoheadrightarrow Y$, there is a Galois connection*

$$f^{-1}(V) \supseteq U \iff V \supseteq f[U]$$

where the preimage function f^{-1} is a homomorphism from $\mathbb{P}^+Y$ to $\mathbb{P}^+X$ and the forward-image function $f[-]\colon \mathbb{P}^+X \to \mathbb{P}^+Y$ is monotonic.

It is straightforward to see that the inequality of Proposition 4.3 is an equality for any change of domain given by a surjective function. That is,

$$f[f^{-1}(U) \cap V] = U \cap f(V)$$

for any U and V by simple calculations.

Proposition 4.8. *Suppose that there are $f_i\colon X_i \twoheadrightarrow Z$ and $g_i\colon Y \twoheadrightarrow X_i$ for $i = 1, 2$ with $g_1 \circ f_1 = g_2 \circ f_2$. Then, (g_i^{-1}, f_i^{-1}) is a linking passage, i.e.*

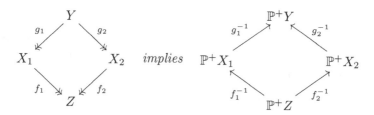

If a linking passage is created by functions $g_i\colon Y \to X_i$, then non-empty subsets $U_i \subseteq X_i$ can be linked as a subset of Y

$$U_1 \boxplus U_2 = g_1^{-1}(U_1) \cap g_2^{-1}(U_2).$$

Example 4.9. Let A be a set of *attributes* and for each $a \in A$ a set Φ_a of values for the attribute i. For example, i can be g for 'gender', p for 'British postcode', s for 'salary', etc., then Φ_g could be the two-element set $\{\sigma, \varphi\}$, $\Phi_p = \mathbf{Post}_{\mathrm{UK}}$ the set of all full British postcodes, and $\Phi_s = \mathbb{N}$ the set of natural numbers. Given any two sets $I, J \subseteq A$ of attributes, we have a commutative diagram

$$
\begin{array}{ccc}
\prod_{k \in I \cup J} \Phi_k & \xrightarrow{\quad g_1 \quad} & \prod_{i \in I} \Phi_i \\
{\scriptstyle g_2}\downarrow & & \downarrow{\scriptstyle f_1} \\
\prod_{j \in J} \Phi_j & \xrightarrow{\quad f_2 \quad} & \prod_{l \in I \cap J} \Phi_l
\end{array}
$$

where g_i and f_i are all projections.

5 Data Sources and Linkage

So far, an OPCM M is an abstract collection of data from a data source for a single domain of discourse that can be combined and compared. A model of data linkage requires a family of PCMs $(M_i, \preceq_i, \oplus_i, 0_i)$, for $i \in I$, and ways to move among various sources and domains. Further, the nature of sources and domains induces a structure to the index set I, typically an ordering $\preceq$, that reflects the relationship between sources and domains such as $i \preceq j$. With these components, we will model and illustrate data linkage using a form of Grothendieck construction for I-indexed OPCMs.

We will develop the theory in two steps and compare our construction with axiomatic frameworks in the community of approximate reasoning such as ordered valuation algebras [10] and information algebras [13,14].

5.1 Grothendieck Construction for Preordered Sets

Let I be a preordered set and P an I-indexed family of preordered sets P_i for $i \in I$ together with order-preserving functions $P_j^i \colon P_i \to P_j$ whenever $i \preceq j$ satisfying

(i) $P_i^i \cong id_{P_i} \colon P_i \to P_i$ is the identity function, and
(ii) $P_k^j \circ P_j^i \cong P_k^i \colon P_i \to P_k$

where $P_k^j \circ P_j^i \cong P_k^i$ means $P_k^j \circ P_j^i(x) \cong P_k^i(x)$ for every x and similarly for $P_i^i \cong id$. Note that P is a *pseudo-functor*. If the above equations hold strictly, then P is a (proper) *functor*.

Definition 5.1. *The* Grothendieck completion *of P consists of*

$$\int P := \{ (i,x) \mid x \in P_i \}$$

with a relation defined by

$$(i,x) \preceq (j,y) \iff i \preceq j \text{ and } P_j^i(x) \preceq y \text{ for } x \in P_i \text{ and } y \in P_j$$

The ordering appears natural in our context: P_j^i is typically a change of domain, and $P_j^i(x)$ is merely an extension of x and $(i,x) \preceq (j,y)$ if and only if j is a larger domain of discourse than i and the extended form of x is still less informative than y.

Proposition 5.2. *The following statements are true:*

(i) The above Grothendieck completion $\int P$ is a preordered set.
(ii) If $(I, \leq)$ and every $(P_i, \leq)$ is partially ordered, then so is $(\int P, \preceq)$.
(iii) The projection $p \colon \int P \to (I, \preceq)$ is functorial.
(iv) p is an opfibration. That is, for every $(i,x) \in \int P$, j with $i \preceq j$ there exists (j,y) such that $(i,x) \preceq (j,y)$ and moreover for any (k,z) with $(i,x) \preceq (k,z)$ and $j \preceq k$ it is also true that $(j,y) \preceq (k,z)$.

(v) If each P^i_j has a right adjoint, then p is an bifibration, i.e. $p^{\mathrm{op}} \colon (\int P, \succeq) \to (I, \succeq)$ is also an opfibration.

Remark 5.3. The construction presented here is a form of Grothendieck construction. The full construction works no only for preordered sets but also categories and beyond. See, e.g., [12], for details.

5.2 Grothendieck Construction for OPCMs

In this section, we extend the Grothendieck construction to OPCMs indexed by a $\vee$-semilattice $(L, \preceq)$, where L is partially ordered with a least element denoted by $\bot$ and for every pair (i, j) of elements there is a least upper bound $i \vee j$. Given a (pseudo-)functor from $(L, \leq)$ to $\mathbf{PCM}_{\preceq}$ we extend the local combination operations $\oplus_i$ for each $i \in L$ to a global combination operation $\boxplus$ for $\int M$.

To simplify our discussion, we confine ourselves to functors instead of pseudofunctors. Indeed, all of our discussion and examples in the remaining section do not require this generality.

Theorem 5.4. *Let $(L, \leq)$ be a bounded $\vee$-semilattice and $M \colon (L, \leq) \to \mathbf{PCM}_{\preceq}$ a functor. Then, the Grothendieck completion $(\int M, \preceq)$ can be equipped with an OPCM given by*

$$(i, x) \boxplus (j, y) := (k, M^i_k(x) \oplus M^j_k(y)) \quad and \quad 0 := (\bot, 0_{\bot})$$

where $k = i \vee j$ and $(i, x) \boxplus (j, y)$ is defined if $M^i_k(x) \oplus M^j_k(y)$ is defined.

The above construction is a slight modification of a form of Grothedieck construction for monoidal categories, see [22] for details.

5.3 Example: Natural Join for Relational Dataset

Before we show our general result of ordered valuation algebras, we proceed with our simplest example—the possibility representation. The linkage operation $\boxplus$ derived from Theorem 5.4 is the *natural join* in relational database theory [4].

First of all, we assume that there is a set $\mathfrak{A}$ of known attribute names and a set Φ_a of values for each attribute $a \in \mathfrak{A}$. For example, $\mathfrak{A}$ may consist of tags for UK postcode, personal information, medical conditions, and so on. By abuse of notation, we denote by Φ_A for $A \subseteq \mathfrak{A}$ the cartesian product $\Phi_A := \prod_{a \in A} \Phi_a$. Whenever $A \subseteq B$, we have projections $p_{B,A}$ from Φ_B to Φ_A which sends $(x_b)_{b \in B}$ to $(x_a)_{a \in A}$. A functor P from the powerset $\mathbb{P}(\mathfrak{A}, \subseteq)$ to $\mathbf{PCM}_{\preceq}$ is defined by

$$(A \subseteq \mathfrak{A}) \mapsto (\mathbb{P}^+ \Phi_A, \supseteq, \cap, \Phi_A) \quad and \quad (A \subseteq B) \mapsto \left(p^{-1}_{B,A} \colon \mathbb{P}^+ \Phi_A \to \mathbb{P}^+ \Phi_B \right).$$

In our interpretation, any set $S \in \mathbb{P}^+ \Phi_A$ is a set of possibilities where only one of them is true, so having more elements in S means less specific information. If $A \subseteq B$, then $p^{-1}_{B,A}(S)$ is merely the set S padded with all combinations, i.e. $S \times \prod_{b \in B-A} \Phi_b$. So, $p^{-1}_{B,A}(S)$ contains no information about attributes $B - A$.

Therefore the ordering on the Grothendieck completion $\int \Phi$

$$(A, S) \le (B, T) \iff A \subseteq B \text{ and } S \times \prod_{b \in B - A} \Phi_b \supseteq T$$

simply means that (A, S) is less informative than (B, T) if (B, T) contains more attributes and is more specific on those already known in A.

By Theorem 5.4, the derived operation $\boxplus$ is given as $(A, S) \boxplus (B, T) = (A \cup B, S \bowtie T)$ for $A, B \subseteq \mathfrak{A}$, $S \in \mathbb{P}^+(\Phi_A)$, and $T \in \mathbb{P}^+(\Phi_B)$ where

$$S \bowtie T = \{ x \in \prod_{a \in A \cup B} \Phi_a \mid p_{A \cup B, A}(x) \in S \wedge p_{A \cup B, B}(x) \in T \}$$

which is by definition the natural join in relational database theory.

5.4   Ordered Valuation Algebras

It is observed in the community of approximate reasoning that with two algebraic operations of combination and marginalization a number of approximating inference techniques can be formalized under reasonable assumptions. The axiomatic approach is pursued by Shenoy and Shafer [21], Shenoy and Kohlas [15], Haenni [10], etc. In this section, we show that a variant of their axiomatic frameworks can be derived by our Grothendieck construction for ordered (total) commutative monoids, clarifying the relationship between our approach and theirs.

The following concept is derived from [10]:

Definition 5.5. *A (stable) ordered valuation algebra is a two-sorted algebra* $(\Phi, \le, D)$, *consisting of a partially ordered set* $(\Phi, \le)$ *of valuations and a bounded lattice* D *of domains with operations*

(i) $\otimes \colon \Phi \times \Phi \to \Phi$ *called* combination,
(ii) $d \colon \Phi \to D$ *such that* $d(\varphi)$ *is called the* domain *of* φ,
(iii) $(-)^{\downarrow -} \colon \Phi \times D \rightharpoonup \Phi$ *called* focusing *where* $\varphi^{\downarrow x}$ *is defined for* $x \le d(\varphi)$,
(iv) *and* $e \colon D \to \Phi$ *such that* e_x *is (called) an* identity element

satisfying conditions below. In the following context, $\Phi_x = \{ \varphi \in \Phi \mid d(\varphi) = x \}$.

(i) $(\Phi, \otimes)$ *is a commutative semigroup.*
(ii) *Comparable valuations are of the same domain:* $\varphi \le \psi$ *implies* $d(\varphi) = d(\psi)$.
(iii) *Identity element:* $d(e_x) = x$, $e_x \otimes e_y = e_{x \vee y}$, *and* $\varphi \otimes e_x = \varphi$ *for* $\varphi \in \Phi_x$.
(iv) *Stability of identity under focusing:* $e_y^{\downarrow x} = e_x$ *for* $x \le y$.
(v) *Labelling:* $d(\varphi \otimes \psi) = d(\varphi) \vee d(\psi)$ *and* $\varphi^{\downarrow x} \in \Phi_x$ *if* $x \le d(\varphi)$.
(vi) *Transitivity of focusing* $(\varphi^{\downarrow y})^{\downarrow x} = \varphi^{\downarrow x}$ *for* $x \le y \le d(\varphi)$.
(vii) *Distributivity of focusing over combination:* $(\varphi \otimes \psi)^{\downarrow d(\varphi)} = \varphi \otimes \psi^{\downarrow d(\varphi) \wedge d(\psi)}$.
(viii) *Combination preserves ordering:* $\varphi_1 \otimes \varphi_2 \le \psi_1 \otimes \psi_2$ *whenever* $\varphi_i \le \psi_i$.
(ix) *Focusing preserves ordering:* $\varphi^{\downarrow x} \le \psi^{\downarrow x}$ *for any* $x \le d(\varphi) = d(\psi)$ *and* $\varphi \le \psi$.

The focusing operation $\downarrow$ formalises marginalization in probability theory and projection in relational database theory. The intuitive meaning of every other operation is self-evident. In addition to the focusing operation, a *vacuous extension* operation, coined in [13], $(-)^{\uparrow y} \colon \Phi_x \to \Phi_y$ can be defined for every $y \geq x$ via

$$\varphi^{\uparrow y} := \varphi \otimes e_y$$

We will see that $\downarrow$ and $\uparrow$ form a Galois connection under mild conditions.

Remark 5.6. The original formulation in [10] imposes additional requirements. For example, D is only a powerset instead of a lattice and Φ_x also requires a null (or, absorbing) element which in [10] represents a special inconsistent information. For the sake of brevity, we refrain to discuss these conditions. More variants of (unordered) valuation algebras can be found in [13, 18].

Proposition 5.7. *Let $(\Phi, \leq, D; \otimes, d, \downarrow, e)$ be an ordered valuation algebra. Then, the following statements hold:*

(i) *$(\Phi_x, \leq, \otimes, e_x)$ is an ordered commutative monoid.*
(ii) *For any $x \leq y$, the vacuous extension operation $(-)^{\uparrow y}$ is an order-preserving monoid homomorphism from Φ_x to Φ_y.*
(iii) *$(\Phi, \leq, D; \otimes, d, \downarrow, e)$ gives rise to a functor from D to the category of ordered commutative monoids.*

As we intend to view ordered valuation algebras as Grothendieck completions of families of commutative monoids, an obvious discrepancy is that φ and ψ are comparable only if $d(\varphi) = d(\psi)$ in ordered valuation algebras while elements (x, φ) and (y, ψ) in $\int P$ are comparable even if domains x and y are different. This can be readily mitigated by extending $\leq$ canonically:

$$\varphi \leq' \psi \iff d(\varphi) \leq d(\psi) \quad \text{and} \quad \varphi \otimes e_{d(\psi)} \leq \psi.$$

Proposition 5.8. *The ordered algebraic structure $(\Phi, \leq', D; \otimes, d, \downarrow, e)$ satisfies the conditions[4] of ordered valuation algebra except that $\varphi \leq \psi$ implies $d(\varphi) = d(\psi)$.*

By applying the Grothendieck construction (Theorem 5.4) to the D-indexed family of ordered commutative monoids Φ_x (Proposition 5.7), we have a partially ordered set $(\int \Phi, \preceq)$. The mapping $(x, \varphi) \mapsto \varphi$ is evidently bijective since $d(\varphi) = x$, and $(x, \varphi) \preceq (y, \psi) \iff \varphi \leq' \psi$ by definition. That is, the bijection $(x, \varphi) \mapsto \varphi$ is an order isomorphism between $(\int \Phi, \preceq)$ and $(\Phi, \leq')$.

It is clear that the domain operation $d \colon \Phi \to D$ is the projection $p \colon \int \Phi \to D$ through the isomorphism, i.e. $p(x, \varphi) = d(\varphi)$. Similarly, $e_x \in \Phi_x$ is unique for each x, so it defines $e \colon D \to \int \Phi$.

As for the combination operations $\otimes$ and $\boxtimes$, note that $\boxtimes$ is given by

$$(x, \varphi) \boxtimes (y, \psi) = \left(z, \varphi^{\uparrow z} \otimes \psi^{\uparrow z}\right)$$

---

[4] The order-preservation property of focusing accordingly becomes 'if $\varphi \leq \psi$ and $x \leq d(\varphi)$ then $\varphi^{\downarrow x} \leq \psi^{\downarrow x}$'.

where $z = x \vee y$ and $\varphi^{\uparrow z} \otimes \psi^{\uparrow z} = \varphi \otimes \psi$ by an easy calculation. Henceforth, $\otimes$ is the same as $\boxtimes$ via the isomorphism.

It remains to derive the focusing operation from the Grothendieck construction. To this point, we need a regularity condition:

Lemma 5.9. *For any ordered valuation algebra* $\Phi = (\Phi, \leq, D; \otimes, d, \downarrow, e)$*, the following statements are true:*

(i) $\varphi^{\uparrow y} \leq \psi$ *implies* $\varphi \leq \psi^{\downarrow x}$*.*
(ii) If $e_x \leq \varphi$ *for any* $\varphi \in \Phi_x$ *and* Φ *is regular, i.e. for any* φ *and* $x \leq d(\varphi)$ *there is* $\chi \in \Phi_x$ *such that* $\varphi^{\downarrow x} \otimes \chi \otimes \varphi \leq \varphi$*, then* $\varphi \leq \psi^{\downarrow x}$ *implies* $\varphi^{\uparrow y} \leq \psi$*.*

Remark 5.10. The condition(s) in Lemma 5.9 are studied in [18]. Idempotent valuation algebras are called *information algebras* by Kohlas [13].

Every adjoint is uniquely determined by the other adjoint, so in particular the focusing operation $\downarrow$ is uniquely determined by the vacuous extension $\uparrow$.

To sum up, we have shown that the combination operation $\otimes$ of an ordered valuation algebra can be derived by the Grothendieck construction:

Theorem 5.11. *Every regular ordered valuation algebra* $(\Phi, \leq, D; \otimes, \downarrow, e)$ *with* $e_x \leq \varphi$ *for any* $\varphi \in \Phi_x$ *is isomorphic to the Grothendieck completion* $(\int \Phi, \preceq, \boxtimes, 0)$ *of the functor given by Proposition 5.7.*

Remark 5.12. Both Theorems 5.4 and 5.11 justify our claim that data linkage is made of data combination and changes of domain. The Grothendieck construction is in fact an equivalence of categories so that a pseudo-functor from a preorder to monoidal structures is essentially an opfibration equipped with a global monoidal structure. For interested readers, see [22, Theorem 12.7].

6   Concluding Remarks

Ubiquitous computing has led to ubiquitous data. Technologies exist that explore information content by combining data in a dataset and, in particular, linking data from different datasets. Given the diversity of what passes for data—exact, approximate, erroneous, fictitious—a very abstract conceptual framework is needed to discover any general principles in today's *datafest*.

We have presented an abstract algebraic framework based on axiomatic notions that model a data source, data representations and their combination '$\oplus$', a measure of information content '$\preceq$', and linkage between data sources. By stripping down intuitions we have found that *ordered partial commutative monoids* provide algebraic structures to be found at the heart of many quite disparate data sharing situations.

Our approach could be developed further using category-theoretic notions which have proved successful in database theory, see e.g., [19]. While databases provide useful examples for our theory, the exact connection remains unclear.

Our next steps are to map the scope of ordered partial commutative monoids by exploring new and various

(i) types of data, especially those in approximate reasoning such as belief functions and those discussed in uncertainty reasoning [11], and so on;

(ii) types of operations on and between our algebras.

Returning to our background motivation in the introduction, clearly more attention needs to be paid to the concept of data privacy and how linkage of data can lead to privacy breach, e.g., de-anonymization. This is the subject of ongoing investigations, cf. [25].

Interestingly, there does not seem to be much of a theory of ordered partial commutative monoids so that, too, is something to do.

References

1. Arieli, O., Avron, A.: The value of the four values. Artif. Intell. **102**(1), 97–141 (1998). https://doi.org/10.1016/S0004-3702(98)00032-0

2. Attard, J., Orlandi, F., Scerri, S., Auer, S.: A systematic review of open government data initiatives. Gov. Inform. Q. **32**(4), 399–418 (2015). https://doi.org/10.1016/j.giq.2015.07.006

3. Belnap, N.D.: A useful four-valued logic. In: Dunn, J.M., Epstein, G. (eds.) Modern Uses of Multiple-Valued Logic. Episteme(A Series in the Foundational, Methodological, Philosophical, Psychological, Sociological, and Political Aspects of the Sciences, Pure and Applied), vol. 2, pp. 5–37. Springer, Dordrecht (1977). https://doi.org/10.1007/978-94-010-1161-7_2

4. Codd, E.F.: The Relational Model for Database Management: Version 2. Pearson, London (1990)

5. Coecke, B., Lal, R.: Causal categories: a backbone for a quantum-relativistic universe of interacting processes. In: Proceedings of QPL VII, pp. 17–26 (2010)

6. Davey, B.A., Priestley, H.A.: Introduction to Lattices and Order, 2nd edn. Cambridge University Press, Cambridge (2002)

7. Foulis, D.J., Bennett, M.K.: Effect algebras and unsharp quantum logics. Found. Phys. **24**(10), 1331–1352 (1994). https://doi.org/10.1007/BF02283036

8. Fritz, T.: Resource convertibility and ordered commutative monoids. Math. Struct. Comp. Sci. **27**(06), 850–938 (2017). https://doi.org/10.1017/S0960129515000444

9. Gunter, C.A.: The mixed powerdomain. Theor. Comput. Sci. **103**(2), 311–334 (1992). https://doi.org/10.1016/0304-3975(92)90017-A

10. Haenni, R.: Ordered valuation algebras: a generic framework for approximating inference. Int. J. Approx. Reason. **37**(1), 1–41 (2004). https://doi.org/10.1016/j.ijar.2003.10.009

11. Halpern, J.Y.: Reasoning About Uncertainty, 1st edn. The MIT Press, Cambridge (2003)

12. Jacobs, B.: Categorical Logic and Type Theory. North Holland, Amsterdam (1999)

13. Kohlas, J.: Discrete mathematics and theoretical computer science. Information Algebras. Generic Structures For Inference, vol. 1. Springer-Verlag, London (2003)

14. Kohlas, J., Pouly, M., Schneuwly, C.: Generic local computation. J. Comput. Syst. Sci. **78**(1), 348–369 (2012). https://doi.org/10.1016/j.jcss.2011.05.012

15. Kohlas, J., Shenoy, P.P.: Computation in valuation algebras. In: Kohlas, J., Moral, S. (eds.) Handbook of Defeasible Reasoning and Uncertainty Management Systems. Handbook of Defeasible Reasoning and Uncertainty Management Systems, vol. 5, pp. 5–39. Springer, Dordrecht (2000)

16. Machanavajjhala, A., Kifer, D., Gehrke, J., Venkitasubramaniam, M.: *l*-diversity: Privacy beyond *k*-anonymity. ACM T. Knowl. Discov. D. **1**(1), 3 (2007). https://doi.org/10.1145/1217299.1217302

17. Narayanan, A., Shmatikov, V.: Robust de-anonymization of large sparse datasets. In: 2008 IEEE Symposium on Security and Privacy, pp. 111–125. IEEE (2008). https://doi.org/10.1109/SP.2008.33

18. Pouly, M., Kohlas, J.: Generic Inference. Wiley, Hoboken, USA (2011)

19. Schultz, P., Spivak, D.I., Wisnesky, R.: Algebraic model management: a survey. In: James, P., Roggenbach, M. (eds.) WADT 2016. LNCS, vol. 10644, pp. 56–69. Springer, Cham (2017). https://doi.org/10.1007/978-3-319-72044-9_5

20. Scott, D.S.: Data types as lattices. SIAM J. Comput. **5**(3), 522–587 (1976). https://doi.org/10.1137/0205037

21. Shenoy, P.P., Shafer, G.: Studies in fuzziness and soft computing. In: Yager, R.R., Liu, L. (eds.) Axioms for Probability and Belief-Function Propagation. Classic Works of the Dempster-Shafer Theory of Belief Functions, pp. 499–528. Springer, Heidelberg (2008)

22. Shulman, M.: Framed bicategories and monoidal fibrations. Theory Appl. Categ. **20**(18), 650–738 (2008)

23. Sweeney, L.: Weaving technology and policy together to maintain confidentiality. J. Law. Med. Ethics **25**(2–3), 98–110 (1997). https://doi.org/10.1111/j.1748-720X.1997.tb01885.x

24. Sweeney, L.: *k*-anonymity: a model for protecting privacy. Int. J. Uncertain. Fuzz. **10**(05), 557–570 (2002). https://doi.org/10.1142/S0218488502001648

25. Wang, V., Tucker, J.V.: Surveillance and identity: conceptual framework and formal models. J. Cybersecurity **3**(3), 145–158 (2017). https://doi.org/10.1093/cybsec/tyx010

26. Wang, Y., Huang, Z., Mitra, S., Dullerud, G.E.: Entropy-minimizing mechanism for differential privacy of discrete-time linear feedback systems. In: 53rd IEEE Conference on Decision and Control, pp. 2130–2135. IEEE (2014). https://doi.org/10.1109/CDC.2014.7039713

27. Wehrung, F.: Refinement Monoids, Equidecomposability Types, and Boolean Inverse Semigroups. LNM, vol. 2188. Springer, Cham (2017). https://doi.org/10.1007/978-3-319-61599-8

Institutions for SQL Database Schemas and Datasets

Martin Glauer and Till Mossakowski[✉]

Otto von Guericke University Magdeburg, Magdeburg, Germany
{martin.glauer,till.mossakowski}@ovgu.de

Abstract. Databases and the query language SQL play a major role in modern applications. In this paper we present an institution-based formalisation of relational databases that uses structures close to those used in SQL. This is the essential difference to other category-theoretical formalisations of databases, which often depart quite far from the SQL standard. We also study SQL queries, using institutional monads, and prove cocompleteness and amalgamation results for the institution.

Keywords: Databases · SQL · Category theory · Institutions · Queries · Derived signature morphisms

1 Introduction

Database techniques have a long tradition in computer science and build the foundation for numerous modern applications. The *Structured Query Language* (SQL) [11] forms the fundamental specification for most state-of-the-art query languages for many database systems.[1] Near to all applications that rely on databases use some query language that conforms to the SQL specification, e.g. MySQL or PostgreSQL. This central role made SQL an essential building block of modern database technology that can not be replaced by other languages easily. Thus, formal approaches towards databases should focus this existing standard rather than develop a rivalling query language.

The diversity and heterogeneity of data needed for one specific application raises the need for frictionless interaction and migration between different database schemas. The growing role of Linked Open Data underlines this need. As a result there this a vast landscape of formal approaches towards databases and data migration, including many category-theoretical approaches. The relational make-up of many database schemas makes it natural to model them as categories and yields the intuitive notion of a schema merge as pushouts of functors. In [21–23] tables are represented as categories and values and relations

---

[1] For big data applications, NoSQL databases play an important role, but even there, also SQL databases are used.

© IFIP International Federation for Information Processing 2019
Published by Springer Nature Switzerland AG 2019
J. L. Fiadeiro and I. Ţuţu (Eds.): WADT 2018, LNCS 11563, pp. 67–86, 2019.
https://doi.org/10.1007/978-3-030-23220-7_4

between tables are functors. The Functorial Query Language yields functionalities to query those structures. A similar approach towards schema integration was defined for the first time in an institutional setting in [1]. Institutions were defined in [10] as a framework to cover the vast, heterogeneous landscape of logical formalisms used in computer science. The benefits of a categorical or institutional formalisation are (1) better tools for database structuring, (2) database integration can be achieved via colimits and (3) the possibility of heterogeneous integration of databases with logical languages.

However, previous approaches to category-theoretic formalisation of databases do not well integrate with actual practice of SQL databases. The reasons are that the defined structures are not close to actual relational database structures, the logic is not three-valued as in SQL[2], data tables cannot contain duplicates, the operators are not exactly those of SQL, and more (see also [22] for differences between algebraic and relational databases). Therefore, in this work, we aim at formalising an SQL institution that comes as close as possible to the SQL standard. This means there should be a simple and obvious correspondence between SQL database schemas and theories in the institution. This is particularly important for tool support via the Heterogeneous tool set (Hets) [14], which provides a software interface for institutions. Only with an institution supporting SQL directly, Hets can read in standard SQL database schemas. If needed, these can then be translated to other institutions. The formalisation presented in this paper can be seen a first step towards institution based logical reasoning on relational databases and their heterogeneous integration with logical theories. For example, in [20], using institutions, (a simplified form of) a database schema is heterogeneously integrated with an ontology formulated in the description logic OWL, via a first-order theory playing the role of a bridge theory. Our work will enable the use of real-world SQL database schemas in such heterogeneous integration scenarios.

2   An Institution for Databases

There is a vast landscape of different logics with varying expressiveness, complexity and purpose. Yet, most logics define syntactical entities like signatures (vocabularies) and sentences, as well as concepts of model and satisfaction (of a sentence in a model). Goguen et al defined institutions in [10] as an overarching, abstract framework that covers all those concepts and thus integrates them into a common structure.

Definition 1. *An institution* $\mathcal{I} = (\boldsymbol{Sign}^{\mathcal{I}}, \boldsymbol{Sen}^{\mathcal{I}}, \boldsymbol{Mod}^{\mathcal{I}}, \models^{\mathcal{I}})$ *consists of*

(i) a category of signatures $\boldsymbol{Sign}^{\mathcal{I}}$ *and signature morphisms;*

(ii) a sentence functor $\boldsymbol{Sen}^{\mathcal{I}} : \boldsymbol{Sign}^{\mathcal{I}} \to \boldsymbol{Set}$ *(where* $\boldsymbol{Set}$ *is the category of sets), providing for each signature* Σ *a set of sentences* $\boldsymbol{Sen}^{\mathcal{I}}(\Sigma)$ *and for each signature morphism* $\sigma : \Sigma_1 \to \Sigma_2$ *a sentence translation map* $\boldsymbol{Sen}^{\mathcal{I}}(\sigma) :$ $\boldsymbol{Sen}^{\mathcal{I}}(\Sigma_1) \to \boldsymbol{Sen}^{\mathcal{I}}(\Sigma_2)$ *(also written* $\sigma(-)$*);*

---

[2] This also means that the subtle difference in the semantics of integrity constraints and that of *where* conditions in queries cannot be captured. We capture it: see our discussion on designated truth values below.

(iii) *a contra-variant* model functor $\boldsymbol{Mod}^{\mathcal{I}} : (\boldsymbol{Sign}^{\mathcal{I}})^{\mathrm{op}} \to \mathbf{Cat}$ *(where* $\mathbf{Cat}$ *is the category of categories[3]), providing for each signature* Σ *a category of models* $\boldsymbol{Mod}^{\mathcal{I}}(\Sigma)$ *and for each signature morphism* $\sigma : \Sigma_1 \to \Sigma_2$ *a model reduct functor* $\boldsymbol{Mod}^{\mathcal{I}}(\sigma) : \boldsymbol{Sen}^{\mathcal{I}}(\Sigma_2) \to \boldsymbol{Sen}^{\mathcal{I}}(\Sigma_1)$ *(also written* $-|_\sigma$*); and*

(iv) *a family of satisfaction relations* $\models^{\mathcal{I}}_{\Sigma} \subseteq |\boldsymbol{Mod}^{\mathcal{I}}(\Sigma)| \times \boldsymbol{Sen}^{\mathcal{I}}(\Sigma)$ *indexed over* $\Sigma \in |\boldsymbol{Sign}^{\mathcal{I}}|$,

such that the following satisfaction condition *holds for every signature morphism* $\sigma : \Sigma \to \Sigma'$ *in* $\boldsymbol{Sign}^{\mathcal{I}}$, *every sentence* $\varphi \in \boldsymbol{Sen}^{\mathcal{I}}(\Sigma)$ *and for every* Σ'*-model* $M' \in |\boldsymbol{Mod}^{\mathcal{I}}(\Sigma')|$:

$$M'|_\sigma \models^{\mathcal{I}}_{\Sigma} \varphi \;\Leftrightarrow\; M' \models^{\mathcal{I}}_{\Sigma'} \sigma(\varphi) \;.$$

Definition 2. *A* semi-institution *($\boldsymbol{Sign}, \boldsymbol{Mod}$) (called* specification frame *in [7]) consists of a signature category* $\boldsymbol{Sign}$ *and a model functor* $\boldsymbol{Mod}^{\mathcal{I}} : (\boldsymbol{Sign}^{\mathcal{I}})^{\mathrm{op}} \to \mathbf{Cat}$ *(that is, it is an institution without sentences and satisfaction relation).*

In this section we will define our institution for relational SQL databases. The general structure is as follows: Each object of the signature category defines the schema of a relational database (e.g. tables, their columns and sorts) as well as the building blocks for expressions (i.e. function and predicate symbols). Sentences represent constraints on these tables (e.g. foreign key constraints) that the data in the database must conform to. The data stored in the database are objects of the model category and morphisms amongst these models represent multiset inclusion. Finally, the satisfaction relation checks whether the data the database (i.e. a model) conforms to a specified constraint (i.e. a sentence). As a guidance all parts of the institution will be explained using the following example tables for persons and employees. Both tables feature a primary key that is an integer. The employee table contains a foreign key reference to the person table, with an according constraint (i.e. the `pid` of an employee always must be the `id` of a person). Moreover, the employee table contains a check constraint ensuring that the salary of an employee cannot negative.

Example 1.

Person

id:int	fname:Text	lname:Text

Employee

id:int	salary:int	pid:int

---

[3] Strictly speaking, $\mathbf{Cat}$ lives in a higher set-theoretic universe, such that it is not member of itself.

```
CREATE TABLE Person(
     id    Int,
     fname Text,
     lname Text,
     PRIMARY KEY (id));

CREATE TABLE Employee(
     id Int,
     salary Int,
     pid Int,
     PRIMARY KEY (id),
     FOREIGN KEY (pid) REFERENCES Person(id),
     CHECK (salary >= 0));
```

The database schema describes the general structure of a database. It includes information about all tables in the database, which columns belong to a specific table and their respective datatype. Information about the structure of a database is expressed in the *Data Definition Language* (DDL). Many basic components (e.g. datatypes, operators) of a database are fixed by the underlying database system. Similarly, the SQL Institution is parameterised over $(D\Sigma, DM)$ consisting of a *datatype signature* $D\Sigma$, which is a many-sorted first-order signature $D\Sigma = (\mathbb{S}^{D\Sigma}, \mathcal{F}_{D\Sigma})$ such that

1. there is a sort *bool* $\in \mathbb{S}^{D\Sigma}$
2. for each sort $s \in \mathbb{S}^{D\Sigma}$ there is a constant *null* : s, unary predicates *is_null* : s and *is_not_null* : s, and a binary predicate $=_s$: $s \times s$.

and of a *datatype model* DM, which is a $D\Sigma$-model such that

1. $DM_{bool} = \{\mathsf{T}, \mathsf{F}, \mathsf{U}\}$. (Note that SQL builds upon a 3-valued logic in order do cope with the existence of *null*-values.)
2. All operations are *strict*, i.e. they return $null_{DM}$ (or U, in case of operations with result sort *bool*) if any of the operands is $null_{DM}$. The only exceptions to this rule are *is_null* and *is_not_null*.
3. *is_null*$_{DM}$ is T for $null_{DM}$, and F otherwise.
4. *is_not_null*$_{DM}$ is F for $null_{DM}$, and T otherwise.
5. $a(=_s)_{DM}b = \begin{cases} \mathsf{T} & a = b \neq null_{DM} \\ \mathsf{F} & null_{DM} \neq a \neq b \neq null_{DM} \\ \mathsf{U} & otherwise \end{cases}$

Example 2. A many-sorted first order signature for MySQL-datatypes may consist of the following components:

```
logic CASL.FOL=
spec Mysql_datatypes =
    sorts Bit, Bool, Int, Float, Text, Blob ...
    ops 0 : Int; null : Int; null : Float; null: Text;
    ...
```

```
ops __+__, __*__ : Int * Int -> Int
ops is_null, is_not_null : Int -> Bool; ...
ops __=__, __>=__ Int * Int -> Bool; ...
ops empty : Text -> Bool; ...
```

An extension for the database PostgreSQL (which also features geometrical datatypes, for geo databases) might look as follows:

```
spec Postgresql_datatypes =
Mysql_datatypes then
    sorts Point, Line, Polygon   ...
```

Both signatures can be interpreted with a model in a standard way, following the SQL conventions for datatypes and their built-in operations.

For a given pair $(D\Sigma, DM)$ of a data type signature and a data type model, we now define an institution $\mathcal{SQL}(D\Sigma, DM)$ as follows.

A signature in $\mathcal{SQL}(D\Sigma, DM)$ defines the tables the database contains as well as the corresponding columns and their datatypes.

Definition 3 (Signatures). *An object Σ of the category of signatures $\mathbf{Sign}$ consists of:*

- *a set of table names (or short: tables) $\mathbb{T}^\Sigma$,*
- *for each table $t \in \mathbb{T}^\Sigma$, a set $col^\Sigma(t)$ of columns,*
- *a function $\tau(\cdot, \cdot) : \{(t, c) | t \in \mathbb{T}^\Sigma, c \in col^\Sigma(t)\} \to \mathbb{S}^{D\Sigma}$ assigning sorts (of the datatype signature) to columns in tables, and*
- *for each table $t \in \mathbb{T}^\Sigma$, a primary key $pk^\Sigma(t) \subseteq col^\Sigma(t)$. Note $pk^\Sigma(t) = \emptyset$ is possible, which expresses, in SQL terms, the absence of a primary key.*

We include primary keys into signatures (instead of considering them to be sentences) because for each table there may be at most one primary key.

Definition 4 (Signature Morphisms). *A signature morphism $\sigma : \Sigma \to \Sigma'$ in the category of signatures $\mathbf{Sign}$ consists of*

- *a table translation $\sigma_\mathbb{T} : \mathbb{T}^\Sigma \to \mathbb{T}^{\Sigma'}$, and*
- *a family of column translations $\langle \sigma_{col,t} : col(t) \to col'(\sigma_\mathbb{T}(t)) \rangle_{t \in \mathbb{T}^\Sigma}$,*

such that types of columns are preserved

$$\tau^{\Sigma'}(\sigma_\mathbb{T}(t), \sigma_{col,t}(c)) = \tau^\Sigma(t, c)$$

and for each table $t \in \mathbb{T}^\Sigma$, the primary key (if existing) is preserved

$$pk^{\Sigma'}(\sigma_\mathbb{T}(t)) = \sigma_{col,t}(pk^\Sigma(t)) \text{ if } pk^\Sigma(t) \neq \emptyset$$

Example 3. A signature Σ for the tables shown in Example 1 is as follows:

- $\mathbb{T}^\Sigma = \{\texttt{Employee}, \texttt{Person}\}$
- $col^\Sigma(\texttt{Employee}) = \{\texttt{id}, \texttt{salary}, \texttt{pid}\}$

- $\mathrm{col}^\Sigma(\texttt{Person}) = \{\texttt{id}, \texttt{fname}, \texttt{lname}\}$
- $\tau^\Sigma(\texttt{Employee}, .) = \{\texttt{id} \mapsto \texttt{Int}, \texttt{salary} \mapsto \texttt{Int}, \texttt{pid} \mapsto \texttt{Int}\}$
- $\tau^\Sigma(\texttt{Person}, .) = \{\texttt{id} \mapsto \texttt{Int}, \texttt{fname} \mapsto \texttt{Text}, \texttt{lname} \mapsto \texttt{Text}\}$
- $pk^\Sigma(\texttt{Person}) = \{\texttt{id}\}$
- $pk^\Sigma(\texttt{Employee}) = \{\texttt{id}\}$

The database schema described above yields means to structure data in tables with little limitations regarding the actual content of the data. In order to ensure data integrity, the SQL defines several types of constraints that may be placed on a table. The sentences of the presented institution formulate the most common types of constraints (NOT NULL, UNIQUE, FOREIGN KEY and CHECK) specified in the SQL standard.

Definition 5 (Sentences). *Given a signature Σ, a sentence φ^t is a constraint on a table $t \in \mathbb{T}^\Sigma$ of one of the following forms:*

- *A non-null constraint $notnull(t.c)$ $(c \in col(t))$*
- *A unique constraint $un(t.c_1, \ldots, t.c_n)$ $(c_1, \ldots, c_n \in col(t))$*
- *A foreign-key constraint $fk((t.c_1, u.d_1), \ldots, (t.c_n, u.d_n))$ for some a table $u \in \mathbb{T}^\Sigma$ and $c_i \in col(t)$, $d_i \in col(u)$ for $i = 1, \ldots, n$*
- *A check constraint $ck_t(\varphi)$, where φ is a term of sort Bool over the signature $D\Sigma$ (extended with logical connectives $\neg$, $\vee$, $\wedge$ as operations on Bool) and variables from the set $Var(t) = \{t.c \mid t \in col(t)\}$.*

Definition 6 (Sentence Translation). *Given a signature morphism $\sigma : \Sigma \to \Sigma'$, a constraint φ^t on a table $t \in \mathbb{T}^\Sigma$ is translated along σ to $\sigma(\varphi^t)$ depending on its structure*

- $\sigma(un(t.c_1, \ldots, t.c_n)) = un(\sigma_\mathbb{T}(t).\sigma_{col,t}(c_1), \ldots, \sigma_\mathbb{T}(t).\sigma_{col,t}(c_n))$
- $\sigma(fk((t.c_1, u.d_1), \ldots, (t.c_n, u.d_n))) = fk(\ (\sigma_\mathbb{T}(t).\sigma_{col,t}(c_1), \sigma_\mathbb{T}(u).\sigma_{col,t}(d_1)),$

$$\ldots$$

$$(\sigma_\mathbb{T}(t).\sigma_{col,t}(c_n), \sigma_\mathbb{T}(u).\sigma_{col,t}(d_n)))$$

- $\sigma(ck_t(\varphi))$ *is obtained by mapping all variable names along σ, i.e. the variable $c.t$ is replaced with $\sigma_{col,t}(c).\sigma_\mathbb{T}(t)$.*

Example 4. Primary keys are already part of the signature. Thus, there are only two constraints remaining in Example 1 that can be formulated as sentences:

- The foreign key linking Employees to Persons

$$fk((\texttt{Employee.pid}, \texttt{Person.id}))$$

- The constraint that the salary of an employee must not be negative

$$ck_t(\texttt{Employee.salary} \;\texttt{>=}\; 0)$$

The signature fixes the structural make-up of the database and its tables. A model represents the data that may be stored in a database w.r.t. to the existing tables, columns and their datatypes. Note that in the interpretation of a table in a model, the same row may appear several times. Thus, tables are interpreted as multisets (also called bags) of rows. The use of multisets may seem overly complicated, because normalised databases cannot have duplicate rows. However, note that not all databases are normalised, and moreover duplicate rows can easily occur within views generated by queries.

For a set X, let $\wp_{multi}(X)$ be the set of finite multisets over X. A finite multiset $B \in \wp_{multi}(X)$ can be understood as a map $B : X \to \mathbb{N}$ such that $B(x) > 0$ only for finitely many $x \in X$. For $x \in X$ and $B \in \wp_{multi}(X)$, let $B \# x$ be the multiplicity of x in B. We write $x \in B$ for the fact that $B \# x > 0$. Moreover, we use the abbreviation $\exists ! x \in B. \varphi(x)$ for

$$\left(\sum_{\varphi(x)} B \# x \right) = 1$$

i.e. there exists a unique x in B satisfying $\varphi(x)$, and this x has multiplicity 1. Furthermore, addition on finite multiset is defined element-wise:

$$(B_1 + B_2) \# x = B_1 \# x + B_2 \# x.$$

Finally, inclusion of multisets is defined as $A \subseteq B$ iff for all $x \in X$, $A \# x \leq B \# x$.

Definition 7 (Models). *Given a signature Σ, an object of the model category **Mod**(Σ) is a function mapping tables to multisets of functions that map columns to elements of the datatype model, formally $M : t \in \mathbb{T}^\Sigma \to \wp_{multi}(c \in col(t) \to DM_{\tau(t,c)})$, such that for each $t \in \mathbb{T}^\Sigma$ with $pk^\Sigma(t) = \{c_1, \ldots, c_n\} \neq \emptyset$*

- *$r(c_i) \neq null_{DM}$ for each row $r \in M(t)$ and $i = 1, \ldots, n$, and*
- *for all rows $r_1 \in M(t)$,*

$$\exists ! r_2 \in M(t). r_1(c_1) = r_2(c_1) \wedge \cdots \wedge r_1(c_n) = r_2(c_n)$$

Note that in presence of the satisfaction relation introduced below, these conditions could be rephrased as

- $M \models \{notnull(t.c_1), \ldots, notnull(t.c_n)\}$
- $M \models un(t.c_1, \ldots, t.c_n)$

Morphisms in the category of models represent inclusion of data multisets.

Definition 8 (Model Morphisms). *Given a signature Σ, the model category **Mod**(Σ) is a partially ordered set, where $M_1 \leq M_2$ iff for each $t \in \mathbb{T}^\Sigma$, $M_1(t) \subseteq M_2(t)$.*

Definition 9 (Model Reducts). *Given a signature morphism $\sigma : \Sigma \to \Sigma'$ and a Σ'-model M' and a table $t \in \mathbb{T}^\Sigma$, a row $r' : (c' \in col(\sigma_\mathbb{T}(t))) \to DM_{\tau(\sigma_\mathbb{T}(t),c')}$ can be reduced to a row $r'|_\sigma : (c \in col(t)) \to DM_{\tau(t,c)}$ by defining*

$$r'|_\sigma(c) = r'(\sigma_{col,t}(c)) \text{ for } c \in col^\Sigma(t).$$

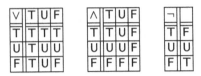

Fig. 1. Boolean operations in SQL's 3-valued logic

Then $M'|_\sigma$, the reduction of M' against σ, is defined by

$$\forall t \in \mathbb{T}^\Sigma, M'|_\sigma(t)\#r = \sum_{r'|_\sigma = r} M'(\sigma_\mathbb{T}(t))\#r' \tag{1}$$

for all $r : (c \in col(t)) \rightarrow DM_{\tau(t,c)})$. Note that $M'|_\sigma(t)\#r = 0$ in case there is no $r' \in M'(\sigma_\mathbb{T}(t))$ with $r'|_\sigma = r$. From M satisfying the primary key and not-null constraints of Σ', it is straightforward to see that $M'|_\sigma$ satisfies those of Σ.

It is easily seen that reducts preserve the partial order on models; hence they are functorial.

Definition 10 (Satisfaction Relation). *For every $M \in \mathbf{Mod}(\Sigma)$ the satisfaction relation is defined depending on the structure the sentence:*

- *$M \models_\Sigma notnull(t.c)$ iff $r(c) \neq null_{DM}$ for each row $r \in M(t)$*
- *$M \models_\Sigma un(t.c_1, \ldots, t.c_n)$ iff for all rows $r_1 \in M(t)$,*

$$\exists! r_2 \in M(t).\, r_1(c_1) = r_2(c_1) \wedge \cdots \wedge r_1(c_n) = r_2(c_n)$$

- *$M \models_\Sigma fk((t.c_1, u.d_1), \ldots, (t.c_n, u.d_n))$ iff for all $r_1 \in M(t)$ there is exactly one $r_2 \in M(u)$ such that $r_1(c_i) = r_2(d_i)$ for $i = 1, \ldots, n$*
- *$M \models_\Sigma ck_t(\varphi)$ iff for all $r \in M(t)$, $[\![\varphi]\!]^M_{\nu(r)} \in \{T, U\}$, where for $r \in M(t)$, $\nu(r)$ is the valuation defined by $\nu(t.c) = r(c)$ for all $c \in col(t)$.*

Here, $[\![\varphi]\!]^{DM}_\nu$ is the evaluation of the term φ in the model DM using a valuation ν of the free variables, defined inductively in a standard way, where Boolean connectives are interpreted as shown in Fig. 1. Note that since $[\![\varphi]\!]^{DM}_\nu$ is of sort Bool, $[\![\varphi]\!]^{DM}_\nu \in \{T, F, U\}$.

While internally, our institution $\mathcal{SQL}(D\Sigma, DM)$ uses a three-valued logic for the semantics of integrity constraints, ultimately, it is a two valued logic. This is achieved by considering sentences evaluating to T or U (the designated truth values, in standard many-valued logic terminology [17]) to hold, and considering those evaluating to F as not to hold. (When eliminating U in the first place, one would obtain a different logic.) Further note that for conditions in queries, SQL takes T as the only designated truth value, see Sect. 3 below. This means that queries impose a stricter regime than integrity constraints, which is pragmatically motivated: missing data should not lead to violation of an integrity constraint, while in queries, all mentioned data should be present.

Proposition 1 (Satisfaction condition). *Let $\sigma : \Sigma \to \Sigma'$ be a signature morphism between two database signatures. For all Σ'-models M' and Σ-constraints φ the following holds:*

$$M'|_\sigma \models \varphi \quad \Leftrightarrow \quad M' \models \sigma(\varphi)$$

Proof. Let M' be a Σ'-model and φ a Σ-sentence. The satisfaction follows directly from the fact that model reducts do not alter the data contained in the tables, apart from altering table and column names:

case $\varphi = notnull(t.c)$:

$$
\begin{aligned}
M'|_\sigma \models notnull(t.c) &\Leftrightarrow \forall r \in M'|_\sigma(t) : r(c) \neq null_{DM} \\
&\overset{Eq.1}{\Leftrightarrow} \forall r' \in M'(\sigma_{\mathbb{T}}(t)) : r'|_\sigma(c) \neq null_{DM} \\
&\Leftrightarrow \forall r' \in M'(\sigma_{\mathbb{T}}(t)) : r'(\sigma_{\mathrm{col},t}(c)) \neq null_{DM} \\
&\Leftrightarrow M' \models \sigma(notnull(t.c))
\end{aligned}
$$

case $\varphi = un(t.c_1, \ldots, t.c_n)$:

$$
\begin{aligned}
&M'|_\sigma \models un(t.c_1, \ldots, t.c_n) \\
&\Leftrightarrow \forall r_1 \in M'|_\sigma(t) : \exists! r_2 \in M'|_\sigma(t) : \bigwedge_{i=1,\ldots,n} r_1(c_i) = r_2(c_i) \\
&\overset{Eq.1}{\Leftrightarrow} \forall r_1 \in M'(\sigma_{\mathbb{T}}(t)) : \exists! r_2 \in M'(\sigma_{\mathbb{T}}(t)) : \bigwedge_{i=1,\ldots,n} r_1|_\sigma(c_i) = r_2|_\sigma(c_i) \\
&\Leftrightarrow \forall r_1 \in M'(\sigma_{\mathbb{T}}(t)) : \exists! r_2 \in M'(\sigma_{\mathbb{T}}(t)) : \bigwedge_{i=1,\ldots,n} r_1(\sigma_{\mathrm{col},t}(c_i)) \\
&\hspace{8cm} = r_2(\sigma_{\mathrm{col},t}(c_i)) \\
&\Leftrightarrow M' \models \sigma(un(t.c_1, \ldots, t.c_n))
\end{aligned}
$$

case $\varphi = fk((t.c_1, u.d_1), \ldots, (t.c_n, u.d_n))$:

$$
\begin{aligned}
M'|_\sigma \models fk((t.c_1, u.d_1), &\ldots, (t.c_n, u.d_n)) \\
&\Leftrightarrow \forall r \in M'|_\sigma(t) \exists! s \in M'|_\sigma(u) : \forall i \in \{1, \ldots, n\} : r(c_i) = s(d_i) \\
&\overset{Eq.1}{\Leftrightarrow} \forall r \in M'(\sigma_{\mathbb{T}}(t)) \exists! s \in M'(\sigma_{\mathbb{T}}(u)) : \forall i \in \{1, \ldots, n\} : \\
&\hspace{2cm} r|_\sigma(c_i) = s|_\sigma(d_i) \\
&\Leftrightarrow \forall r \in M'(\sigma_{\mathbb{T}}(t)) \exists! s \in M'(\sigma_{\mathbb{T}}(u)) : \forall i \in \{1, \ldots, n\} : \\
&\hspace{2cm} r(\sigma_{\mathrm{col},t}(c_i)) = s(\sigma_{\mathrm{col},u}(d_i)) \\
&\Leftrightarrow M' \models \sigma(fk((t.c_1, u.d_1), \ldots, (t.c_n, u.d_n))))
\end{aligned}
$$

Concerning check constraints, one can prove by induction over φ that

$$\llbracket \varphi \rrbracket^{DM}_{\nu(r|_\sigma)} = \llbracket \sigma(\varphi) \rrbracket^{DM}_{\nu(r)}$$

From this, the satisfaction condition for check constraints follows using Eq. 1. $\square$

This completes the definition of the institution $\mathcal{SQL}(D\Sigma, DM)$.

3   Queries and Views

Our institution $\mathcal{SQL}(D\Sigma, DM)$ provides a formalisation of SQL database schemas as logical theories in that institution. Now an important feature of SQL is of course the *Data Query Language* (DQL). Queries cannot be directly represented as logical formulas in the institution, because as an answer, they deliver data and not just logical truth values. Therefore, formalisations for dealing with Prolog-style queries in an institutional setting usually use generalised substitutions [3,5] or derived signature morphisms. The latter are a generalised version of signature morphisms that may map signature symbols not only to other such symbols, but also to complex terms and expressions [13,19]. Then Prolog-style queries can be formalised as open sentences and their answer substitutions as derived signature morphisms[4].

However, it turns out that queries in SQL are different from Prolog-style queries. Indeed, SQL queries do not provide answer substitutions that map variables to terms, and so they cannot naturally be extended to a translation of sentences either. This is because SQL queries have a rich syntax, which in general cannot be reflected in SQL sentences (constraints). Instead, SQL queries provide a mapping of databases, i.e. models (see also Table 1). Compared of abstract substitutions [3,5], the syntactic half of the structure is missing. This means we would need to use abstract *semi*-substitutions. However, we follow a slightly different path. Namely we use Kleisli morphisms in an institutional monad as an institution-independent formalisation of derived signature morphisms. Queries can then be formalised as such Kleisli morphisms, and materialised views (answer to queries) are reducts against these. Moreover, Kleisli composition gives a means to compose queries, which is also called query unfolding in database terminology [6].

Table 1. Different types of queries

	Query	Answer
Prolog-style	Open sentence	Derived signature morphism
Database-style	Derived signature morphism	Reduct against derived signature morphism

The notion of institutional monad [13] has been introduced for formalising the notion of derived signature morphism in an arbitrary institution; we weaken it here to the notion of *semi*-institutional monad, based on the notion of institution semi-morphism. We first recall the latter. Institution semi-morphisms relate two institutions by relating their signatures and models, while sentences are not related. This is useful if the institutions are semantically related, but differ too much in their sentences to have a full institution morphism between them.

---

[4] This way of formalising queries also has been proposed in an informal annex within the DOL language standard [16].

Definition 11 ([10]). *Given institutions $\mathcal{I}$ and $\mathcal{J}$, an institution semi-morphism $\mu = (\Phi, \beta): \mathcal{I} \longrightarrow \mathcal{J}$ consists of*

- *a functor $\Phi: \mathbf{Sign}^{\mathcal{I}} \longrightarrow \mathbf{Sign}^{\mathcal{J}}$ and*
- *a natural transformation $\beta: \mathbf{Mod}^{\mathcal{I}} \longrightarrow \Phi^{op}; \mathbf{Mod}^{\mathcal{J}}$.*

Definition 12 ([5]). *Given two institution semi-morphisms $\mu_1, \mu_2: \mathcal{I} \longrightarrow \mathcal{J}$ with $\mu_i = (\Phi_i, \beta_i)$, a (discrete) institution semi-morphism modification $\tau: \mu_1 \longrightarrow \mu_2$ is a natural transformation $\tau: \Phi_1 \longrightarrow \Phi_2$ such that*

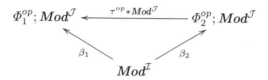

commutes.

Definition 13 (Semi-institutional monad). *Let $\mathcal{I}$ be an institution. A semi-institutional monad (T, η, μ) consists of*

- *An institution semi-morphism $T: \mathcal{I} \to \mathcal{I}$*
- *A institution semi-morphism modification $\eta: id \to T$ (the unit of the monad)*
- *A institution semi-morphism modification $\mu: TT \to T$ (the multiplication of the monad)*

such that the usual laws of a monad are satisfied:

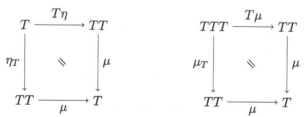

The semi-institutional monad for the SQL data query language can now be sketched as follows. The institution semi-morphism $(\Phi, \beta) : \mathcal{SQL}(D\Sigma, DM) \to \mathcal{SQL}(D\Sigma, DM)$ of the semi-institutional monad maps a signature Σ to $\Phi(\Sigma)$, which extends Σ with tables q, where q is an SQL query over Σ. The tables q are also called *views*, because the table resulting from a query represents a new view on the database. Resulting in such a view, an SQL query naturally has an associated set of (result) columns (=materialised view), this will act as q's set of columns in $\Phi(\Sigma)$. q will not have a primary key. β maps an SQL-model (aka database) M into the model $\beta_\Sigma(M)$ which interprets each query q as the multiset of solutions of q over M. The monad unit η_Σ is simply the inclusion of Σ into $\Phi(\Sigma)$. The monad multiplication μ_Σ maps queries over queries to normal SQL queries. This is straightforward, because SQL allows to insert queries in positions where tables can occur (after all, views are special forms of tables), which is a form of query composition.

Since SQL is a rich language, the detailed formalisation of the complete SQL query language along the lines sketched above is beyond the scope of this paper. Instead, we concentrate on one particular form of SQL query, involving select, where and join. In a system, information is often distributed amongst multiple tables in order to prevent redundancies. In order to retrieve distributed data multiple tables can be joined into a view, using a query. When employing this restriction on queries, the above sketched semi-institutional monad can be detailed as follows, where the monad action given by the institution semi-morphism is denoted as $T = (\Phi, \beta)$:

- The signature functor $\Phi : \mathbf{Sign}^{SQL} \to \mathbf{Sign}^{SQL}$ extends a signature Σ by tables of form

$$t_1 \times \cdots \times t_n|_{\varphi_1,\ldots,\varphi_k} \to c_1 \blacktriangleright e_1, \ldots, c_m \blacktriangleright e_m$$

written in SQL notation as

```
SELECT e_1 AS c_1, ..., e_m AS c_m
FROM t_1 JOIN ... JOIN t_n
WHERE φ_1 AND ... AND φ_k
```

where $t_1, \ldots, t_n \in \mathbb{T}^\Sigma$, $\varphi_1, \ldots, \varphi_k$ are check constraints with the columns of $t_1, \ldots, t_n$ as variables, $c_1, \ldots, c_m$ are new column names, and each c_i is attached with a λ-expression e_i

$$\lambda(t_1.c_1, \ldots, t_1.c_{n_1}, \ldots, t_n.c_1, \ldots, t_n.c_{n_m}).t$$

that specifies the computation rules for this column depending on all columns of the joined tables. The type of t is called result type of e_i.
The columns of these tables are given as

$$\mathrm{col}(t_1 \times \cdots \times t_n|_{\varphi_1,\ldots,\varphi_k} \to c_1 \blacktriangleright e_1, \ldots, c_m \blacktriangleright e_m) = \{c_1, \ldots, c_m\}.$$

Sorts of columns are set w.r.t to the column expressions:

$$\tau(t_1 \times \cdots \times t_n|_{\varphi_1,\ldots,\varphi_k} \to c_1 \blacktriangleright e_1, \ldots, c_m \blacktriangleright e_m, c_i) = s_i$$

where s_i is the result type of e_i.
- $\beta_\Sigma(M)$ preserves the models behaviour on tables from Σ, i.e. $\beta_\Sigma(M)(t) = M(t)$ for $t \in \mathbb{T}^\Sigma$. In order to construct the interpretation of the new tables in $\Phi(\Sigma)$, we define $e_i(r_1, \ldots, r_n)$ as the evaluation of an expression e_i ($i = 1, \ldots, m$) w.r.t. to rows $r_1, \ldots, r_n$, i.e.

$$e_i(r_1, \ldots, r_n) :=$$
$$(\lambda(c_1^1, \ldots, c_{m_1}^1, \ldots, c_1^n, \ldots, c_{m_n}^n).t)(r_1(\mathrm{col}(t_1)), \ldots, r_n(\mathrm{col}(t_n)))$$

Each of the constructed rows has to conform to the constraints specified in $\varphi_1, \ldots, \varphi_k$. This can be easily guaranteed by checking whether the model $M^{r_1,\ldots,r_m}$ satisfies the set of constraints $(\varphi_1, \ldots, \varphi_k)$ where $M^{r_1,\ldots,r_n}$ contains just the row r_i for each table t_i $(i = 1, \ldots, n)$ and no data for other tables. For a table $t = t_1 \times \cdots \times t_n|_{\varphi_1,\ldots,\varphi_k} \to c_1 \blacktriangleright e_1, \ldots, c_m \blacktriangleright e_m$ we construct the dataset as the evaluations of the corresponding column expressions:

$$\beta_\Sigma(M)(t) = \{r|\; r(c_i) = e_i(r_1, \ldots, r_n)(i = 1, \ldots, m),$$
$$r_1 \in M(t_1), \ldots, r_n \in M(t_n),$$
$$[\![\varphi_j]\!]^{M^{r_1,\ldots,r_n}}_{\nu_{r(\varphi_j)}} = \mathsf{T} \; (j = 1, \ldots, k)\}$$

Here $\nu_{r(\varphi_j)}$ is the valuation determined by the unique row r_i in table t_i, where t_i is the table over which φ_j has been formulated. As stated above (after Definition 10), for constraints in queries, T is the only designated truth value.

- η_Σ is the inclusion
- μ_Σ maps tables by collapsing an (outer) query over (inner) queries into a simple query. The result is the outer query, modified by substituting λ-terms for the inner queries into the column variables in λ-terms and check constraints of the outer query, and adding check constraints of the inner queries.

Example 5.
   The tables from Example 1. A query

```
SELECT Person.salary AS salary,
       Person.fname AS fname,
       Person.lname AS lname
FROM Person JOIN Employee
ON Employee.pid = Person.id
WHERE Employee.salary >= 10000;
```

would correspond to the table in the monad

$\text{Person} \times \text{Employee}|_{\texttt{Employee.pid = Person.id,Employee.salary >= 10000}} \to$
$\text{salary} \blacktriangleright e_1, \text{fname} \blacktriangleright e_2, \text{lname} \blacktriangleright e_3$

where

$$e_1 = \lambda \text{p\_id}, \text{p\_fname}, \text{p\_lname}, \text{e\_id}, \text{e\_salary}, \text{e\_pid}. \text{e\_salary}$$
$$e_2 = \lambda \text{p\_id}, \text{p\_fname}, \text{p\_lname}, \text{e\_id}, \text{e\_salary}, \text{e\_pid}. \text{e\_fname}$$
$$e_3 = \lambda \text{p\_id}, \text{p\_fname}, \text{p\_lname}, \text{e\_id}, \text{e\_salary}, \text{e\_pid}. \text{e\_lname}$$

In the sequel, we work with an arbitrary but fixed semi-institutional monad (T, η, μ) over an institution $\mathcal{I}$ (with $T = (\Phi, \beta)$). We can define several derived notions:

Definition 14 (Kleisli semi-institution, adapted from [13]). *The Kleisli signature category has a objects $\mathcal{I}$-signatures, and its morphisms $\Sigma_1 \to \Sigma_2$ are $\mathcal{I}$-signature morphisms $\Sigma_1 \to \Phi(\Sigma_2)$. Kleisli composition is defined by*

$$\Sigma_1 \xrightarrow{\sigma_1} \Phi(\Sigma_2) \; ; \; \Sigma_2 \xrightarrow{\sigma_2} \Phi(\Sigma_3) \;=$$

$$\Sigma_1 \xrightarrow{\sigma_1} \Phi(\Sigma_2) \xrightarrow{\Phi(\sigma_2)} \Phi(\Phi(\Sigma_3)) \xrightarrow{\mu_{\Sigma_3}} \Phi(\Sigma_3)$$

Model categories are inherited from $\mathcal{I}$. Model reduct against $\sigma : \Sigma_1 \to \Phi(\Sigma_2)$ is given by $\beta_{\Sigma_2}; \mathbf{Mod}^{\mathcal{I}}(\sigma)$. This gives a semi-institution in the sense of Definition 2.

Due to the "semi"-nature of the monad, we do not have sentence translations along Kleisli signature morphisms. This reflects the fact that queries use a much more powerful language than constraints, and constraints are not closed under queries.

Queries are just Kleisli signature morphisms:

Definition 15 (Query). *A* query *is a signature morphism $q : \Sigma^Q \to \Phi(\Sigma)$.*

Here, Σ^Q typically is a "small" or "singleton" signature. In the case of $\mathcal{SQL}(D\Sigma, DM)$, Σ^Q will typically consist of a single table only, providing a name and column types for the result of the query. The query itself is then given by $q(\Sigma^Q)$, which singles out one particular query in the space $\Phi(\Sigma)$ of all Σ-queries. The semantics of a query q as above is given by the Kleisli reduct $\beta_\Sigma; \mathbf{Mod}^{\mathcal{I}}(q)$, mapping Σ-models (aka Σ-databases) to Σ^Q-models (aka materialised views of signature Σ^Q).

Two queries $q_1, q_2 : \Sigma^Q \to \Phi(\Sigma)$ are *equivalent* [6] if their semantics agree, i.e. $\beta_\Sigma; \mathbf{Mod}(q_1) = \beta_\Sigma; \mathbf{Mod}(q_2)$. q_1 is *contained in* q_2 if for each $M \in \mathbf{Mod}(\Sigma)$, there is a model monomorphism $\beta_\Sigma(M)|_{q_1} \to \beta_\Sigma(M)|_{q_2}$.[5]

Next, we consider composition of queries, also known as query unfolding, which is an important tool for data base integration [6]. Given two queries $q_1 : \Sigma_1^Q \to \Phi(\Sigma_1)$ and $q_2 : \Sigma_2^Q \to \Phi(\Sigma_2)$, we cannot compose them directly. Rather, we have (assuming the existence of signature coproducts) to assume that the first query is built over the second database enriched with the result of the second query, i.e. that $\Sigma_1 = \Sigma_2^Q + \Sigma_2$. Then we can pair the second query with η and take the Kleisli composition

$$\Sigma_1^Q \xrightarrow{q_1} \Phi(\Sigma_1) \; ; \; \Sigma_1 = \Sigma_2 + \Sigma_2^Q \xrightarrow{[\eta, q_2]} \Phi(\Sigma_2)$$

We can also obtain a semi-substitution from a query. Substitutions have been introduced in [3,5]. They run between variable sets that are represented as signature morphisms (extending a base signature with some constants playing the role of variables). We weaken the notion as follows:

Definition 16. *Given two signature morphisms ("variable sets") $\chi_1 : \Sigma \to \Sigma_1$ and $\chi_2 : \Sigma \to \Sigma_2$, a Σ-semi-substitution $\psi : \chi_1 \to \chi_2$ is a functor*

$$\mathbf{Mod}(\psi) : \mathbf{Mod}(\Sigma_2) \to \mathbf{Mod}(\Sigma_1)$$

---

[5] For $\mathcal{SQL}(D\Sigma, DM)$ this means multiset inclusion; and query equivalence is the same as containment in both directions.

such that the following diagram commutes:

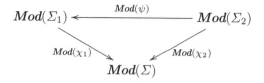

For a query $q : \Sigma^Q \to \Phi(\Sigma)$, we consider the coproduct injection $\iota_1 : \Sigma \to \Sigma + \Sigma^Q$ as "variable set", and define the semi-substitution $\psi : \iota_1 \to 1_\Sigma$ via

$$\mathbf{Mod}(\psi) = \beta_\Sigma; \mathbf{Mod}^\mathcal{I}(\Sigma + \Sigma^Q \xrightarrow{[\eta_\Sigma, q]} \Phi(\Sigma)) \ .$$

Commutativity of the above diagram for semi-substitutions is ensured by the modification property of η (see Definition 12).

Another view on (general) Kleisli morphisms is that they correspond to (complex) schema mappings [22], because they map table names to queries. This means that we can compose schema mappings, and also (via the Kleisli model functor) compute their semantics.

4   Database Integration via Colimits

The formalisation of SQL databases as an institution allows the use of colimits for database integration.

Proposition 2. *Consider finite diagram $D : I \to \mathbf{Sign}^{SQL}$, where for any span $j \xleftarrow{m} i \xrightarrow{n} k$ in I with $j \neq k$ and any $t \in \mathbb{T}^{D(i)}$, the following holds: if $D(m)_\mathbb{T}(t)$ and $D(n)_\mathbb{T}(t)$ both have a primary key, then so does t. Then D has a colimit.*

Proof. Let a finite diagram $D : I \to \mathbf{Sign}^{SQL}$ with the above property be given. We construct its colimit signature Σ together with colimit injections $(\mu_i : D(i) \to \Sigma)_{i \in |I|}$ as follows. Let $D_\mathbb{T}$ be the projection of D to tables and table translations. Then let $\mathbb{T}^\Sigma$ be the colimit of $D_\mathbb{T}$ (in **Set**), and let $(\mu_i)_\mathbb{T} : \mathbb{T}^{D(i)} \to \mathbb{T}^\Sigma$ (for $i \in |I|$) be the colimit injections. This gives us the table part of the colimit. Concerning the column part, let $\mathbb{S}^{D\Sigma}$-**Set** be the category of $\mathbb{S}^{D\Sigma}$-sorted sets, which is given by the comma category **Set** $\downarrow \mathbb{S}^{D\Sigma}$. For a table $t \in \mathbb{T}^\Sigma$, we construct a diagram of $\mathbb{S}^{D\Sigma}$-sorted column sets as follows. The index category I_t has objects

$$|I_t| = \{(i, u) \mid u \in \mathbb{T}^{D(i)}, (\mu_i)_\mathbb{T}(u) = t\},$$

i.e. the set of tables that are mapped (by some colimit injection) to t. I_t has a morphism $m : (i, u_1) \to (j, u_2)$ whenever $m : i \to j \in I$ and $D(m)_\mathbb{T}(u_1) = u_2$. The diagram functor $D_t : I_t \to \mathbb{S}^{D\Sigma}$-**Set** acts on objects as

$$D_t(i, u) = \mathrm{col}^{D(i)}(u),$$

which is $\mathbb{S}^{D\Sigma}$-sorted using $\tau^{D(i)}(u,\cdot)$, and on morphisms as

$$D_t(m : (i, u_1) \to (j, u_2)) = D(m)_{\text{col},u_1} : \text{col}^{D(i)}(u_1) \to \text{col}^{D(j)}(u_2)$$

Let $(C_t, (\theta^t_{(i,u)})_{(i,u)\in|I_t|})$ be the colimit of D_t in $\mathbb{S}^{D\Sigma}$-**Set** (recall that colimits in comma categories are constructed component-wise). Then C_t is the sorted set of columns of table t in Σ. The column translation of $\mu_i : D(i) \to \Sigma$ is given by

$$(\mu_i)_{\text{col},u} = \theta^{(\mu_i)_{\mathbb{T}}(u)}_{(i,u)} \qquad (u \in \mathbb{T}^{D(i)}).$$

Finally, the primary key of $C(t)$ is determined as $(\mu_i)_{\text{col},u}(pk^{D(i)}(u))$ for any $(i, u) \in |I_t|$ with $pk^{D(i)}(u) \neq \emptyset$. Since any two such (i, u) are connected via a zigzag path in I_t, the assumption about spans in I together with preservation of primary keys along signature morphisms ensures that this is independent of the choice of (i, u). This completes the construction of the colimit $(\Sigma, (\mu_i : D(i) \to \Sigma)_{i\in|I|})$. Its universal property follows from the universal properties of the colimits involved in its construction. $\square$

Example 6. Coproducts put database tables side by side:

Address(name:string,address:string)

Address(name:string,address:string)
Birthdate(name:string,dob:date)

Birthdate(name:string,dob:date)

Here, signature morphisms are inclusions.

An integration of tables can be achieved using pushouts:

Example 7.

Address(name:string,address:string)

Person(name:string Person1(name:string,address:string,dob:date)

Birthdate(name:string,dob:date)

Here, signature morphisms map tables in the unique way and leave columns as they are. If table Person has primary key name, then this is also the primary key in the colimit. However, if Person does not have a primary key, but Birthdate and Address have one consisting of both of their respective columns, then the diagram does not have a colimit, because its primary key cannot be determined.

Since tables in one signature do not interact, the same effect can also be achieved with a coequaliser

Example 8.

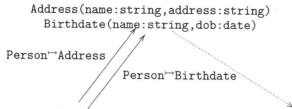

```
      Address(name:string,address:string)
        Birthdate(name:string,dob:date)
```

Person↪Address

Person↪Birthdate

```
Person(name:string)   Person(name:string,address:string,dob:date)
```

Here, signature morphisms leave columns as they are. For table `Person`, at the table level, we have the coequaliser (in **Set**)

$$\text{Person} \rightrightarrows \text{Address}, \text{ Birthdate} \dashrightarrow \text{Person}$$

At the column level, we obtain a pushout

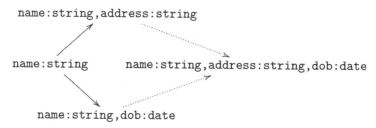

```
      name:string,address:string
```

```
name:string      name:string,address:string,dob:date
```

```
      name:string,dob:date
```

So the coequaliser involves a coequaliser at the level of tables plus a pushout at the level of columns.

The amalgamation property is a major technical assumption in the study of specification semantics [18] and is important in many respects. For example, it allows the computation of normal forms for specifications [2], and it is a prerequisite for good behaviour w.r.t. parameterization [8] and conservative extensions [4] and for soundness of proof systems for structured specification [15]. Intuitively, amalgamation of databases is just a rearrangement of the (partially shared) tables.

Definition 17. *A cocone for a diagram in $\textbf{Sign}^{\mathcal{I}}$ is called (weakly) amalgamable if it is mapped to a (Weak) limit under $\textbf{Mod}^{\mathcal{I}}$. This can be characterised in more elementary terms as follows: Given a diagram $D: I \longrightarrow \textbf{Sign}^{\mathcal{I}}$, a family of models $(M_i)_{i \in |I|}$ is called D-consistent if $M_j|_{D(m)} = M_i$ for each $m: i \longrightarrow j \in I$. Then a cocone $(\Sigma, (\mu_i)_{i \in |I|})$ over the diagram in $D: I \longrightarrow \textbf{Sign}^{I}$ is weakly amalgamable if for each D-consistent family of models $(M_i)_{i \in |I|}$, there is a Σ-model M with $M|_{\mu_i} = M_i$ ($i \in |I|$) (and moreover, an analogous condition holds for model morphisms). In case M is unique with these properties, the cocone is amalgamable.*

An institution $\mathcal{I}$ admits (weak) finite amalgamation if all finite colimit cocones are (weakly) amalgamable.

Proposition 3. *For colimit cocones as in Proposition 2, $\mathcal{SQL}(D\Sigma, DM)$ admits weak finite amalgamation, and if all diagram signatures have a primary key, then also finite amalgamation.*

Proof. Let $(\Sigma, (\mu_i)_{i\in|I|})$ be a colimit cocone as in Proposition 2. Moreover, let $(M_i)_{i\in|I|}$ a D-consistent family of models. We need to define its amalgamation $M \in \mathbf{Mod}^{\mathcal{SQL}}(\Sigma)$. Given $t \in \mathbb{T}^\Sigma$, consider the diagram $D_t : I_t \to \mathbb{S}^{D\Sigma}\text{-}\mathbf{Set}$ defined in the proof of Proposition 2. Recall that $\mathrm{col}^\Sigma(t)$ is the colimit of this diagram. The carrier sets of the model DM form an $\mathbb{S}^{D\Sigma}$-sorted set $|DM|$, and any row is an $\mathbb{S}^{D\Sigma}$-sorted map into $|DM|$. Hence, any compatible family of rows $(r_{(i,u)} \in M_i(u))_{(i,u)\in|I_t|}$ is a cocone for D_t, and by the colimit property of $\mathrm{col}^\Sigma(t)$, it can be amalgamated to a row $r : (c \in \mathrm{col}(t)) \to DM_{\tau(t,c)}$. If all diagram signatures have a primary key, then let $M(t)\#r = 1$ for any such r, and M is the unique amalgamation. If not, then proceed with the following algorithm (working on a copy of $(M_i)_{i\in|I|}$ that is modified):

1. initially, set all multiplicities $M(t)\#r$ to 0.
2. Choose a compatible family of rows $(r_{(i,u)} \in M_i(u))_{(i,u)\in|I_t|}$, and for its amalgamation r, increase $M(t)\#r$ by one.
3. Decrease the multiplicities $M_i(u)\#r_{(i,u)}$ by one.
4. Repeat steps 2 and 3 until all multiplicities $M_i(u)\#r_{(i,u)}$ are zero. By Eq. 1, all $M_i(u)\#r_{(i,u)}$ will reach zero simultaneously. $\quad\square$

By very general results [10,19], Propositions 2 and 3 carry over from signatures to presentations, i.e. signatures equipped with axioms, e.g. foreign key constraints.

5 Conclusion

We presented an institutional approach towards a formalisation of relational databases and their integration via colimits and amalgamation. Building on a foundation of a many-sorted first-order structure, the signatures and sentences reflect SQL's Data Description Language, including tables, their columns and various constraints. The models of this institution capture the data that can be stored in those tables. Queries on a database can be formalised as a semi-institutional monad. Syntactic and semantic components of this institution were designed to closely follow those used in SQL, which allows an easy application of this new formalisation to existing database-related tools.

Many other categorical approaches define a new query language (e.g. FQL [24]). This limits the frictionless application of those approaches in real-world scenarios, as SQL is used in most software solutions that involve database communication. Therefore, we designed the presented institutional formalisation of databases to closely reflect the existing structures from the SQL specification.

Many open questions remain, e.g. whether model reducts have left and right adjoints as in [22], or whether colimits can be expressed as queries. Also, the existence of colimits in the Kleisli category should be studied, because these correspond to database integrations using queries. Note that by the results of [13], these colimits do not always exist.

Future work should also investigate the manipulation of data by insert and delete statements. Model morphisms could be used to capture a structure similar to those used in a categorical theory of patches [12], which may yield a logical framework for version tracking of databases.

Operations that involve multiple tables are present in most database-related application. The introduction of a suitable institutional semi-monad (and its Kleisli morphisms) enhances the presented institution for databases with functionalities such as inner joins that combine multiple tables. Yet, the current formalisation allows only inner joins. Full formalisations of all different types of joins (e.g. left join, outer join) and other principles (e.g. aggregations, unions) are yet to be done. The introduction of other join types can be achieved by introducing multiple join operators with appropriate model interpretations. A similar approach could be chosen for unions. Aggregations will pose a tougher problem. They require an adaption of the notion of reduct of a Kleisli morphism, because a single row in a query result would stem from multiple rows of a single base table.

Institutions were defined as a framework that allows integration of different logics. Similarly, one may define institution comorphisms [9] to different logics (including logics for algebraic databases) and thus open the doors for the vast and powerful landscape of logic reasoning tools. The Heterogeneous tool set (Hets) [14] offers functionalities for reasoning and proving not only across logics, but also integrates languages like UML. The integration of the SQL-institution into this tool set can be a step towards a logics-founded approach for model-driven development for databases with automated checks for coherence. Integration of queries could be done by representing Kleisli morphisms[6], implementing their composition as well as checks for query containment and equivalence.

References

1. Alagić, S., Bernstein, P.A.: A model theory for generic schema management. In: Ghelli, G., Grahne, G. (eds.) DBPL 2001. LNCS, vol. 2397, pp. 228–246. Springer, Heidelberg (2002). https://doi.org/10.1007/3-540-46093-4_14
2. Borzyszkowski, T.: Generalized interpolation in CASL. Inf. Process. Lett. **76**(1–2), 19–24 (2000)
3. Diaconescu, R.: Herbrand theorems in arbitrary institutions. Inf. Process. Lett. **90**, 29–37 (2004)
4. Diaconescu, R., Goguen, J., Stefaneas, P.: Logical support for modularisation. In: Huet, G., Plotkin, G. (eds.) Proceedings of a Workshop on Logical Frameworks (1991)
5. Diaconescu, R.: Institution-Independent Model Theory. SUL. Birkhäuser, Basel (2008). https://doi.org/10.1007/978-3-7643-8708-2
6. Doan, A., Halevy, A.Y., Ives, Z.G.: Principles of Data Integration. Morgan Kaufmann, San Francisco (2012). http://research.cs.wisc.edu/dibook/

---

[6] Note that the signatures $\Phi(\Sigma)$ are generally infinite and cannot be easily represented, but for a Kleisli morphism, only the mapped symbols need to be represented.

7. Ehrig, H., Große-Rhode, M.: Functorial theory of parameterized specifications in a general specification framework. Theor. Comput. Sci. **135**, 221–266 (1994)
8. Ehrig, H., Mahr, B.: Fundamentals of Algebraic Specification 2. EATCS, vol. 21. Springer, Heidelberg (1990). https://doi.org/10.1007/978-3-642-61284-8
9. Goguen, J., Roşu, G.: Institution morphisms. Form. Asp. Comput. **13**, 274–307 (2002)
10. Goguen, J.A., Burstall, R.M.: Institutions: abstract model theory for specification and programming. J. ACM (JACM) **39**(1), 95–146 (1992)
11. Melton, J.: ISO/IEC 9075-2: 2003 (SQL/foundation). ISO standard (2003)
12. Mimram, S., Di Giusto, C.: A categorical theory of patches. Electron. Notes Theor. Comput. Sci. **298**, 283–307 (2013)
13. Mossakowski, T., Krumnack, U., Maibaum, T.: What is a derived signature morphism? In: Codescu, M., Diaconescu, R., Ţuţu, I. (eds.) WADT 2015. LNCS, vol. 9463, pp. 90–109. Springer, Cham (2015). https://doi.org/10.1007/978-3-319-28114-8_6
14. Mossakowski, T., Maeder, C., Lüttich, K.: The heterogeneous tool set. In: Grumberg, O., Huth, M. (eds.) TACAS 2007. LNCS, vol. 4424, pp. 519–522. Springer, Heidelberg (2007). https://doi.org/10.1007/978-3-540-71209-1_40
15. Mossakowski, T., Tarlecki, A.: A relatively complete calculus for structured heterogeneous specifications. In: Muscholl, A. (ed.) FoSSaCS 2014. LNCS, vol. 8412, pp. 441–456. Springer, Heidelberg (2014). https://doi.org/10.1007/978-3-642-54830-7_29
16. Object Management Group: The distributed ontology, modeling, and specification language (DOL) (2018). oMG standard available at http://www.omg.org/spec/DOL/
17. Rosser, J.B., Turquette, A.: Many-Valued Logics. North-Holland, Amsterdam (1952)
18. Sannella, D., Tarlecki, A.: Specifications in an arbitrary institution. Inf. Comput. **76**, 165–210 (1988)
19. Sannella, D., Tarlecki, A.: Foundations of Algebraic Specification and Formal Software Development. EATCS. Springer, Heidelberg (2012). https://doi.org/10.1007/978-3-642-17336-3
20. Schorlemmer, W.M., Kalfoglou, Y.: Institutionalising ontology-based semantic integration. Appl. Ontol. **3**(3), 131–150 (2008). https://doi.org/10.3233/AO-2008-0041
21. Schultz, P., Spivak, D., Vasilakopoulou, C., Wisnesky, R.: Algebraic databases. Theory Appl. Categ. **32**(16), 547–619 (2017)
22. Schultz, P., Spivak, D.I., Wisnesky, R.: Algebraic model management: a survey. In: James, P., Roggenbach, M. (eds.) WADT 2016. LNCS, vol. 10644, pp. 56–69. Springer, Cham (2017). https://doi.org/10.1007/978-3-319-72044-9_5
23. Schultz, P., Wisnesky, R.: Algebraic data integration. J. Funct. Program. **27**, e24 (2017). https://doi.org/10.1017/S0956796817000168
24. Spivak, D.I., Wisnesky, R.: Relational foundations for functorial data migration. In: Proceedings of the 15th Symposium on Database Programming Languages, pp. 21–28. ACM (2015)

Finite Limits and Anti-unification
in Substitution Categories

Wolfram Kahl[(✉)]

McMaster University, Hamilton, ON, Canada
kahl@cas.mcmaster.ca

Abstract. It is well-known that coequalisers and pushouts of substitutions correspond to solutions of unification problems, and therefore do not always exist. But how about equalisers and pullbacks? If the literature contains the answers, they are well-hidden.

We provide explicit details and proofs for these constructions in categories with substitutions as morphisms, and in particular work out the details of categorial products for which the universal arrow construction turns out to correspond exactly to anti-unification.

1 Introduction

Substitutions occur in the formal study of syntactic systems, and are mappings from "variables" to "terms" (or "expressions"). Terms may contain variables, and "application" of substitution to terms produces terms again. Rydeheard and Stell (1987) introduced (based on closely related ideas by Lawvere (1963)) a categorial treatment of substitutions, where objects are sets considered as sets of variables, and morphisms from V_1 to V_2 are substitutions that map each element of V_1 to a term containing only variables from V_2. They say: "In this case variables are *localized*." This is in contrast with most of the conventional literature on substitutions, were mostly a single global set of variables is assumed. For example, Eder (1985) investigates a "more general than" order on idempotent substitutions.

Rydeheard and Stell (1987) used their category-theoretic formulation in particular for the construction of a unification algorithm, where unification is defined as coequaliser of substitutions. Since unification problems are not always solvable, coequalisers do not always exist in substitution categories, but since unification problems are important, coequalisers (and pushouts which correspond to unification problems with disjoint variable sets) have received much attention in the literature. However, I have not been able to find explicit statements about equalisers, pullbacks, or products in substitution categories. Since substitution categories are a concrete instance of Kleisli categories, Szigeti's (1983) study on limits and colimits in Kleisli categories using adjunctions is related, but, in his own words: "Mention must be made that these results are powerless in concrete instances." Hosseini and Qasemi Nezhad (2016) tackle the problem of existence

© IFIP International Federation for Information Processing 2019
Published by Springer Nature Switzerland AG 2019
J. L. Fiadeiro and I. Ţuţu (Eds.): WADT 2018, LNCS 11563, pp. 87–102, 2019.
https://doi.org/10.1007/978-3-030-23220-7_5

of equalisers in Kleisli categories for a number of more concrete monads, but still without covering the term monad.

One motivation for studying finite limits in substitution categories comes from the fact that substitutions can be components of homomorphisms of attributed graphs (Kahl 2014, 2015), and the properties of the resulting categories are key to the applicability of categorial approaches to graph transformation (Ehrig et al. 2006) in the spirit of the "high level replacement (HLR) systems" introduced by Ehrig et al. (1991). In particular for the "adhesive categories" introduced by Lack and Sobociński (2004, 2005) as a useful abstraction for frequently-studied HLR properties, existence of pullbacks becomes a key property. Another important question in that context is whether pushouts along all monomorphisms exist, or whether at least useful classes of monomorphisms can be defined along which pushouts exist.

In this paper, we provide concrete constructions and detailed proofs for equalisers, products, and pullbacks in substitution categories. In summary, the instances of basic category-theoretic concepts for the substitution category for a fixed signature take the following shapes, where well-known general facts are included in parentheses for completeness:

1. Epimorphisms are those substitutions where all target variables occur in the image.
2. Monomorphisms are those substitutions for which the image of any variable does not result from applying that substitution to any term different from that variable, as previously shown in (Kahl 2015).
3. Equalisers of two substitutions in the substitution category always exist, and are the variable subset injections for the subset on which the two substitutions have the same images—these are the equalisers of the two substitutions in *Set*, but the proof of the universal property is substitution-specific.
4. Regular monomorphisms are precisely the injective variable renamings.
5. (Coequalisers are most general unifiers, and do not always exist.)
6. Products have as objects the sets of all pairs of not-equally-headed terms; the construction of the universal morphism is essentially anti-unification. Products of finite (variable) sets are in general infinite.
7. (Coproducts are inherited from *Set* as for every monad.)
8. Pullbacks always exist (since they can be obtained from products and equalisers). Pullbacks of substitutions between finite (variable) sets have finite pullback objects.
9. (Pushouts correspond to most general unifiers of substitutions with disjoint ranges, and do not always exist.) Pushouts along regular monomorphisms do exist, and regular monomorphisms are stable under pushout.

We are working on a mechanisation of this theory in the dependently-typed programming language and proof assistant Agda (Norell 2007); at the time of writing, proofs for items 2, 3, and 6 are already complete.

Overview

After some background in Sects. 2 and 3 about monads and the term monad, we will work through the list above, except for the items in parentheses, which are well-known. We devote Sect. 4 to epimorphisms, Sect. 5 to monomorphisms, Sect. 6 to equalisers and regular monomorphisms, Sect. 7 to products, Sect. 8 to pullbacks, and Sect. 9 to pushouts.

2 Notation and Background: Categories and Monads

We assume familiarity with the basics of category theory; for notation, we write "$f : A \to B$" to declare that morphism f goes from object A to object B, or we may refer to the source and target objects of f as $\mathsf{src}\, f = A$ and $\mathsf{trg}\, f = B$. We use ";" as the associative binary *forward composition* operator that maps two morphisms $f : A \to B$ and $g : B \to C$ to $(f\,;g) : A \to C$. The identity morphism for object A is written $\mathbb{I}_A$. We assign ";" higher priority than other binary operators, and assign unary operators higher priority than all binary operators.

The category of sets and functions is denoted by *Set*. For a function $f : A \to B$ and an element $x : A$, we normally denote function application by juxtaposition "$f\ a$". (We may need to add parentheses to either subexpression, "$(f)\ a$" or "$f(a)$".) This juxtaposition has higher precedence than all visible operators.

A *functor* $\mathcal{F}$ from one category to another maps objects to objects and morphisms to morphisms respecting the structure that src, trg, $\mathbb{I}$, and composition constitute; we denote functor application by juxtaposition both for objects, $\mathcal{F}\, A$, and for morphisms, $\mathcal{F}\, f$.

A *monad* on a category $\mathcal{C}$ consists is a functor $\mathcal{M} : \mathcal{C} \to \mathcal{C}$ for which there are two natural transformations ("polymorphic morphisms") $\mathsf{return}_A : A \to \mathcal{M}\, A$ and $\mathsf{join}_A : \mathcal{M}\,(\mathcal{M}\, A) \to \mathcal{M}\, A$ satisfying $\mathsf{return}_{\mathcal{M}\, A}\,;\mathsf{join}_A = \mathbb{I}$ and $\mathcal{M}\mathsf{return}_A\,;$ $\mathsf{join}_A = \mathbb{I}$ and $\mathcal{M}\, \mathsf{join}_A\,;\mathsf{join}_A = \mathsf{join}_{\mathcal{M}\, A}\,;\mathsf{join}_A$. Important monads are the List monad, and the term monad $\mathcal{T}_\Sigma$ for any (algebraic) signature Σ. For the former, $\mathsf{join}_{\mathsf{List},A} : \mathsf{List}\,(\mathsf{List}\, A) \to \mathsf{List}\, A$ is the function that flattens (or concatenates) lists of lists.

Each monad $\mathcal{M}$ on $\mathcal{C}$ induces the so-called *Kleisli category* $\mathbb{K}_\mathcal{M}$ that has the same objects as $\mathcal{C}$, but $\mathcal{C}$-morphisms $A \to \mathcal{M}\, B$ as morphisms from A to B. Kleisli composition of $f : A \to \mathcal{M}\, B$ with $g : B \to \mathcal{M}\, C$ will be written $f\,\fatsemi\, g$; this is defined by $f\,\fatsemi\, g = f\,;(\mathcal{M}\, g)\,;\mathsf{join}_C$. In the Kleisli category, return is the identity for Kleisli composition, that is, for each Kleisli morphism f from A to B we have $\mathsf{return}_A\,\fatsemi\, f = f$ and $f = f\,\fatsemi\, \mathsf{return}_B$.

Note the different symbols ";" for composition in the base category and "$\fatsemi$" for composition in the Kleisli category! Both will occur frequently, and also together. They satisfy, among others, the equations $(f\,;g)\,\fatsemi\, h = f\,;(g\,\fatsemi\, h)$ and $f\,\fatsemi\,(g\,;\mathsf{return}) = f\,;\mathcal{M}\, g$ and $(f\,\fatsemi\, g)\,;\mathcal{M}\, h = f\,\fatsemi\,(g\,;\mathcal{M}\, h)$.

3 Substitution Categories as Kleisli Categories of Term Monads

Let $\mathcal{T}_\Sigma$ denote the term functor for signature Σ, that is, $\mathcal{T}_\Sigma\, X$ is the set of Σ-terms with elements of set X as variables. As usual, $\mathcal{T}_\Sigma\, X$ is defined inductively by the following:

- Each variable $v : X$ is a term, that is, $v \in \mathcal{T}_\Sigma\, X$.
- If $t_1, \ldots, t_n \in \mathcal{T}_\Sigma\, X$ are n terms, and f is an n-ary function symbol provided by Σ, then the resulting function symbol application is a term, too: $f(t_1, \ldots, t_n) \in \mathcal{T}_\Sigma\, X$.

$\mathcal{T}_\Sigma$ is an endofunctor on the category *Set*, and naturally extends to a monad, the *term monad*. Its "join" natural transformation, $\mathsf{join}_{\mathcal{T}_\Sigma}$, produces for each set A (of variables) the function $\mathsf{join}_{\mathcal{T}_\Sigma, A} : \mathcal{T}_\Sigma\, (\mathcal{T}_\Sigma\, A) \to \mathcal{T}_\Sigma\, A$ which "flattens" nested terms over variables in A (that is, terms over $\mathcal{T}_\Sigma\, A$ as their set of variables). The "return" natural transformation of the term monad, $\mathsf{return}_{\mathcal{T}_\Sigma}$, maps each variable v to the term v. (We will omit the subscript $\mathcal{T}_\Sigma$ for join and return.)

The Kleisli category of the term monad $\mathcal{T}_\Sigma$ will be denoted $\mathbb{T}_\Sigma$; its morphisms from set X to set Y are substitutions, that is, functions $X \to \mathcal{T}_\Sigma\, Y$, that is, the sets X and Y are "interpreted" as sets of *variables*.

The definition of Kleisli composition instantiated for the term monad $\mathcal{T}_\Sigma$ takes two arbitrary substitutions $F : X \to \mathcal{T}_\Sigma\, Y$ and $G : Y \to \mathcal{T}_\Sigma\, Z$ to their composed substitution

$$F \,\mathbin{\fatsemi}\, G \;\; = \;\; F \,\mathbin{;}\, \mathcal{T}_\Sigma\, G \,\mathbin{;}\, \mathsf{join}_Z \; .$$

Conventionally, this would be described via "application" of substitutions to terms: We write $F \triangleright t$ for the application of substitution $F : X \to \mathcal{T}_\Sigma\, Y$ to term $t : \mathcal{T}_\Sigma\, X$, and the substitution composition $F \mathbin{\fatsemi} G$ can alternatively be defined by

$$(F \mathbin{\fatsemi} G)\, v \;\; = \;\; G \triangleright (F\, v), \qquad \text{for all } v : X.$$

When starting from the monadic setting, application of substitutions can be defined as follows:

$$F \triangleright t = ((\mathcal{T}_\Sigma\, F) \,\mathbin{;}\, \mathsf{join}_Y)(t)$$

For most signatures Σ and most variable sets V, the set of terms $\mathcal{T}_\Sigma\, V$ is infinite, but there are a few exceptions, which are important to keep in mind:

- The set $\mathcal{T}_\Sigma\, \emptyset$ of ground terms (i.e., terms without variables) is empty iff Σ has no constant symbols (that is, no zero-ary function symbols).
- The set $\mathcal{T}_\Sigma\, \emptyset$ of ground terms has exactly n elements for $n > 0$ iff Σ has no function symbols with arity at least one, and exactly n constant symbols.
- For a one-element variable set $\mathbb{1}$, the set $\mathcal{T}_\Sigma\, \mathbb{1}$ has at most one element iff Σ has no symbols at all.

We shall need the following definitions:

Definition 3.1. For a substitution $\sigma : V_1 \to T_\Sigma V_2$, its *range* $\mathrm{ran}\ \sigma : \mathbb{P}\ V_2$ is the set of all variables occurring in $\sigma\ v$ for some $v : V_1$. ☐

Definition 3.2. A *position* is a finite sequence of positive natural numbers, with ϵ denoting the empty sequence and $k.p$ denoting the sequence with first element k and tail sequence p.

Positions are used to select subterms:

$$f(t_1, \ldots, t_n)|_{k.p} = t_k|_p \qquad \text{if } f \text{ has arity } n, \text{ and } 1 \leq k \leq n; \qquad t|_\epsilon = t \ . \qquad ☐$$

4 Epimorphisms in Substitution Categories

For every monad over category $\mathcal{C}$ we have that, if f is epi in $\mathcal{C}$, then $f \,\mathring{,}\, \mathsf{return}$ is epi in the Kleisli category. Substitutions of shape $f \,\mathring{,}\, \mathsf{return}$ only map to variables. However, not all epis in $\mathbb{T}_\Sigma$ are of this shape:

Theorem 4.1. A substitution $\sigma : V_1 \to T_\Sigma V_2$ is epi in $\mathbb{T}_\Sigma$ iff all variables in V_2 occur in the range of σ, that is, $\mathrm{ran}\ \sigma = V_2$.

Proof. Recall that σ is epi iff for all $\tau_1, \tau_2 : V_2 \to T_\Sigma V_3$ we have that $\sigma \,\mathring{,}\, \tau_1 = \sigma \,\mathring{,}\, \tau_2$ implies $\tau_1 = \tau_2$.

Assume σ is epi. Choose $V_3 = \{x, y\}$, and define τ_1 and τ_2 as follows:

$$\tau_1(v) = x \qquad \text{and} \qquad \tau_2(v) = \begin{cases} x & \text{if } v \in \mathrm{ran}\ \sigma \\ y & \text{if } v \notin \mathrm{ran}\ \sigma \end{cases}$$

Then $\sigma \,\mathring{,}\, \tau_1 = \sigma \,\mathring{,}\, \tau_2$, and since σ is epi, also $\tau_1 = \tau_2$, which implies that $\mathrm{ran}\ \sigma = V_2$.

Conversely, if $\mathrm{ran}\ \sigma = V_2$, and any V_3 and any $\tau_1, \tau_2 : V_2 \to T_\Sigma V_3$ with $\sigma \,\mathring{,}\, \tau_1 = \sigma \,\mathring{,}\, \tau_2$ are given, then for each variable v in V_2, there is at least one $u \in V_1$ and position p in the term $\sigma\ u$ such that $(\sigma u)|_p = v$; then

$$\tau_1\ v = \tau_1\ ((\sigma u)|_p) = (\tau_1 \triangleright (\sigma u))|_p = (\tau_2 \triangleright (\sigma u))|_p = \tau_2\ ((\sigma u)|_p) = \tau_2\ v,$$

and therefore $\tau_1 = \tau_2$. ☐

5 Monomorphisms in Substitution Categories

A first version of the following analysis of monomorphisms in substitution categories appeared in the appendix of (Kahl 2015).

In any monad, if the "return" natural transformation produces monomorphisms (which it does for T_Σ), then monomorphisms in the Kleisli category of this monad are also monomorphisms in the underlying category. Monomorphisms F of the underlying category that are preserved by the monad functor give rise to monomorphisms $F \,\mathring{,}\, \mathsf{return}$ in the Kleisli category.

The term functor preserves all monomorphisms: An injective variable mapping $F : V_1 \to V_2$ gives rise to an injective term mapping $T_\Sigma F : T_\Sigma V_1 \to T_\Sigma V_2$ that only renames variables. The resulting substitution $F \mathbin{\text{\textsemicolon}} \text{return} : V_1 \to T_\Sigma V_2$ is an injective variable renaming, which is therefore a mono in the category of substitutions, too—this also can easily be seen directly.

However, not all monos in $\mathbb{T}_\Sigma$ are of this simple shape.

For σ, being a monomorphism in the category of substitutions exactly means that *substitution application* of σ does not unify any two different terms. That is, σ is a monomorphism in the category of substitutions iff for any two terms t_1 and t_2 we have

$$\sigma \triangleright t_1 = \sigma \triangleright t_2 \qquad \text{implies} \qquad t_1 = t_2.$$

Due to the quantification over arbitrary terms t_1 and t_2, this condition is not easy to check directly.

It is easy to see that monomorphisms in the category of substitutions, as a consequence of this condition, cannot map any variables to ground terms. However, this by itself does not constitute a characterisation of monomorphisms.

Fortunately a much simpler condition is (necessary and) sufficient: We can show that monomorphisms in the $\mathbb{T}_\Sigma$ are those substitutions that do not identify variables with different terms:

Theorem 5.1. A substitution $\sigma : V_1 \to T_\Sigma V_2$ is a monomorphism in the category of substitutions iff for every variable $v : V_1$ and every term $t : T_\Sigma V_1$, we have:

$$\sigma \triangleright t = \sigma\, v \qquad \text{implies} \qquad t = v \ .$$

Proof. "$\Rightarrow$" follows directly by applying the monomorphism property to the two terms v and t.

"$\Leftarrow$": Assume that σ satisfies the given condition. To show that σ is a monomorphism in the category of substitutions it suffices to show that for any two terms $t, u : T_\Sigma V_1$ with $\sigma \triangleright t = \sigma \triangleright u$, we have $t = u$. We show this by induction on the structure of t and u:

- If $t = v$ is a variable, then $\sigma\, v = \sigma \triangleright t = \sigma \triangleright u$, from which the given property yields $v = u$.
- The case where u is a variable is analogous.
- If $t = f(t_1, \ldots, t_n)$ and u is not a variable, then $\sigma \triangleright t = \sigma \triangleright u$ implies that there are terms $u_1, \ldots, u_n$ such that $u = f(u_1, \ldots, u_n)$ and $\sigma \triangleright t_i = \sigma \triangleright u_i$, from which the induction hypothesis yields $t_i = u_i$ for all i, implying $t = u$.
$\qquad\qquad\square$

For finite substitutions, the condition of Theorem 5.1 directly translates into a decision procedure that for each variable $v : V_1$ checks whether for any *different* variable $u : V_1$, its image $\sigma\, u$ occurs as a subterm in $\sigma\, v$. Due to the observation above, this can be further sped up for the negative case by first checking whether $\sigma\, v$ is ground, in which case σ cannot be a monomorphism.

6 Equalisers

In any category $\mathcal{C}$, an equaliser of two parallel morphisms $f, g : A \to B$ is an object S together with a morphism $\zeta : S \to A$ such that $\zeta \,\mathring{,}\, f = \zeta \,\mathring{,}\, g$, and for every other candidate morphism h with $h \,\mathring{,}\, f = h \,\mathring{,}\, g$ there us a unique morphism u such that $h = u \,\mathring{,}\, \zeta$. An equaliser morphism ζ is always mono.

   In *Set*, an equaliser for two functions f and g is a subobject monomorphism selecting the subset of A on which f and g coincide.

   Kleisli categories do not automatically inherit equalisers from the underlying category.

   For two substitutions $\sigma, \tau : V_1 \to \mathcal{T}_\Sigma\, V_2$, let V_0 together with $\zeta : V_0 \to V_1$ be their equaliser in *Set*. We now show that V_0 together with $\zeta \,\mathring{,}\, \mathsf{return}_{V_1}$ is an equaliser for σ and τ in $\mathbb{T}_\Sigma$.

   Commutativity follows from the monad laws:

$$(\zeta \,\mathring{,}\, \mathsf{return}_{V_1}) \,\mathring{,}\, \sigma = \zeta \,\mathring{,}\, \sigma = \zeta \,\mathring{,}\, \tau = (\zeta \,\mathring{,}\, \mathsf{return}_{V_1}) \,\mathring{,}\, \tau$$

For the universal property, we need to resort to substitution-specific reasoning. Assume a substitution $h : Z \to V_1$ with $h \,\mathring{,}\, \sigma = h \,\mathring{,}\, \tau$.

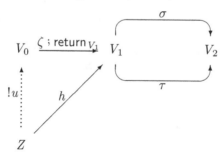

If $\mathsf{ran}\, h$ is empty, then we can define $u\, z = h\, z$ since the latter is a closed term, and since $\mathsf{ran}\, u$ is then also empty, we obtain $u \,\mathring{,}\, (\zeta \,\mathring{,}\, \mathsf{return}_{V_1}) = u \,\mathring{,}\, \mathcal{T}_\Sigma\, \zeta = h$.

   If $\mathsf{ran}\, h$ is non-empty, let $z : Z$ be a variable, and p a position such that $(h\, z)|_p = v$ for some variable $v : V_1$. Then

$$\sigma\, v = \sigma\, ((h\, z)|_p) = (\sigma \triangleright h\, z)|_p = ((h \,\mathring{,}\, \sigma)\, z)|_p$$
$$= ((h \,\mathring{,}\, \tau)\, z)|_p = (\tau \triangleright h\, z)|_p = \tau\, ((h\, z)|_p) = \tau\, v \ ,$$

so v has to be in the range of ζ. Since ζ is a monomorphism in *Set*, that is, injective, there is exactly one variable $u_0 : V_0$ such that $\zeta\, u_0 = v$. Let $\nu : V_1 \rightarrow V_0$ be an arbitrary mapping such that $\zeta\,\mathbin{;}\nu = \mathbb{I}_{V_0}$—such a mapping exists since V_0 is non-empty. Then we have:

$$(\nu\,\mathbin{;}\zeta)\, v = v \qquad \text{for all } v \in \operatorname{ran} \zeta. \tag{$\dagger$}$$

We define $u = h\,\mathbin{;}\mathcal{T}_\Sigma\, \nu$, and obtain:

$\quad u\,\mathbin{\S}\,(\zeta\,\mathbin{;}\operatorname{return}_{V_1})$

$=\quad\{ \text{ Definition of } u \}$

$\quad (h\,\mathbin{;}\mathcal{T}_\Sigma\, \nu)\,\mathbin{\S}\,(\zeta\,\mathbin{;}\operatorname{return}_{V_1})$

$=\quad\{ \text{ Monad properties } \}$

$\quad h\,\mathbin{;}\mathcal{T}_\Sigma\, (\nu\,\mathbin{;}\zeta)$

$=\quad\{\ (\dagger)\text{ with } \operatorname{ran} h \subseteq \operatorname{ran} \zeta\ \}$

$\quad h$

In both cases, u is uniquely determined due to the fact that $\zeta\,\mathbin{;}\operatorname{return}_{V_1}$ is a monomorphism in $\mathbb{T}_\Sigma$.

This shows that $\zeta\,\mathbin{;}\operatorname{return}_{V_1}$ is an equaliser for σ and τ in $\mathbb{T}_\Sigma$, and we have:

Theorem 6.1. $\mathbb{T}_\Sigma$ has equalisers: For two substitutions σ, τ from V_1 to V_2, an equaliser in $\mathbb{T}_\Sigma$ can be obtained as $\zeta\,\mathbin{;}\operatorname{return}_{V_1}$, where ζ is the equaliser in *Set* of σ and τ as functions in $V_1 \rightarrow \mathcal{T}_\Sigma\, V_2$. $\qquad\square$

If we consider any other $\mathbb{T}_\Sigma$-equaliser h of σ and τ, with $h : Z \rightarrow \mathcal{T}_\Sigma\, V_1$, then there must also be a substitution $q : V_0 \rightarrow \mathcal{T}_\Sigma\, Z$ such that $\zeta\,\mathbin{;}\operatorname{return}_{V_1} = q\,\mathbin{\S}\,h$. This equation implies that in particular h must be of shape $h_0\,\mathbin{;}\operatorname{return}_{V_1}$ for some (variable renaming) function $h_0 : Z \rightarrow V_1$.

Since *regular monomorphisms* are defined to be those that are equalisers of some pair of parallel morphisms, and since in *Set* all monomorphisms are regular, we now also have:

Theorem 6.2. The regular mononorphisms in $\mathbb{T}_\Sigma$ are precisely the morphisms obtained as $\zeta\,\mathbin{;}\operatorname{return}$ from some mononorphism ζ in *Set*. $\qquad\square$

7 Products

For every monad, a coproduct (S, ι, κ) for A and B in the base category give rise to the coproduct $(S,\ \iota\,\mathbin{;}\operatorname{return}S,\ \kappa\,\mathbin{;}\operatorname{return}S)$ in the Kleisli category.

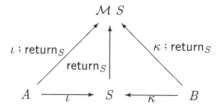

For the term monad, coproducts are just disjoint unions of variable sets.

However, starting from a product (P, π, ρ) for A and B in the base category and trying the same construction does not produce a product in the substitution category:

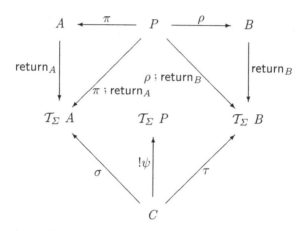

Given σ and τ, we would need to be able to construct a substitution ψ such that $\psi \,\mathbin{\text{\fontfamily{}\selectfont\textsemicolon}}\, (\pi \,\mathbin{\text{\textsemicolon}}\, \mathsf{return}_A) = \sigma$ and $\psi \,\mathbin{\text{\textsemicolon}}\, (\rho \,\mathbin{\text{\textsemicolon}}\, \mathsf{return}_B) = \tau$. Let $v : C$ be a variable. Then $\psi\, v$ must be some term $u : \mathcal{T}_\Sigma\, P$ (over the variable set $P = A \times B$) for which $(\pi \,\mathbin{\text{\textsemicolon}}\, \mathsf{return}_A) \vartriangleright u = \sigma\, v$ and $(\rho \,\mathbin{\text{\textsemicolon}}\, \mathsf{return}_B) \vartriangleright u = \tau\, v$. Using the monad laws, these equations are equivalent to the following equations, where π and ρ are mapped over the variables of u:

$$(\mathcal{T}_\Sigma\, \pi)\, u = \sigma\, v \qquad \text{and} \qquad (\mathcal{T}_\Sigma\, \rho)\, u = \tau\, v \qquad\qquad (*)$$

If u is not a variable, then the two left-hand sides of these equations will have the same outermost function symbol.

If we choose, for example, $\sigma\, v = a$ and $\tau\, v = b$ for different constant symbols a and b, then no appropriate u can be chosen, and no substitution ψ can be constructed.

The argument above, slightly modified, actually shows that for any product of A and B in $\mathbb{T}_\Sigma$, the choice $\sigma\, v = a$ and $\tau\, v = b$ for different constant symbols a and b implies that $\psi\, v$ must be a variable, and analogously in the more general case where $\sigma\, v$ and $\tau\, v$ have different outermost function symbols. We therefore define:

Definition 7.1. Given two (variable) sets V_1 and V_2, two terms $t_1 : \mathcal{T}_\Sigma \, V_1$ and $t_2 : \mathcal{T}_\Sigma \, V_2$ are called *strong-head-equal*, written $t_1 \simeq t_2$, if there are an (n-ary) function symbol f and terms $s_{1,1}, \ldots, s_{1,n} : \mathcal{T}_\Sigma \, V_1$ and $s_{2,1}, \ldots, s_{2,n} : \mathcal{T}_\Sigma \, V_2$ such that $t_1 = f(s_{1,1}, \ldots, s_{1,n})$ and $t_2 = f(s_{2,1}, \ldots, s_{2,n})$.

We will write $t_1 \not\simeq t_2$ for $\neg(t_1 \simeq t_2)$. $\qquad\qquad\square$

The discussion above also shows that, since $\psi \, v$ is a variable w from the product set P, the information that $\sigma \, v = a$ and $\tau \, v = b$ must be contained in that variable.

One might consider to use $P = \mathcal{T}_\Sigma \, A \times \mathcal{T}_\Sigma \, B$, which makes the projection definitions easy: $\pi : P \to \mathcal{T}_\Sigma \, A$ with $\pi(t_1, t_2) = t_1$ and analogously for ρ. However, now we have several choices for $u = \psi \, v$ if $\sigma \, v = f(a)$ and $\tau \, v = f(b)$: We could set $u = f((a, b))$ or $u = (f(a), f(b))$. (Remember that "variables" in P are pairs of terms!) Both choices would satisfy the required equations $(*)$.

This shows that, more generally, pairs (t_1, t_2) with $t_1 \simeq t_2$ should not be "variables" in P.

We obtain that $\mathbb{T}_\Sigma$ always has products:

Theorem 7.2. For any to sets A and B, the set $P = \{(t_1, t_2) : \mathcal{T}_\Sigma \, A \times \mathcal{T}_\Sigma \, B \mid t_1 \not\simeq t_2\}$ together with the projections $\pi : P \to \mathcal{T}_\Sigma \, A$ with $\pi(t_1, t_2) = t_1$ and $\rho : P \to \mathcal{T}_\Sigma \, B$ with $\rho(t_1, t_2) = t_2$ forms a product in $\mathbb{T}_\Sigma$.

Proof. Let a set C be given, and two substitutions $\sigma : C \to \mathcal{T}_\Sigma \, A$ and $\tau : C \to \mathcal{T}_\Sigma \, B$.

We need to show that there is a unique substitution $\psi : C \to \mathcal{T}_\Sigma \, P$ such that $\psi \, \natural \, \pi = \sigma$ and $\psi \, \natural \, \rho = \tau$.

Recall that the *anti-unifier* of two terms t and u is the most specific generalisation g of the two terms, together with two substitutions ξ_1 and ξ_2 such that $\xi_1 \triangleright g = t$ and $\xi_2 \triangleright g = u$. We shall write:

$$(g, \xi_1, \xi_2) = \mathsf{antiUnif}(t, u)$$

Now let G be the variable set of g (that is, $g \in \mathcal{T}_\Sigma \, G$), and define $\xi : G \to P$ with $\xi \, z = (\xi_1 \, z, \xi_2 \, z)$ for every $z : G$; this is well-defined since $\xi_1 \, z \not\simeq \xi_2 \, z$ by the definition of anti-unification. We use this to define a variant of anti-unification

$$\mathsf{AntiUnif} : (\mathcal{T}_\Sigma \, A \times \mathcal{T}_\Sigma \, B) \to \mathcal{T}_\Sigma \, P$$
$$\mathsf{AntiUnif}(t, u) = (\mathcal{T}_\Sigma \, \xi) \, g$$

that produces a single term with the structure of g over variables from P, which are pairs of terms in $\not\simeq$.

For every variable $x : C$, we now define $\psi \, x = \mathsf{AntiUnif}(\sigma \, x, \tau \, x)$ and $(g_x, \xi_{x,1}, \xi_{x,2}) = \mathsf{antiUnif}(\sigma \, x, \tau \, x)$. Then:

$(\psi \mathbin{\raisebox{0.2ex}{\scriptsize$\S$}} \pi)\, x$

$=$ { Definition of substitution composition }

   $\pi \rhd (\psi\, x)$

$=$ { Definition of ψ }

   $\pi \rhd (\mathsf{AntiUnif}(\sigma\, x, \tau\, x))$

$=$ { Definition of $\mathsf{AntiUnif}$ }

   $\pi \rhd ((\mathcal{T}_\Sigma\ \xi_x)\ g_x)$

$=$ $\{\ \pi(\xi_x\ z) = \xi_{x,1}\ z\ \}$

   $\xi_{x,1} \rhd g_x$

$=$ { Definition of antiUnif }

   $\sigma\, x$

and analogously $(\psi \mathbin{\raisebox{0.2ex}{\scriptsize$\S$}} \rho)\, x = \tau\, x$.

Furthermore, if $\chi : C \to \mathcal{T}_\Sigma\, P$ is given such that $\chi \mathbin{\raisebox{0.2ex}{\scriptsize$\S$}} \pi = \sigma$ and $\chi \mathbin{\raisebox{0.2ex}{\scriptsize$\S$}} \rho = \tau$, then, for every variable $x : C$:

- If $\chi\, x = (t_1, t_2)$ is a variable from P, then $t_1 \neq t_2$ and $\sigma\, x = (\chi \mathbin{\raisebox{0.2ex}{\scriptsize$\S$}} \pi)\, x = t_1$ and $\tau\, x = (\chi \mathbin{\raisebox{0.2ex}{\scriptsize$\S$}} \rho)\, x = t_2$, and therefore by definition of anti-unification also $\psi\, x = (t_1, t_2)$
- If $\chi\, x = f(s_1, \ldots, s_n)$, then

$$\sigma\, x = (\chi \mathbin{\raisebox{0.2ex}{\scriptsize$\S$}} \pi)\, x = f(\pi \rhd s_1, \ldots, \pi \rhd s_n)$$
$$\tau\, x = (\chi \mathbin{\raisebox{0.2ex}{\scriptsize$\S$}} \rho)\, x = f(\rho \rhd s_1, \ldots, \rho \rhd s_n)$$

and therefore $\psi\, x = f\,(\mathsf{AntiUnif}(\pi \rhd s_1, \rho \rhd s_1), \ldots, \mathsf{AntiUnif}(\pi \rhd s_n, \rho \rhd s_n))$.

By induction over the structure of terms we then obtain $\chi = \psi$. □

From the proof, it is obvious that P is infinite as soon as at least one of $\mathcal{T}_\Sigma\, A$ and $\mathcal{T}_\Sigma\, B$ is infinite. Therefore, we have:

Corollary 7.3

1. Over the category of finite sets, a substitution category has all products only if the signature has no function symbols with arity at least one.
2. Over arbitrary sets, the substitution category $\mathbb{T}_\Sigma$ has all products. □

8 Pullbacks of Substitutions

Since $\mathbb{T}_\Sigma$ has products and equalisers, the standard definition of pullbacks from these can be used.

Let a cospan of substitutions $B \xrightarrow{\tau_1} D \xleftarrow{\tau_2} C$ in the Kleisli category of $\mathcal{T}_\Sigma$ be given, that is, two functions $\tau_1 : B \to \mathcal{T}_\Sigma D$ and $\tau_2 : C \to \mathcal{T}_\Sigma D$.

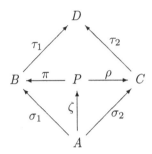

The equaliser of $\zeta : A \to \mathcal{T}_\Sigma P$ of $\pi \, \mathring{\,}\, \tau_1$ and $\pi \, \mathring{\,}\, \tau_2$ gives rise to the pullback $B \xleftarrow{\sigma_1} A \xrightarrow{\sigma_2} C$ with $\sigma_1 = \zeta \, \mathring{\,}\, \pi$ and $\sigma_2 = \zeta \, \mathring{\,}\, \rho$; the proof for this is a popular exercise in many introductions to category theory.

Corollary 8.1. For every signature, the resulting substitution category over *Set* has all pullbacks.   □

The equaliser ζ selects those pairs (t_1, t_2) from P for which $\tau_1 \triangleright t_1 = \tau_2 \triangleright t_2$. Since $t_1 \neq t_2$, at least one of t_1 and t_2 must be a variable, since if both were constructed from (necessarily different) function symbols, the equality $\tau_1 \triangleright t_1 = \tau_2 \triangleright t_2$ would not be possible.

For the case that t_1 is the variable v_1, we obtain:

$$\tau_2 \triangleright t_2 = \tau_1 \triangleright t_1 = \tau_1 \, v_1$$

Since $\tau_1 \, v_1$ is a finite term, there are only finitely many choices of t_2 satisfying this. Analogously, if t_2 is a variable, then there are only finitely many choices for t_1. Therefore, if the variable sets B, C, and D are all finite, then also A will be finite, even though P is (in general) infinite.

Theorem 8.2. For every signature, the resulting substitution category over the category of finite sets has all pullbacks.   □

9   Pushouts

The question whether $V_1 \xleftarrow{\sigma} V_0 \xrightarrow{\tau} V_2$ has a pushout in $\mathbb{T}_\Sigma$ can be seen as a unification problem for two substitutions with disjoint variables, which corresponds to the standard construction of pushouts from coproducts and coequalisers. Therefore, obviously not all spans in $\mathbb{T}_\Sigma$ have pushouts.

An important special case are pushouts along monomorphisms, or even along monomorphisms belonging to a particular class. We have seen in Sect. 5 that in $\mathbb{T}_\Sigma$, monomorphisms may map variables to non-variable terms, and since independent monomorphisms σ and τ may map the same variable to non-unifiable terms, just restricting to monomorphisms does not help here.

We therefore have to restrict our attention to monomorphisms that map variables only to variables, that is, regular monomorphisms in $\mathbb{T}_\Sigma$, which are according to Theorem 6.2 the monomorphisms of shape $m \mathbin{\text{\fontfamily{cmss}\selectfont ;}} \mathsf{return}$ where m is a monomorphism in the base category, that is, an injective variable mapping.

Let a substitution $\sigma : V_0 \to \mathcal{T}_\Sigma\, V_1$ and an injective function $\iota_2 : V_0 \to V_2$ be given. Since this is in Set, we can see ι_2 as the first injection of a coproduct $V_0 \xrightarrow{\iota_2} V_2 \xleftarrow{\kappa_2} U$, where U needs to be isomorphic to the set $V_2 - \mathrm{ran}\, \iota_2$. Then define V_3 via another coproduct $V_1 \xrightarrow{\iota_3} V_3 \xleftarrow{\kappa_3} U$ in Set.

Now we define $\tau : V_2 \to \mathcal{T}_\Sigma\, V_3$ as a universal morphism associated with the coproduct V_2, namely:

$$\tau = [\sigma \mathbin{;} \mathcal{T}_\Sigma\, \iota_3, \quad \kappa_3 \mathbin{;} \mathsf{return}_{V_3}]$$

Then the following diagram is a pushout in $\mathbb{T}_\Sigma$:

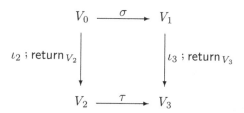

Commutativity follows easily:
$$(\iota_2 \mathbin{;} \mathsf{return}_{V_2}) \mathbin{\text{\textfontstyle ;}} \tau$$
$=$ $\{$ Monad properties $\}$
$$\iota_2 \mathbin{;} \tau$$
$=$ $\{$ Definition of τ $\}$
$$\iota_2 \mathbin{;} [\sigma \mathbin{;} \mathcal{T}_\Sigma\, \iota_3, \quad \kappa_3 \mathbin{;} \mathsf{return}_{V_3}]$$
$=$ $\{$ Coproduct properties $\}$
$$\sigma \mathbin{;} \mathcal{T}_\Sigma\, \iota_3$$
$=$ $\{$ Monad properties $\}$
$$\sigma \mathbin{\text{\textfontstyle ;}} (\iota_3 \mathbin{;} \mathsf{return}_{V_3})$$

Assume another cospan $V_1 \xrightarrow{\varphi} V_4 \xleftarrow{\psi} V_2$ in $\mathbb{T}_\Sigma$ with

$$\sigma \mathbin{\text{\textfontstyle ;}} \varphi = (\iota_2 \mathbin{;} \mathsf{return}_{V_2}) \mathbin{\text{\textfontstyle ;}} \psi \ . \qquad\qquad (\ddagger)$$

Then define $\chi : V_3 \to \mathcal{T}_\Sigma\, V_4$ as a universal morphism associated with the coproduct V_3, namely $\chi = [\varphi, \quad \kappa_2 \mathbin{;} \psi]$. The resulting triangles commute:
$$(\iota_3 \mathbin{;} \mathsf{return}_{V_3}) \mathbin{\text{\textfontstyle ;}} \chi$$
$=$ $\{$ Monad properties, definition of χ $\}$
$$\iota_3 \mathbin{;} [\varphi, \quad \kappa_2 \mathbin{;} \psi]$$
$=$ $\{$ Coproduct properties $\}$
$$\varphi$$

and:

$$\tau \,\mathring{,}\, \chi$$
$$= \quad \{ \text{ Definition of } \tau, \text{ coproduct properties } \}$$
$$[(\sigma \,\mathring{,}\, \mathcal{T}_\Sigma \,\iota_3) \,\mathring{,}\, \chi, \quad (\kappa_3 \,\mathring{,}\, \mathsf{return}_{V_3}) \,\mathring{,}\, \chi]$$
$$= \quad \{ \text{ Monad properties } \}$$
$$[\sigma \,\mathring{,}\, (\iota_3 \,\mathring{,}\, \chi), \quad \kappa_3 \,\mathring{,}\, \chi]$$
$$= \quad \{ \text{ Definition of } \chi, \text{ coproduct properties } \}$$
$$[\sigma \,\mathring{,}\, \varphi, \quad \kappa_2 \,\mathring{,}\, \psi]$$
$$= \quad \{ (\ddagger), \text{ monad properties } \}$$
$$[\iota_2 \,\mathring{,}\, \psi, \quad \kappa_2 \,\mathring{,}\, \psi]$$
$$= \quad \{ \text{ Coproduct properties } \}$$
$$\psi$$

Furthermore, for every other substitution $\xi : V_3 \to \mathcal{T}_\Sigma \, V_4$ with $(\iota_3 \,\mathring{,}\, \mathsf{return}_{V_3}) \,\mathring{,}\, \xi = \varphi$ and $\tau \,\mathring{,}\, \xi = \psi$ we have:

$$\chi$$
$$= \quad \{ \text{ Definition of } \chi \}$$
$$[\varphi, \quad \kappa_2 \,\mathring{,}\, \psi]$$
$$= \quad \{ \text{ Assumptions about } \xi \}$$
$$[(\iota_3 \,\mathring{,}\, \mathsf{return}_{V_3}) \,\mathring{,}\, \xi, \quad \kappa_2 \,\mathring{,}\, (\tau \,\mathring{,}\, \xi)]$$
$$= \quad \{ \text{ Monad properties } \}$$
$$[(\iota_3 \,\mathring{,}\, \xi, \quad (\kappa_2 \,\mathring{,}\, \tau) \,\mathring{,}\, \xi)]$$
$$= \quad \{ \text{ Definition of } \tau, \text{ coproduct properties } \}$$
$$[(\iota_3 \,\mathring{,}\, \xi, \quad (\kappa_3 \,\mathring{,}\, \mathsf{return}_{V_3}) \,\mathring{,}\, \xi)]$$
$$= \quad \{ \text{ Monad properties } \}$$
$$[(\iota_3 \,\mathring{,}\, \xi, \quad \kappa_3 \,\mathring{,}\, \xi)]$$
$$= \quad \{ \text{ Coproduct properties } \}$$
$$\xi$$

Altogether, this shows:

Theorem 9.1. $\mathbb{T}_\Sigma$ has pushouts along regular monomorphisms. $\qquad\square$

Such a pushout just adds the variables of V_2 outside the range of m as additional "unused" target variables to σ.

Already if m is not a monomorphism, pushouts for $V_1 \xleftarrow{\;\sigma\;} V_0 \xrightarrow{m \,\mathring{,}\, \mathsf{return}} V_2$ in $\mathbb{T}_\Sigma$ will not exist if there are two variables $u, v : V_0$ with $m\,u = m\,v$, but for which $\sigma\,u$ and $\sigma\,v$ are not unifiable.

In the context of the proof above, if the $\mathbb{T}_\Sigma$-cospan $V_1 \xrightarrow{\;\varphi\;} V_4 \xleftarrow{\;\psi\;} V_2$, too, is a $\mathbb{T}_\Sigma$-pushout for $V_1 \xleftarrow{\;\sigma\;} V_0 \xrightarrow{\iota_2 \,\mathring{,}\, \mathsf{return}} V_2$, then $\chi : V_3 \to \mathcal{T}_\Sigma \, V_4$ has to be an isomorphism between the two pushout objects V_3 and V_4, with the inverse satisfying in particular $\varphi \,\mathring{,}\, \chi^{-1} = \iota_3 \,\mathring{,}\, \mathsf{return}_{V_3}$. Due to this equality, the image of φ can only contain variable terms, and since $\varphi = (\iota_3 \,\mathring{,}\, \mathsf{return}_{V_3}) \,\mathring{,}\, \chi$ is a composition of a monomorphism with an isomorphism, it altogether has to be a regular monomorphism, so we have:

Theorem 9.2. In $\mathbb{T}_\Sigma$, regular monomorphisms are stable under pushout. □

10 Conclusion and Outlook

For categories with variable sets as objects and substitutions as morphisms, we provided explicit characterisations and constructions of monomorphisms, epimorphisms, equalisers, regular monomorphisms, products, pullbacks, and of pushouts along regular monomorphisms. These can be useful in contexts where categories of substitutions become building blocks of more complicated categories, as for example in transformation of symbolically attributed graphs.

While in settings with global variable sets, such as that of Eder (1985), anti-unification appears as dual to unification, we identified the construction of the universal morphisms for products as corresponding to anti-unification. This, interestingly, is not at all categorially-dual to the coequalisers or pushouts that correspond to unification.

Acknowledgement. I would like to express my gratitude to the anonymous referees for their constructive comments, which helped significantly to improve the presentation.

References

Eder, E.: Properties of substitutions and unifications. J. Symbolic Comput. **1**, 31–46 (1985). https://doi.org/10.1016/S0747-7171(85)80027-4

Ehrig, H., Habel, A., Kreowski, H.-J., Parisi-Presicce, F.: From graph grammars to high level replacement systems. In: Ehrig, H., Kreowski, H.-J., Rozenberg, G. (eds.) Graph Grammars 1990. LNCS, vol. 532, pp. 269–291. Springer, Heidelberg (1991). https://doi.org/10.1007/BFb0017395

Ehrig, H., Ehrig, K., Prange, U., Taentzer, G.: Fundamentals of Algebraic Graph Transformation. MTCSAES. Springer, Heidelberg (2006). https://doi.org/10.1007/3-540-31188-2

Hosseini, S., Qasemi Nezhad, Y.: Equalizers in Kleisli categories. Cahiers de Topologie ed Géométrie Différentielle Catégoriques **57**(1), 51–76 (2016). http://cahierstgdc.com/index.php/volumes/volume-lii-2016/

Kahl, W.: Categories of coalgebras with monadic homomorphisms. In: Bonsangue, M.M. (ed.) CMCS 2014. LNCS, vol. 8446, pp. 151–167. Springer, Heidelberg (2014). https://doi.org/10.1007/978-3-662-44124-4_9. Agda theories at http://RelMiCS.McMaster.ca/RATH-Agda/

Kahl, W.: Graph transformation with symbolic attributes via monadic coalgebra homomorphisms. ECEASST **71**, 5:1–5:17 (2015). https://doi.org/10.14279/tuj.eceasst.71.999

Lack, S., Sobociński, P.: Adhesive categories. In: Walukiewicz, I. (ed.) FoSSaCS 2004. LNCS, vol. 2987, pp. 273–288. Springer, Heidelberg (2004). https://doi.org/10.1007/978-3-540-24727-2_20

Lack, S., Sobociński, P.: Adhesive and quasiadhesive categories. RAIRO Inform. Théor. Appl. **39**(3), 511–545 (2005). https://doi.org/10.1051/ita:2005028

Lawvere, F.W.: Functorial semantics of algebraic theories. Proc. Nat. Acad. Sci. USA **50**, 869–872 (1963). https://doi.org/10.2307/2272673

Norell, U.: Towards a practical programming language based on dependent type theory. Ph.D. thesis, Department of Computer Science and Engineering, Chalmers University of Technology (2007). See also http://wiki.portal.chalmers.se/agda/pmwiki.php

Rydeheard, D.E., Stell, J.G.: Foundations of equational deduction: a categorical treatment of equational proofs and unification algorithms. In: Pitt, D.H., Poigné, A., Rydeheard, D.E. (eds.) Category Theory and Computer Science. LNCS, vol. 283, pp. 114–139. Springer, Heidelberg (1987). https://doi.org/10.1007/3-540-18508-9_23

Szigeti, J.: On limits and colimits in the Kleisli category. Cahiers de Topologie ed Géométrie Différentielle Catégoriques **24**(4), 381–391 (1983). http://www.numdam.org/item?id=CTGDC_1983_24_4_381_0

A Flexible Categorial Formalisation
of Term Graphs as Directed Hypergraphs

Wolfram Kahl[(⊠)] and Yuhang Zhao

McMaster University, Hamilton, ON, Canada
{kahl,zhaoy36}@mcmaster.ca

Abstract. Term graphs are the concept at the core of important implementation techniques for functional programming languages, and are also
used as internal data structures in many other symbolic computation setting, including in code generation back-ends for example in compilers. To
our knowledge, there are no formally verified term graph manipulation
systems so far; we present an approach to formalising term graphs, as
a relatively complex example of graph structures, in the dependently-
typed programming language and proof system Agda in a way that both
the mathematical theory and useful executable implementations can be
obtained as instances of the same abstract definition.

1   Introduction

Terms (or expressions) are the conceptual data structure at the heart of almost
all symbol manipulation for mathematical reasoning and programming language
implementation. Terms as a data structure are a kind of trees, and in many
applications, intermediate or result terms arise that contain multiple copies of
equal subterms. To save space in software implementations of such applications,
all these copies are frequently represented by references to a single copy: Conceptually, the tree is replaced by a (directed, and for the purposes of the current
paper always acyclic) graph, a *term graph*. Nowadays, term graphs are typically
considered as *jungles*, a kind of directed hypergraphs introduced for this purpose
by Hoffmann and Plump (1991) and Corradini and Rossi (1993).

For the purpose of creating a toolset for term graph manipulation supported
by machine-checked correctness proofs, we develop a flexible formalisation of
term graphs in a categorial setting, with the following goals:

- We want to use the formalisation to develop mathematical theories of term
  graph transformation and how it can be used in particular for correct-by-
  construction compiler optimisation passes.
- We want to use **that same** formalisation as basis for executable implementations of these compiler optimisation passes.

As our formalisation setting, we use the dependently-typed programming language and proof assistant Agda (Norell 2007). Agda permits us to write definitions essentially in the way they are written for mathematical purposes, and

© IFIP International Federation for Information Processing 2019
Published by Springer Nature Switzerland AG 2019
J. L. Fiadeiro and I. Țuțu (Eds.): WADT 2018, LNCS 11563, pp. 103–118, 2019.
https://doi.org/10.1007/978-3-030-23220-7_6

prove properties about them, but all function definitions are also executable, making this a good environment for correct-by-construction tool development.

The body of this paper will start from a sequence of mathematical definitions (expressed in Agda) of datatypes for somewhat simplified term graphs, then consider also an implementation-oriented definition, and proceed to abstract both to a common generalisation. The full complexity of term graphs is the recovered in a few more refinements.

The result is a simple language for defining not only term graphs, but any of a large class of different kind of graph datastructures, when recognising these as coalgebras possibly including dependently-typed operations, as far as dependencies are used with a certain discipline.

2   Jungle Representation of Term Graphs

We think of term graphs as a kind of data-flow graphs, and we draw the flow from inputs (labelled by their positions in triangles) at the top to output positions at the bottom. We use the jungle approach of Hoffmann and Plump (1991); Corradini and Rossi (1993): We define term graphs as hypergraphs, where each (hyper-)edge is labelled with an operation name, and connected via "input tentacles" (drawn as arrows to the box representing the hyperedge) to the edge's input nodes, and via a single "output tentacle" (pointing away from the edge) to its output node. Term graph inputs correspond to variables in terms; so if we map each input position i to the variable x_i, then the term graph in the following drawing to the left represents the term $(x_1 + x_2) * x_2$:

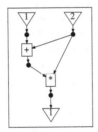
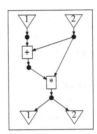

The term graph drawn above to the right has two output positions, and therefore should be interpreted as a pair of terms; in this case the two output positions are "fed" from the same node, so this is just the pair $\langle (x_1 + x_2) * x_2, \ (x_1 + x_2) * x_2 \rangle$. (We could easily switch to considering multi-output edges, but for the purposes of the current paper this would only result in some duplication, without introducing any additional interesting aspects, so we stick with single-output edges.)

The pure "directed hypergraph" aspect of term graph structure, without considering inputs and outputs, and without restricting the edge output assignment to be bijective onto non-input nodes, can be captured via the following signature:

$$\text{sigDHG} := \langle \; \textbf{sorts:} \; \text{N}, \text{E}$$
$$\textbf{ops:} \; \text{src} : \text{E} \to \text{List N}$$
$$\text{trg} : \text{E} \to \text{N}$$
$$\text{eLab} : \text{E} \to L \qquad \rangle$$

This is a coalgebraic signature in the sense used in (Kahl 2014, 2015): the argument type of each operation symbol is a single sort, and the result type is a term in a language of functor symbols (here including the constant symbol L and the unary List functor symbol) over the sorts (as variables).

3 Directed Hypergraphs—Simplified

To proceed towards capturing the full term graph structure and reduce ad-hoc notations, we now switch to using Agda Norell (2007) as our mathematical notation. The following Agda record type definition defines the type DHG_{00} to be the type of tuples containing the four sets[1] Input, Output, Inner, and Edge, together with the five functions gOut, eOut, eArity, eLabel, and eIn. The choice to have separate functions for assigning each edge its arity (number of edge input positions), its label, and its actual input node sequence has been made to introduce the right kind of problems for discussion in the current paper.

Different input positions need to be associated with different nodes — for simplicity, we identify input positions and input nodes, and introduce a separate carrier set for "inner" nodes, that is, nodes that are not input nodes. Both input nodes and inner nodes can be used as edge inputs, so we introduce the abbreviation[2] "Node" for the set of all nodes, constructed as the disjoint sum of the input node set and the inner node set:

```
record DHG₀₀ : Set₁ where
    field Input : Set                -- set of input nodes/positions
          Output : Set               -- set of output interface positions
          Inner : Set                -- set of inner (non-input) nodes
        Node = Input ⊎ Inner          -- derived set of all nodes
    field gOut   : Output → Node      -- graph output assignment
          Edge   : Set                -- set of edges
          eOut   : Edge → Inner       -- edge output node
          eArity : Edge → ℕ           -- edge arity
          eLabel : Edge → Label₀₀     -- edge label
          eIn    : Edge → List Node   -- edge input nodes
```

This models directed hypergraphs with input and output interfaces, but not yet term graphs where eOut needs to be bijective—we will come back to that only in Sect. 11. Dealing with directed hypergraphs is motivated by the fact that we use

---

[1] We gloss over the fact that in any real Agda development of these mathematical definitions, Setoid types will normally be used instead of Set. A variant using setoids of the definitions of the current section can be found in (Kahl 2011, Sect. 3).

[2] Agda **record** declarations simultaneously define modules, and as such can contain other definitions besides field declarations.

them as setting for double-pushout (DPO) rewriting of term graphs—directed hypergraphs include the "term graphs with holes" that occur as gluing and host graphs in DPO rewriting steps.

The DHG_{00} record type declaration corresponds again to a coalgebraic signature in the sense explained above, after expanding the Node abbreviation, as can be seen in the following reformulation:

```
record DHG₀₁ : Set₁ where
    field Input   : Set              -- set of input nodes
          Output  : Set              -- set of output interface positions
          Inner   : Set              -- set of inner (non-input) nodes
          Edge    : Set              -- set of edges
    field gOut    : Output → Input ⊎ Inner    -- graph output assignment
          eOut    : Edge → Inner                -- edge output node
          eArity  : Edge → ℕ                    -- edge arity
          eLabel  : Edge → Label₀₀              -- edge label
          eIn     : Edge → List (Input ⊎ Inner) -- edge input nodes
```

Since the presence of the local definition for Node may perhaps be confusing for readers unfamiliar with Agda, we will stick with continue our development from this expanded version.

4   Interface-Parameterised Directed Hypergraphs

We will need to implement several operations on our directed hypergraphs, in particular sequential composition: If the set of output positions of G_1 coincides with the set of input positions of G_2, then their sequential composition $G_1 \,\mathring{,}\, G_2$ results from "gluing them together" along this common interface.

Since we want type-checking to guarantee well-definedness of any applications of $\_\mathring{,}\_$ we use in programs manipulating term graphs, the input and output interfaces need to be part of the type of G_1 and G_2. In Agda, this is achieved by making the record type parameterised:

```
record DHG₀₂ (Input : Set) (Output : Set) : Set₁ where
    field Inner  : Set              -- set of inner (non-input) nodes
          Edge   : Set              -- set of edges
    field gOut   : Output → Input ⊎ Inner    -- graph output assignment
          eOut   : Edge → Inner                -- edge output node
          eArity : Edge → ℕ                    -- edge arity
          eLabel : Edge → Label₀₀              -- edge label
          eIn    : Edge → List (Input ⊎ Inner) -- edge input nodes
```

(Mathematically, this corresponds to defining a functor from trivial two-sort coalgebras to coalgebras of shape DHG_{01}.)

5   Implemented Directed Hypergraphs

So far, the record types we defined are mathematical datatypes, with sets as components, exactly in the way used for mathematical studies of term graphs. Since we used Agda as our mathematical language, and Agda can be used as a proof checker, we can build a mathematical theory of directed hypergraphs and term graphs on top of these definitions.

However, since Agda is also a programming language, we would like to also use our definitions for data structures used in programs that manipulate term graphs. However, records containing Set fields are hard to use—how do you save one of those to a file? The field Edge could be a set of functions. . .

To come from the opposite perspective, consider now what a plausible implementation datatype for directed hypergraphs might look like. We present a "proof-of-concept" implementation based on arrays, using the Vec datatype constructor for dependently-typed vectors from the Agda standard library (Danielsson et al. 2018)—the type "Vec A n" is the type of n-element vectors with elements of type A. (A "production" implementation might for example use some kind of binary trees, or a type of arrays with constant-time access.)

A plausible design is then to use as carrier sets only sets constructed by Fin; for a natural number n, the type "Fin n" is the type of natural numbers less than n. The elements of "Fin n" are precisely the indices that can be used with vectors of type "Vec A n".

However, where the mathematical data structure contains Sets of size n, the implementation data structure will contain only the index n:

$$
\begin{aligned}
&\textbf{record } \mathsf{VecDHG_1} \ (\mathsf{input} : \mathbb{N}) \ (\mathsf{output} : \mathbb{N}) : \mathsf{Set_1} \ \textbf{where} \\
&\quad \textbf{field } \mathsf{inner} \quad : \mathbb{N} \\
&\qquad\quad\ \, \mathsf{edge} \quad : \mathbb{N} \\
&\quad \textbf{field } \mathsf{gOut} \quad : \mathsf{Vec} \ (\mathsf{Fin} \ \mathsf{input} \uplus \mathsf{Fin} \ \mathsf{inner}) \ \mathsf{output} \\
&\qquad\quad\ \, \mathsf{eOut} \quad : \mathsf{Vec} \ (\mathsf{Fin} \ \mathsf{inner}) \ \mathsf{edge} \\
&\qquad\quad\ \, \mathsf{eArity} : \mathsf{Vec} \ \mathbb{N} \ \mathsf{edge} \\
&\qquad\quad\ \, \mathsf{eLabel} : \mathsf{Vec} \ \mathsf{Label_{00}} \ \mathsf{edge} \\
&\qquad\quad\ \, \mathsf{eIn} \qquad : \mathsf{Vec} \ (\mathsf{List} \ (\mathsf{Fin} \ \mathsf{input} \uplus \mathsf{Fin} \ \mathsf{inner})) \ \mathsf{edge}
\end{aligned}
$$

It is straight-forward to write a function that maps each element of "VecDHG$_1$ m n" to the mathematical representation of that graph in the type "DHG$_{02}$ (Fin m) (Fin n)", and this would populate also the Inner and Edge fields with Fin types. However, it is quite cumbersome to attempt to define even a partial inverse to that, which makes it essentially infeasible to use operations defined on the "mathematical implementation" DHG$_{02}$ to induce operations on the "executable implementation" VecDHG$_1$.

Perhaps more importantly, there is no good way to "obtain" the definition of VecDHG$_1$ "from" that of DHG$_{02}$, or even more generally, to adapt DHG$_{02}$ to finite node and edge sets—one could do this via an extension that adds finiteness proofs. But using this approach to restrict DHG$_{02}$s to those having node and edge sets of shape "Fin n" would involve a type-level propositional equality that would be extremely awkward to use.

The solution to this problem is to obtain both as instances of a generalised, *abstract* definition, with essentially the goal of being able to

– instantiate with Set and → to obtain the mathematical theory, and
– instantiate with $\mathbb{N}$ and flip Vec to obtain the desired implementation.

After putting it this way, the natural option is to use a category as parameter.

6   Abstract Directed Hypergraphs—First Attempt

We now assume that we are in a setting where $\mathcal{C}$ is an arbitrary but fixed category with coproducts—the Agda way of expressing this is to locate the development in a parameterised module (with additional parameters for ListF etc.):

> **module** _ ($\mathcal{C}$: Category) (hasCoproduct : HasCoproducts $\mathcal{C}$) [. . .] **where**
> [. . .] -- bring _ ⊞ _ and other useful material into scope. . .

Then occurrences of Set in DHG_{02} are replaced with the type of objects of category $\mathcal{C}$, and operations become morphisms instead of functions:

> **record** $ADHG_0$ (Input : $\mathcal{C}$.Obj) (Output : $\mathcal{C}$.Obj) : Set _ **where**
> **field Inner**   : $\mathcal{C}$.Obj   -- inner (non-input) nodes
>   Edge   : $\mathcal{C}$.Obj   -- edges
> **field gOut**   : $\mathcal{C}$.Mor Output (Input ⊞ Inner)   -- graph output assignment
>   eOut   : $\mathcal{C}$.Mor Edge Inner   -- edge output node
>   eArity : $\mathcal{C}$.Mor Edge obj$\mathbb{N}$ -- edge arity
>   eLabel : $\mathcal{C}$.Mor Edge Label$_{10}$ -- edge label
>   eIn   : $\mathcal{C}$.Mor Edge (ListF (Input ⊞ Inner))   -- edge input nodes

We shall use the name vecCategory for the category with natural numbers as objects, and where the type of morphisms from m to n is "Vec (Fin n) m"; the coproduct there is just addition.

Trying to instantiate $\mathcal{C}$ with vecCategory presents the problem that that even if obj$\mathbb{N}$ and ListF are supplied as module parameters in [. . .], we will not find any n such that Fin n represents $\mathbb{N}$ respectively List (Input ⊞ Inner). (For the sake of the argument, we will ignore the option to restrict to some maximal arity that might be sufficient for some particular application.)

7   Abstract Directed Hypergraphs—Second Attempt

The solution to this problem is to make use of the type discipline of a coalgebra: Only sorts occur as argument types; infinite types like $\mathbb{N}$ and List (Input ⊞ Inner) only occur in the result types. We translate this into a setting where we do not need morphisms starting from all types—we embed the parameter $\mathcal{C}$ (that we plan to instantiate with vecCategory), used for the morphisms between all relevant finite sets, including the carrier sets, in a *semigroupoid*[3] S that provides objects also for $\mathbb{N}$ and List (Input $\boxplus$ Inner).

The semigroupoid S will need to have morphisms from objects of C to the object objℕ implementing $\mathbb{N}$, and in the context of our implementation, these can all be implemented as vectors of the types "Vec $\mathbb{N}$ k" for natural numbers k. However, S does not need any morphisms starting at objℕ, so we can characterise S in a way that precisely fits this vector-based implementation: Vectors can contain elements of infinite types, but vectors cannot be infinite.

The (full and faithful, coproduct-preserving, . . .) semigroupoid functor $\mathcal{F}$ embedding C in S becomes another important part of the setting we now adopt:

> **module** _ (C : Category) (hasCoproduct : HasCoproducts C)
> (S : Semigroupoid) ($\mathcal{F}$: SGFunctor' C S)
> (objℕ : S.Obj) (ListF : SGFunctor S S) [. . .] **where**

Functions "between sorts", here gOut and eOut, are now morphisms in the parameter category C, while functions from a sort to an "arbitrary" (potentially infinite) type are morphisms in the parameter semigroupoid S, starting from the $\mathcal{F}$-image of the sort.

> **record** ADHG_1 (Input : C.Obj) (Output : C.Obj) : Set _ **where**
>   **field** Inner   : C.Obj   -- inner nodes
>   Edge   : C.Obj   -- edges
>   **field** gOut   : C.Mor Output (Input $\boxplus$ Inner)   -- graph output
>   eOut   : C.Mor Edge Inner   -- edge output
>   eArity : S.Mor ($\mathcal{F}$ Edge) objℕ   -- edge arity
>   eLabel : S.Mor ($\mathcal{F}$ Edge) Label_{11} -- edge label
>   eIn   : S.Mor ($\mathcal{F}$ Edge) (ListF ($\mathcal{F}$ (Input $\boxplus$ Inner))) -- edge input

Instantiating C with the category *Set* and S with the underlying semigroupoid makes the resulting ADHG_1 directly equivalent with DHG_{02}.

Instantiating C with vecCategory and S with a carefully constructed semigroupoid ($S^{\mathcal{F}}$ in Appendix B) with arbitrary vectors as morphisms resulting ADHG_1 directly equivalent with VecDHG_1.

Other easy instantiations are useful, too: For example, instantiating C with the category of all finite sets and S with the semigroupoid of all sets gives us the variant of DHG_{02} restricted to finite carrier sets.

---

[3] A semigroupoid is a "category without identity morphisms", analogous to how a semigroup is a "monoid without identity element".

8   Directed Hypergraphs—Dependently Typed

A different issue with DHG_{02} is the fact that the types do not enforce that the length of an edge's input node list corresponds to its arity: In terms of DHG_{02}, we want to add the following restriction:

$$\forall\ (e : Edge) \rightarrow eArity\ e \equiv length\ (eIn\ e)$$

It would be possible to add this in the spirit of datatype invariants as the type of an additional **field** to the record, which then induces a proof obligation at every record construction site. Therefore it is far more attractive to move this invariant into the type system, which is possible in Agda due to its support for dependent types: A **dependent function type** "$(e : Edge) \rightarrow R\ e$" contains functions mapping each e : Edge to an element of type "$R\ e$", where R : Edge $\rightarrow$ Set is assumed to be some "result" type constructor depending on an Edge argument.

We use the additional expressivity provided by dependent types to move from List to Vec in the result type of eIn, and for each result vector we supply the arity of the edge in question as length:

record DHG_1 (Input : Set) (Output : Set) : Set_1 **where**
    field Inner   : Set   -- set of inner (non-input) nodes
            Edge   : Set   -- set of edges
    Node = Input $\uplus$ Inner   -- set of all nodes
    field gOut : Output $\rightarrow$ Input $\uplus$ Inner   -- graph output assignment
           eOut : Edge $\rightarrow$ Inner   -- edge output node
           eArity : Edge $\rightarrow \mathbb{N}$ -- edge arity
           eLabel : (e : Edge) $\rightarrow Label_1$ (eArity e)   -- edge label
           eIn   : (e : Edge) $\rightarrow$ Vec Node (eArity e) -- edge input nodes

At the same time, we also switched the type of edge labels to come from an arity-indexed label set $Label_1 : \mathbb{N} \rightarrow Set$.

Although this is not anymore of the shape of a coalgebra signature as described in Sect. 2, this is still a type of coalgebras mathematically, due to the fact that the dependent arguments are used only as arguments to other operations.

9   Implementation of Dependently-Typed Fields

The implementation type $VecDHG_1$ is easily adapted to such dependent fields, exploiting the presence of dependent pair types (Σ-types): The type "$\Sigma\,a : A \bullet B\,a$" is inhabited by pairs "a , b" where a : A and b : B a (where B : A $\rightarrow$ Set is a type constructor taking an argument of type A).

Straight-forwardly embedding the type constructors for labels and input vectors in Σ-types yields the following refined implementation type:

```
record VecDHG₂ (input : ℕ) (output : ℕ) : Set₁ where
   field inner  : ℕ
         edge   : ℕ
   field gOut   : Vec (Fin input ⊎ Fin inner) output
         eOut   : Vec (Fin inner) edge
         eArity : Vec ℕ edge
         eLabel : Vec (Σ n : ℕ • Label₀₁ n) edge
         eIn    : Vec (Σ n : ℕ • Vec (Fin input ⊎ Fin inner) n) edge
```

Such structures will then be subject to the following datatype invariants:

$$\forall\ (e\ :\ \mathsf{Edge})\ \to\ \mathsf{fst}\ (\mathsf{lookup}\ e\ \mathsf{eLabel})\ \equiv\ \mathsf{eArity}\ e$$
$$\forall\ (e\ :\ \mathsf{Edge})\ \to\ \mathsf{fst}\ (\mathsf{lookup}\ e\ \mathsf{eIn})\ \quad \equiv\ \mathsf{eArity}\ e$$

A more rational implementation (which can easily be obtained by a systematic transformation from $\mathsf{VecDHG_2}$) would store these three equal values only once, and at the same time also be closer to directly representing the functor underlying the coalgebra type here:

```
record VecDHG₃ (input : ℕ) (output : ℕ) : Set₁ where
   field inner : ℕ
         edge  : ℕ
   field gOut  : Vec (Fin input ⊎ Fin inner) output
         eOut  : Vec (Fin inner) edge
         eInfo : Vec (Σ n : ℕ • Label₀₁ n × Vec (Fin input ⊎ Fin inner) n) edge
```

10 Dependently-Typed Abstract Directed Hypergraphs

For abstracting dependently-typed operations into the category-semigroupoid setting of Sect. 7, we introduce an minimal interface to *dependent objects* that can be seen as individual building blocks of a *type-category* as described by Pitts (2001), adapted so that it "does not demand existence of too many morphisms" for our semigroupoid:

Definition 10.1. *For an object I of S, an object D of S is a dependent object indexed over I iff for every object $Y : C.Obj$ and every morphism f from $\mathcal{F}\,Y$ to D in S there is a morphism $ind_D\ f$ from $\mathcal{F}\,Y$ to I in S such that the operation ind_D commutes with C-pre-composition, that is, for every object X of C and every morphism g from X to Y in C, the following holds:*

$$ind_D\ (\mathcal{F}\,g\ \mathring{,}\ f)\quad =\quad \mathcal{F}\,g\ \mathring{,}\ ind_D\ f$$

□

The Σ-types of Sect. 9 are an instance of dependent objects by virtue of implementing ind_D f as $(\mathsf{Vec.map\,proj_1}\ f)$, extracting the index from dependent pairs. The "trick" of dependent objects is that the dependent-pair-projection $\mathsf{proj_1}$ used here does not need to be a morphism of the semigroupoid $\mathcal{S}$, making it possible to define $\mathcal{S}$ in a way that all its morphisms can be implemented based on vectors.

For the abstract variant, we assume a dependent objects Label and a "dependent functor" VecF; the latter needs to map any object A of $\mathcal{S}$ to a dependent object with the common index objN. (The dependent functor image of a morphism f can be implemented as f itself tagged with a name of the functor, see Appendix B.)

We introduce two new abbreviations, so that operation types now can be of the following three kinds (due to the coalgebra nature, all have to "conceptually start" at sorts, which are objects of $\mathcal{C}$):

$\mathcal{C}.\mathsf{Mor}\ \mathsf{X}\ \mathsf{Y}$ (straight morphisms in $\mathcal{C}$)

$\mathsf{X} \hookrightarrow \mathsf{A}$ abbreviates $\mathcal{S}.\mathsf{Mor}\ (\mathcal{F}\ \mathsf{X})\ \mathsf{A}$, where $\mathsf{X} : \mathcal{C}.\mathsf{Obj}$ and $\mathsf{A} : \mathcal{S}.\mathsf{Obj}$

$\mathsf{f} \nearrow \mathsf{D}$ abbreviates $\Sigma\,\mathsf{g} : \mathsf{X} \hookrightarrow \mathsf{D} \bullet (\mathrm{ind}_D\ \mathsf{g} = \mathsf{f})$, where $\mathsf{f} : \mathsf{X} \hookrightarrow \mathsf{I}$

That is, $\mathsf{f} \nearrow \mathsf{D}$ contains pairs of shape $(\mathsf{g}\,,\,\mathsf{p})$ where $\mathsf{g} : \mathsf{X} \hookrightarrow \mathsf{D}$ and p is a proof for the morphism equality of $\mathrm{ind}_D\ \mathsf{g}$ with f.

For the instance $\mathsf{VecDHG_2}$, these proofs are exactly proofs for the datatype invariants mentioned there. The final abstract version of our directed hypergraph type therefore also starts closer to $\mathsf{VecDHG_2}$ than to $\mathsf{VecDHG_3}$:

```
module _ [...] (objN : S.Obj) (Label : DepObj objN)
                              (VecF : DepFunctor objN) [...] where
  [...]
  record ADHG₂ (Input : C.Obj) (Output : C.Obj) : Set _ where
    field Inner Edge : C.Obj
    field gOut   : C.Mor Output (Input ⊞ Inner)
          eOut   : C.Mor Edge Inner
          eArity : Edge ↪ objN
          ELabel : eArity ↗ Label
          EIn    : eArity ↗ VecF (F (Input ⊞ Inner))
```

While $\hookrightarrow$ is essentially just a kind of "casting" that emphasises the "starting at a sort" intention, the type constructor $\nearrow$ is the real innovation here; thanks to $\nearrow$, the presentation of $\mathsf{ADHG_2}$ does not require local variable binders; $\nearrow$ therefore introduces the possibility of result type dependencies on the result of other operations into coalgebraic signatures while preserving the overall character of traditional signatures. (Technically, $\hookrightarrow$ and $\nearrow$ can be considered as parts of a shallowly-embedded DSL for a novel kind of coalgebra signatures.)

Expanding definitions, we see that $\mathsf{ELabel} : \mathsf{eArity} \nearrow$ from above is a dependent pair of type $\Sigma\,\mathsf{g} : \mathsf{Edge} \hookrightarrow \mathsf{Label} \bullet (\mathrm{ind}_{\mathsf{Label}}\ \mathsf{g} = \mathsf{eArity})$; for convenience, we give individual names to the two constituents of this pair, which then have the following types, the second of which corresponds to the first datatype invariant in Sect. 9 (where fst implements $\text{ind}_{\text{Label}}$).

$$
\begin{array}{ll}
\text{eLabel} & : \text{Edge} \hookrightarrow \text{Label} \\
\text{eLabel-ind} & : \text{ind}_{\text{Label}} \ \text{eLabel} = \text{eArity}
\end{array}
$$

11   GS-Monoidal Categories of Abstract Term Graphs

The definition of abstract directed hypergraphs we actually use also has the Node definition again, and therefore is even more readable:

```
module _ [...] (objℕ : S.Obj) (Label : DepObj objℕ)
                             (VecF : DepFunctor objℕ) [...] where
   [...]
      record ADHG₃ (Input : C.Obj) (Output : C.Obj) : Set _ where
         field Inner Edge : C.Obj
         Node = Input ⊞ Inner
         field gOut   : C.Mor Output Node
               eOut   : C.Mor Edge Inner
               eArity : Edge ↪ objℕ
               ELabel : eArity ↗ Label
               EIn    : eArity ↗ VecF (F Node)
```

As mentioned in Sect. 2, we are really interested in jungles, which are directed hypergraphs with a one-to-one correspondence between edges and inner nodes established by eOut. Since we need directed hypergraphs as common substrate for an adapted kind of double-pushout term graph rewriting, we define jungles separately as "ADHG₃s where eOut is an isomorphism in C", in Agda:

```
   record AJungle (m n : C.Obj) : Set _ where
      field dhg         : ADHG₃ m n
      open ADHG₃ dhg              -- bringing Inner, Edge, eOut, etc. into scope
      field eOutIsIso : C.IsIso eOut
      eOut⁻¹ : C.Mor Inner Edge   -- providing a nice name for the inverse
      eOut⁻¹ = eOutIsIso C.IsIso.⁻¹
```

The full setting used as context for this includes a few properties not yet mentioned in Sect. 7; it consists of the following items:

- A category C intended to have (representations of) all possible carrier sets as objects, and (representations of) functions between these as morphisms.
  C needs to have coproducts, a terminal object, and a strict initial object.
- A semigroupoid S intended to have (representations of) all possible value sets (including label sets, $\mathbb{N}$, vector sets) as objects.
  S is only required to contain the morphisms associated with the additional structure below; it can be quite "sparse".
- A full and faithful *semigroupoid functor* $\mathcal{F}$ from the semigroupoid underlying C to S that preserves identity morphisms, coproducts, and initial objects.
  This functor is understood as embedding C into S.

– Specifically as setting for the ADHG definitions, a natural number object objℕ, an objℕ-indexed dependent object Label, and an objℕ-indexed dependent functor VecF for vectors satisfying an appropriate vector specification.

In this setting, we have implemented large parts of the theory of gs-monoidal categories introduced by Corradini and Gadducci (1999): For term graphs, monoidal composition $\otimes$ is "parallel composition" that "concatenates" (via coproduct) the input and output interfaces; gs-monoidal categories are monoidal categories with additional transformations ! and ∇:

– $!_A : A \to \mathbb{1}$ is the *terminator* and introduces **g**arbage, and
– $\nabla_A : A \to (A \otimes A)$ is the *duplicator* and introduces s*haring*.

These are present also in cartesian categories such as Lawvere theories, and there they are natural transformations. In **gs**-monoidal categories they do not need to be natural, which is important for term graphs, where **g**arbage and **s**haring make a difference.

We have implemented (Zhao 2018a,b) Agda-verified gs-monoidal categories with ADHGs respectively Jungles as morphisms fully at the abstract level in the category-semigroupoid setting described above. We also implemented Jungle decomposition and proved it correct, which is the core of the result of Corradini and Gadducci (1999) that term graphs (i.e., jungles) form a free gs-monoidal category. For this part, we followed Corradini and Gadducci's set-up, which specialises $\mathcal{C}$.obj to $\mathbb{N}$, interpreting n : $\mathbb{N}$ as the type Fin n—this is justified by the fact that there will be a forgetful functor from every practically useful gs-monoidal category mapping the object monoid to $\mathbb{N}$, and this functor will reflect decomposition. We used this specialisation for decomposition of wiring graphs (which have no edges); apart from that, we elaborated the proofs at the abstract category-semigroupoid level as far as we found feasible. An improved library of dependent functors will make fully abstract proofs possible in the future. We also started to develop a rewriting mechanism for these Jungles via constrained DPO rewriting steps in the category of ADHG matchings, see (Kahl and Zhao 2019).

12 Conclusion

An important observation arising from the development of our ADHG formalisations is that categorial abstraction is frequently enhanced by embedding a "nice" category in a "big" semigroupoid. Careful choices then allow us to develop theory and implementations at the abstract level, and obtain the conventional *Set*-based mathematical theory as one instantiation, while correct-by-construction executables can be generated via instantiations with concrete datatypes. In this way, we achieve re-usability of theoretical developments as implementations that are tunable for efficiency.

A Representation Contexts

We now provide a more fine-grained abstraction for the category-semigroupoid setting of Sections Sects. 7 and 11. Recall that the key idea is to provide a separate interface, the category C, for objects that can be used as carriers of coalgebra sorts, and "extend" this category to an encompassing semigroupoid S that can contain also other objects that may be used to interpret the result type expressions of coalgebra function symbols. For example, the (conceptually) infinite datatype String will never be used as node set of a graph, but it may well be used for node labels. In addition, a type of "representations" for S-morphisms that "start at C-objects" is assumed—these are the morphisms that may serve as interpretations of coalgebra function symbols. The "upwards arrows" are motivated by visualising the semigroupoid S *above* the category C, which is "embedded" into S via $\mathcal{R}$.

Definition A.1. *A* representation context $\mathcal{X} = (C, S, \mathcal{R}, \nearrow, \mathbb{S}, \mathbb{R}, \nearrow)$ *consists of*
- *a category C*
- *a semigroupoid S*
- *a full and faithful semigroupoid functor $\mathcal{R} : C \to S$ that preserves identities*
- *for each object k of C and each object A of S, a collection $k \nnearrow A$ of representations, together with a bijection $\mathbb{S}_{k,A}$ between $k \nnearrow A$ and the S-homset $\mathcal{R}\, k \to A$,*
- *for any two objects k and m of C, a bijection $\mathbb{R}_{k,m}$ between the C-homset $k \to m$ and $k \nnearrow \mathcal{R}\, m$, and*
- *for each representation $U : k \nnearrow A$ and each S-morphism $g : A \to B$ a composition $U \nearrow g$ in $k \nnearrow B$*

such that the following are satisfied:

$$
\begin{aligned}
\mathbb{S}_{k,B}\, (U \nearrow g) &= (\mathbb{S}_{k,A}\, U)\, ;\, g && \text{for } U : k \nnearrow A, \text{ and } g : A \to B \text{ in } S \\
\mathbb{S}_{k,B}^{-1}\, (f\, ;\, g) &= (\mathbb{S}_{k,A}^{-1}\, f) \nearrow g && \text{for } f : \mathcal{R}\, k \to A \text{ and } g : A \to B \text{ in } S \\
\mathcal{R}\, f &= \mathbb{S}_{k, \mathcal{R}\, m}\, (\mathbb{R}_{k,m}\, f) && \text{for } f : k \to m \text{ in } C
\end{aligned}
$$

The implementation setting described in Sect. 7 for obtaining VecDHG_1 from ADHG_1 can be explained as a representation context where
- C has $\mathbb{N}$ as object collection, and Fin $m \to$ Fin n as homset from m to n;
- S is the semigroupoid underlying *Set*;
- $\mathcal{R} : C \to S$ maps $n : \mathbb{N}$ to the set Fin n, and is the identity on morphisms;
- for each $k : \mathbb{N}$ and each set A, the type of representations is $k \nnearrow A = \mathsf{Vec}\, A\, k$, and $\mathbb{S}_{k,A}$ is the canonical isomorphism between Vec A k and Fin $k \to A$;
- for each $k, m : \mathbb{N}$, the canonical isomorphism between Fin $k \to$ Fin m and Vec (Fin m) k is used as $\mathbb{R}_{k,m}$;
- for each vector $U : \mathsf{Vec}\, A\, k$ and each *Set*-morphism $g : A \to B$, the composition is $U \nearrow g = \mathsf{mapVec}\, g\, U$.

Note that there are "more" vectors than there are morphisms in C, and yet more set functions in S than there are vectors.

    Theoretically, one could choose to identify $k \nnearrow A$ with the S-homset $\mathcal{R}\, k \to A$, but we consider it useful to keep the two separate: The point of having $\nnearrow$ as a separate component of representation contexts is that it can be instantiated with *morphism implementations* for which $\mathbb{S}$ provides the semantics in terms of the semigroupoid $\mathcal{S}$, which in turn is intended to provide the connection to *Set*.

For interpretation of coalgebra signatures (as shown in Sect. 2), we assume a fixed interpretation function $\mathcal{F}$ that maps n-ary functor symbols to semigroupoid functors from $\mathcal{S}^n$ to $\mathcal{S}$ that preserve identities (and correspond to meet-preserving relators). If a structure A provides an interpretation of sort symbols as objects in $\mathcal{C}$, then let $[\![t]\!]_A$ be the resulting interpretation of the type expression t, where each sort s is interpreted as $[\![s]\!]_A = \mathcal{R}\, s_A$, and functor symbol applications are interpreted as the corresponding functor applications:

$$[\![F(t_1, \ldots, t_n)]\!]_A = (\mathcal{F}\ F)([\![t_1]\!]_A, \ldots, [\![t_n]\!]_A)$$

For each type expression T, this gives rise to an identity-preserving semigroupoid functor, written $[\![t]\!]$, from the sort-indexed product category $\mathcal{C}^{Sort_\Sigma}$ to $\mathcal{S}$.

Definition A.2. *Let a coalgebraic signature Σ and a representation context $\mathcal{X} = (\mathcal{C}, \mathcal{S}, \mathcal{R}, \nearrow, \mathbb{S}, \mathbb{R}, \nearrow)$ be given. A Σ-$\mathcal{X}$-coalgebra A consists of*

– for each sort s an object s_A of $\mathcal{C}$
– for each function symbol $f : s \to t$ a representation $f_A : s_A \nearrow [\![t]\!]_A$

Given two such coalgebras A and B, a Σ-$\mathcal{X}$-coalgebra homomorphism ϕ from A to B consists of

– for each sort s a representation $\phi_S : s_A \nearrow (\mathcal{R}\, s_B)$ of the $\mathcal{C}$ morphism $(\mathbb{R}^{-1}_{s_A,s_B} \phi_S) : s_A \to s_B$,
– such that for each function symbol $f : s \to t$, the following homomorphism property *holds:*

$$f_A \ \nearrow \ [\![t]\!]\ (\mathbb{R}^{-1}\ \phi) \quad = \quad \phi_s \ \nearrow \ (\mathbb{S}_{s_B, [\![t]\!]_B}\ f_B)$$

This homomorphism property is an equality of representations; in concrete applications this will be a decidable equivalence.

It is easy to see that the Σ-$\mathcal{X}$-coalgebra homomorphisms of Definition A.2 form a category; this is a "good implementation" of Σ-coalgebras in the following sense:

Theorem A.3. *Let a coalgebraic signature Σ, and a representation context $\mathcal{X} = (\mathcal{C}, \text{Set}, \mathcal{R}, \nearrow, \mathbb{S}, \mathbb{R}, \nearrow)$ using the full category Set for $\mathcal{S}$ be given. For each Σ-$\mathcal{X}$-coalgebra A, applying $\mathcal{R}$ to each carrier object s_A, and applying $\mathbb{S}$ to each function symbol interpretation f_A maps the Σ-$\mathcal{X}$-coalgebra A to a conventional Set-based coalgebra in a way that gives rise to a full and faithful functor.* □

In the setting of Sect. 7, the category of Σ-$\mathcal{X}$-coalgebras is therefore equivalent to the subcategory of Σ-coalgebras over *Set* which results from restriction to finite carrier sets.

B   Concretised Representation Context

For an implementation based on, for example, the vectors of Sect. 5, the question arises how to represent not only the components of coalgebras and of morphisms, both of which are representations, but also the results of functor application to morphisms, which are used in the context of the dependent functors mentioned in Sect. 10.

We now assume a language $\mathcal{F}$ of functor symbols (with arity). Our goal is to move from an abstract semigroupoid $\mathcal{S}$, such as *Set*, to one that has a concrete representation amenable to implementation using finite datastructures. (Objects of *Set*, as far as relevant in this context, are considered to be implemented as datatype identifiers or type expressions.)

Given a representation context $\mathcal{X} = (\mathcal{C}, \mathcal{S}, \mathcal{R}, \nearrow, \mathbb{S}, \mathbb{R}, \nearrow)$ and a functor symbol semantics that maps each functor symbol $F : \mathcal{F}$ to a semigroupoid endofunctor $[\![F]\!]$ (of corresponding arity) on $\mathcal{S}$, we construct a new *concretised representation context* $\mathcal{X}^{\mathcal{F}} = (\mathcal{C}, \mathcal{S}^{\mathcal{F}}, \mathcal{R}^{\mathcal{F}}, \nearrow^{\mathcal{F}}, \mathbb{S}^{\mathcal{F}}, \mathbb{R}^{\mathcal{F}}, \nearrow^{\mathcal{F}})$ over the same base category $\mathcal{C}$, where:

- A $\mathcal{S}^{\mathcal{F}}$ object is
  - either LIFT k for a $\mathcal{C}$ object k,
  - or EMBED A for an $\mathcal{S}$ object A,
  - or WRAP F $(Q_1, \dots, Q_n)$ for an n-ary functor symbol F and $\mathcal{S}^{\mathcal{F}}$ objects $Q_1, \dots, Q_n$.

  $\mathcal{S}^{\mathcal{F}}$ objects are assigned a straightforward "semantics" as $\mathcal{S}$ objects:

$$[\![\text{LIFT } k]\!] = \mathcal{R}\, k$$
$$[\![\text{EMBED } A]\!] = A$$
$$[\![\text{WRAP } F\, (Q_1, \dots, Q_n)]\!] = [\![F]\!]([\![Q_1]\!], \dots, [\![Q_n]\!])$$

- $\mathcal{S}^{\mathcal{F}}$ morphisms are
  - either $\mathbb{S}^{\mathcal{F}}_{k,Q}\, U : \text{LIFT } k \to Q$ for a representation $U : k \nearrow^{\mathcal{F}} Q$, which is a representation in $k \nearrow [\![Q]\!]$,
  - or MAP F $(g_1, \dots, g_n) : \text{WRAP } F\, (Q_1, \dots, Q_n) \to \text{WRAP } F\, (P_1, \dots, P_n)$ for an n-ary functor symbol F and morphisms $g_i : Q_i \to P_i$.

  (There are no morphisms starting from EMBED objects.)

  Morphisms are also given a straightforward semantics in $\mathcal{S}$.
- $\mathbb{R}^{\mathcal{F}}$, the composition $;^{\mathcal{F}}$ in $\mathcal{S}^{\mathcal{F}}$, and the composition $\nearrow^{\mathcal{F}}$ are determined by the semantics; $\mathcal{R}^{\mathcal{F}}$ is induced by LIFT.

$\mathcal{X}^{\mathcal{F}}$ is a well-defined representation context, and if $\mathcal{R}$ preserves finite colimits, so does $\mathcal{R}^{\mathcal{F}}$. Note that $\mathcal{S}^{\mathcal{F}}$ is only a semigroupoid, and cannot be a category, since there are no morphisms starting at EMBED objects, not even identity morphisms. This fact is the motivation for asking only for a semigroupoid in this place in a representation context.

For signatures Σ over the functors in $\mathcal{F}$, the concretised representation context $\mathcal{X}^{\mathcal{F}}$ generates the same Σ-coalgebras as the (possibly abstract) context $\mathcal{X}$, but extends the concretely implementable morphisms to "exactly all morphisms ever required while reasoning about Σ-coalgebra transformation".

Theorem B.1. *The category of Σ-$\mathcal{X}^{\mathcal{F}}$-coalgebras is equivalent to the subcategory of the corresponding category of Σ-coalgebras in $\mathcal{S}$ restricted to carriers in $\mathcal{C}$.* □

References

Corradini, A., Gadducci, F.: An algebraic presentation of term graphs, via GS-monoidal categories. Appl. Categ. Struct. **7**(4), 299–331 (1999). https://doi.org/10.1023/A:1008647417502. ISSN 1572–9095

Corradini, A., Rossi, F.: Hyperedge replacement jungle rewriting for term-rewriting systems and logic programming. Theor. Comput. Sci. **109**(1–2), 7–48 (1993). https://doi.org/10.1016/0304-3975(93)90063-Y

Danielsson, N.A., Daggit, M., et al.: Agda standard library, version 0.17 (2018). http://tinyurl.com/AgdaStdlib

Hoffmann, B., Plump, D.: Implementing term rewriting by jungle evaluation. Informatique théorique et applications/Theor. Inform. Appl. **25**(5), 445–472 (1991). https://doi.org/10.1051/ita/1991250504451

Kahl, W.: Dependently-typed formalisation of typed term graphs. In: Echahed, R. (ed.) Proceedings of 6th International Workshop on Computing with Terms and Graphs, TERMGRAPH 2011. EPTCS, vol. 48, pp. 38–53 (2011). https://doi.org/10.4204/EPTCS.48.6

Kahl, W.: Categories of coalgebras with monadic homomorphisms. In: Bonsangue, M.M. (ed.) CMCS 2014 2014. LNCS, vol. 8446, pp. 151–167. Springer, Heidelberg (2014). https://doi.org/10.1007/978-3-662-44124-4_9. Agda theories at http://RelMiCS.McMaster.ca/RATH-Agda/

Kahl, W.: Graph transformation with symbolic attributes via monadic coalgebra homomorphisms. ECEASST **71**, 5.1–5.17 (2015). https://doi.org/10.14279/tuj.eceasst.71.999

Kahl, W., Zhao, Y.: Dependently-typed formalisation of typed term graphs. In: Fernández, M., Mackie, I. (eds.) Proceedings of Tenth International Workshop on Computing with Terms and Graphs, TERMGRAPH 2018. EPTCS, vol. 288, pp. 26–37 (2019). https://doi.org/10.4204/EPTCS.288.3

Norell, U.: Towards a practical programming language based on dependent type theory. Ph.D. thesis, Department of Computer Science and Engineering, Chalmers University of Technology (2007). See also http://wiki.portal.chalmers.se/agda/pmwiki.php

Pitts, A.M.: Categorical logic. In: Abramsky, S., Gabbay, D.M., Maibaum, T.S.E. (eds.) Handbook of Logic in Computer Science, vol. 5, pp. 39–128. Oxford University Press, Oxford (2001)

Zhao, Y.: A machine-checked categorial formalisation of term graph rewriting with semantics preservation. Ph.D. thesis, McMaster University (2018a)

Zhao, Y.: A formalisation of term graph rewriting in Agda – TGR1. Mechanically checked Agda development, with 283 pages literate document output (2018b). http://relmics.mcmaster.ca/RATH-Agda/TGR1/

Term Charters

Alexander Knapp[(✉)] and María Victoria Cengarle

Universität Augsburg, Augsburg, Germany
knapp@informatik.uni-augsburg.de, mv.cengarle@gmail.com

Abstract. Expressions in specification and programming languages often extend algebraic terms by additional term formation rules and enlarged evaluation domains. For use in different contexts, the semantics of these expressions must allow for interface modification, that is, evaluation must be compatible with signature translation and with variable renaming. This work introduces term charters as an abstract framework for terms and expressions following the slogan "evaluation is invariant under change of notation". Several examples illustrate the use of term charters. Different term charter representations are discussed and morphisms between term charters are defined. Finally, the relation of term charters with institutions in general and with context institutions in particular is demonstrated.

1 Introduction

Algebraic signatures are customarily connected with a fixed grammar for term construction as well as a canonical accompanying procedure for term evaluation; what may vary is the term representation when using different names for function symbols. More often than not, expressions of specification or programming languages build on algebraic signatures and evaluation, but exceed the boundaries of such a tightly connected syntactical and semantical scheme. For instance, the "Object Constraint Language" (OCL [10]) is mainly based on order-sorted algebra with function symbols like + and `append` giving rise to expressions like $1 + 2$ and c_1->`append`(c_2) as well as their usual evaluation.

The OCL grammar, however, also offers a general iteration construct c->`iterate`$(i : s;\ a : s' = e_0 \mid e)$ for applying the expression e over the successive elements of the sequence c using the iterator i and accumulating the partial results in a initialised by e_0. Here, e has to be evaluated multiple times for different valuations of its bound variables i and a. This would be at least cumbersome to comprise into order-sorted terms using a different function symbol for every possible iteration expression. Alternatively, full higher-order algebras [14] could be employed, which yet would seem rather generous for such a small excursion. A more direct solution is to use a special evaluation rule for the iteration construct with only one local auxiliary semantic function of higher order.

Another set of language features of the OCL that stretches order-sorted algebras is `undef` representing undefinedness, its corresponding undefinedness test

© IFIP International Federation for Information Processing 2019
Published by Springer Nature Switzerland AG 2019
J. L. Fiadeiro and I. Ţuţu (Eds.): WADT 2018, LNCS 11563, pp. 119–138, 2019.
https://doi.org/10.1007/978-3-030-23220-7_7

e.isUndef(), and the conditional if e then e_1 else e_2 endif that is only strict in its first argument. A change to the setting of partial algebras [14] could be considered, but also sticking with order-sortedness and just extending the value domains of the algebras by a semantic value † and providing a special evaluation rule for the conditional presents a viable alternative.

These examples suggest that it is sometimes necessary to consider special expression construction and evaluation rules added to algebraic languages. In order to be applicable in varying contexts and to allow for different representations of the underlying algebraic signature, evaluation still has to be compatible with changes to the interface of expressions, i.e., the function symbols and the free variables. In the following, we discuss a notion of evaluation for generalised terms in an abstract framework that we call *term charter*. It captures the fundamental properties of evaluation w.r.t. variables, signatures, variable renamings, and signature translations along the slogan "evaluation is invariant under change of notation". Using this as a guideline, the present account of term charters provides a simplification and rational reconstruction of our previous rendition in [6].

We first review the motivational OCL examples and the principal evaluation properties more precisely in Sect. 2, though starting, for simplicity, from many-sorted algebras. Based on indexed categories [15,17], we then present term charters in Sect. 3. Term charters are built over *term charter domains* consisting of values and variables, structures, and the underlying values of structures, all indexed over signatures. A *term charter* itself consists of a term constructor, a variable embedding, and evaluation maps for terms over a signature and variables using valuations; the interaction of these ingredients is regulated by three axioms for variable evaluation, variable renaming, and signature translations such that indeed evaluation is invariant under change of notation. We also discuss two more compact alternative presentations of term charters using comma categories [8] and the Grothendieck construction [17] in Sect. 4. The latter lets us directly construct an *institution* [3,5] from a term charter as shown in Sect. 5; again, this new construction simplifies [6]. The generation of an institution conveniently embeds term charters into the landscape of logical systems. What is more, the induced institution is closely related to the notion of *context institutions* by Pawłowski [12], which has been introduced in a similar effort to capture open formulæ over variables in institutions. We finally discuss different notions of *morphisms* between term charter domains and term charters in Sect. 6. We conclude in Sect. 7 with some application scenarios of term charters to OCL. Mainly for fixing notation, some categorical prerequisites are briefly summarised in Appendix A.

2   Extending Algebraic Term Evaluation

The evaluation of terms over a many-sorted *signature* $\Sigma = (S, F)$ of sorts and function symbols directly follows term formation. Given S-sorted *variables* $X = (X_s)_{s \in S}$, the family of terms $\mathscr{T}_\Sigma^{\mathrm{m}}(X) = (\mathscr{T}_\Sigma^{\mathrm{m}}(X)_s)_{s \in S}$ over Σ and X is inductively defined by

- $x \in \mathscr{T}_\Sigma^m(X)_s$ if $x \in X_s$;
- $f(t_1, \ldots, t_n) \in \mathscr{T}_\Sigma^m(X)_s$ if $f \in F_{s_1 \ldots s_n\, s}$ and $t_i \in \mathscr{T}_\Sigma^m(X)_{s_i}$ for $1 \leq i \leq n$.

For a Σ-*structure* $M = (S^M, F^M)$ and a *valuation* $\beta = (\beta_s : X_s \to s^M)_{s \in S} : X \to U_\Sigma(M)$ from the variables X to the *underlying sets* $U_\Sigma(M) = S^M$ of the structure, *term evaluation* $[\![-]\!]_{(\Sigma,X)}^m(M,\beta) = ([\![-]\!]_{(\Sigma,X)}^m(M,\beta)_s : \mathscr{T}_\Sigma^m(X)_s \to s^M)_{s \in S} : \mathscr{T}_\Sigma^m(X) \to U_\Sigma(M)$ is inductively defined in correspondence with term formation of the grammar:

- $[\![x]\!]_{(\Sigma,X)}^m(M,\beta)_s = \beta_s(x)$ for $x \in X_s$, and
- $[\![f(t_1, \ldots, t_n)]\!]_{(\Sigma,X)}^m(M,\beta)_s = f^M([\![t_1]\!]_{(\Sigma,X)}^m(M,\beta)_{s_1}, \ldots, [\![t_n]\!]_{(\Sigma,X)}^m(M,\beta)_{s_n})$ for $f \in F_{s_1 \ldots s_n\, s}$ and $t_i \in \mathscr{T}_\Sigma^m(X)_{s_i}$ for $1 \leq i \leq n$.

If, however, other term formation rules are considered that transcend the boundaries of the compliance of the function symbols f with the interpreting functions f^M or that require values besides the sorted universes s^M of the structure M for evaluation, recourse to an extended notion of structures has to be taken.

Example 1. Consider the many-sorted signature $\Sigma^\circ = (S, F)$ showing as sorts S, Bool for the booleans, Int for the integers, and, for every sort $s \in S$, Seq(s) for the (finite) lists, together with some function symbols F like $0 \in F_{\text{Int}}$ for zero and $+ \in F_{\text{Int Int Int}}$ for addition; and the Σ°-structure $M^\circ = (S^{M^\circ}, F^{M^\circ})$ interpreting these sorts and function symbols of Σ° in the standard way, such that, in particular, $\text{Bool}^{M^\circ} = \{f\!f, t\!t\}$, $\text{Int}^{M^\circ} = \mathbb{Z}$, $\text{Seq}(s)^{M^\circ} = (s^{M^\circ})^*$, $0^{M^\circ} = 0$, and $+^{M^\circ} = \lambda v_1, v_2 . v_1 + v_2$. Besides the usual term formation rules from the variables and the function symbols above, we want to include an OCL-like *iteration* construct

$$c\text{->iterate}(i : s;\, a : s' = e_0 \mid e)$$

in the grammar of iteration terms $\mathscr{T}_\Sigma^{it}(X)$: Starting with the accumulator variable a of sort s' initialised with the evaluated term $e_0 \in \mathscr{T}_\Sigma^{it}(X)_{s'}$, each entry in the evaluated term $c \in \mathscr{T}_\Sigma^{it}(X)_{\text{Seq}(s)}$ is successively assigned to the iterator variable i of sort s updating the accumulator a with the result of evaluating the term $e \in \mathscr{T}_\Sigma^{it}(X \uplus \{i : s, a : s'\})_{s'}$, which thus may contain i and a as fresh local variables, and finally, the last value of a is returned; such that, e.g., evaluation of Seq$\{$1, 2, 3$\}$->iterate(i : Int; a : Int = 0 | i+a) yields 6. Evaluation of iterations could rely on an extended Σ° with function symbols $it_{\lambda i:s, a:s'\,.\,e} \in F_{\text{Seq}(s)\, s'}$ for every possible iteration expression (and a correspondingly extended M°), or an embedding of the whole language into higher-order algebra. As a more moderate alternative, the evaluation of iterations can also be directly expressed using M° based on an intermediate, ad hoc higher-order function it^{M°:

$$[\![c\text{->iterate}(i : s;\, a : s' = e_0 \mid e)]\!]_{(\Sigma^\circ,X)}^{it}(M^\circ,\beta)_{s'} =$$
$$it^{M^\circ}([\![c]\!]_{(\Sigma^\circ,X)}^{it}(M^\circ,\beta)_{\text{Seq}(s)}, [\![e_0]\!]_{(\Sigma^\circ,X)}^{it}(M^\circ,\beta)_{s'},$$
$$\{(v_i, v_a) \mapsto [\![e]\!]_{(\Sigma^\circ,X \uplus \{i:s,a:s'\})}^{it}(M^\circ,\beta\{i : s \mapsto v_i, a : s' \mapsto v_a\})_{s'}\}) ,$$

where $it^{M^\circ} : \mathsf{Seq}(s)^{M^\circ} \times s'^{M^\circ} \times (s^{M^\circ} \times s'^{M^\circ} \to s'^{M^\circ}) \to s'^{M^\circ}$, like Haskell's foldr, is defined by $it^{M^\circ}(\varepsilon, v_a, h) = v_a$ and $it^{M^\circ}(v_i::\ell, v_a, h) = it^{M^\circ}(\ell, h(v_i, v_a), h)$.

In order to obtain a proper evaluation, the basic properties of algebraic term evaluation w.r.t. the interface of terms must be retained also for extended term formation rules and structures, i.e., compatibility with variable renamings and signature translations has to be ensured. For the many-sorted case a *variable renaming* $\xi = (\xi_s : X_{1,s} \to X_{2,s})_{s \in S} : X_1 \to X_2$ induces a *term renaming* $\mathscr{T}_\Sigma^{\mathrm{m}}(\xi) = (\mathscr{T}_\Sigma^{\mathrm{m}}(\xi)_s : \mathscr{T}_\Sigma^{\mathrm{m}}(X_1)_s \to \mathscr{T}_\Sigma^{\mathrm{m}}(X_2)_s)_{s \in S} : \mathscr{T}_\Sigma^{\mathrm{m}}(X_1) \to \mathscr{T}_\Sigma^{\mathrm{m}}(X_2)$, which usually is denoted again by ξ; then for each $t \in \mathscr{T}_\Sigma^{\mathrm{m}}(X_1)_s$ a "renaming lemma" holds:

$$(\mathrm{R_m}) \quad [\![\xi_s(t)]\!]_{(\Sigma,X_2)}^{\mathrm{m}}(M, \beta)_s = [\![t]\!]_{(\Sigma,X_1)}^{\mathrm{m}}(M, \beta \circ \xi)_s \ .$$

Moreover, a *signature translation* $\sigma = (\sigma_{\mathrm{S}} : S \to S', \sigma_{\mathrm{F}} : F \to F')$: $\Sigma = (S, F) \to \Sigma' = (S', F')$ and the corresponding *reducts* of variables $X'|\sigma = (X'_{\sigma_{\mathrm{S}}(s)})_{s \in S}$ and terms $\mathscr{T}_{\Sigma'}^{\mathrm{m}}(X')|\sigma = (\mathscr{T}_{\Sigma'}^{\mathrm{m}}(X')_{\sigma_{\mathrm{S}}(s)})_{s \in S}$ induce a *term translation* $\mathscr{T}_\sigma^{\mathrm{m}}(X') : \mathscr{T}_\Sigma^{\mathrm{m}}(X'|\sigma) \to \mathscr{T}_{\Sigma'}^{\mathrm{m}}(X')|\sigma$ inductively defined by

- $\mathscr{T}_\sigma^{\mathrm{m}}(X')_s(x') = x'$ for $x' \in (X'|\sigma)_s$;
- $\mathscr{T}_\sigma^{\mathrm{m}}(X')_s(f(t_1, \ldots, t_n)) = \sigma_{\mathrm{F}}(f)(\mathscr{T}_\sigma^{\mathrm{m}}(X')_{s_1}(t_1), \ldots, \mathscr{T}_\sigma^{\mathrm{m}}(X')_{s_n}(t_n))$
  for $f \in F_{s_1 \ldots s_n \, s}$ and $t_i \in \mathscr{T}_\Sigma^{\mathrm{m}}(X'|\sigma)_{s_i}$ for $1 \le i \le n$.

Then, for the σ-*reduct* of structures $M'|\sigma = ((\sigma_{\mathrm{S}}(s)^{M'})_{s \in S}, (F'^{M'}_{\sigma_{\mathrm{S}}(\bar{s})})_{\bar{s} \in S^+})$ and valuations $\beta'|\sigma = (\beta'_{\sigma_{\mathrm{S}}(s)})_{s \in S}$, and abbreviating $\mathscr{T}_\sigma^{\mathrm{m}}(X')$ by just σ, a "translation lemma" for each $t \in \mathscr{T}_\Sigma^{\mathrm{m}}(X'|\sigma)_s$ holds:

$$(\mathrm{T_m}) \quad [\![\sigma_s(t)]\!]_{(\Sigma',X')}^{\mathrm{m}}(M', \beta')_{\sigma_{\mathrm{S}}(s)} = [\![t]\!]_{(\Sigma,X'|\sigma)}^{\mathrm{m}}(M'|\sigma, \beta'|\sigma)_s \ .$$

These properties $(\mathrm{R_m})$, $(\mathrm{T_m})$ can be straight forwardly transferred to properties $(\mathrm{R_{it}})$, $(\mathrm{T_{it}})$ for the evaluation of iterations in Example 1: The signatures and structures are taken to be restricted to the forms of Σ° and M° such that signature translations preserve `Bool`, `Int`, `Seq`, `0`, etc., and $\mathscr{T}_\Sigma^{\mathrm{it}}(\xi)$ and $\mathscr{T}_{\sigma,X'}^{\mathrm{it}}$ are defined to preserve the grammar also of `iterate` such that, in particular, the additional clause for variable renamings becomes

$$\mathscr{T}_\Sigma^{\mathrm{it}}(\xi)_{s'}(c\texttt{->iterate}(i : s;\ a : s' = e_0 \mid e)) =$$
$$\mathscr{T}_\Sigma^{\mathrm{it}}(\xi)_{\mathsf{Seq}(s)}(c)\texttt{->iterate}(i : s;\ a : s' = \mathscr{T}_\Sigma^{\mathrm{it}}(\xi)_{s'}(e_0) \mid$$
$$\mathscr{T}_\Sigma^{\mathrm{it}}(\xi\{i : s \mapsto i : s, a : s' \mapsto a : s'\})_{s'}(e)) \ .$$

Name capturing of the bound variables i and a is avoided due to the explicit provision of fresh variables in $X \uplus \{i : s, a : s'\}$ and the corresponding extension of ξ.

Example 2. Again inspired by the OCL, consider the addition of a term former **undef** denoting *undefinedness* over the signature Σ° and the Σ°-structure M° from above. The predefined function symbols are to be interpreted strictly, i.e., if any of the argument terms of a function symbol is undefined, the overall result shall be undefined. Additionally, we want to include the non-strict term former e.isUndef() for testing for undefinedness, and the conditional if e then e_1 else e_2 endif which is only strict in its first argument. Here, a first option is to change the interpreting structure M° into a partial algebra. As an alternative to such a pervasive adaptation, we may also opt for just including a semantic value † into the underlying sets of M° by defining $U^\dagger(M^\circ) = (s^{M^\circ} \uplus \{\dagger\})_{s \in S}$. The valuations then are of the form $\beta^\dagger : X \to U^\dagger(M^\circ)$ and the evaluation becomes $[\![-]\!]^u_{(\Sigma^\circ, X)}(M^\circ, \beta^\dagger) : \mathcal{T}^u_{\Sigma^\circ}(X) \to U^\dagger(M^\circ)$ defined by

- $[\![x]\!]^u_{(\Sigma^\circ, X)}(M^\circ, \beta^\dagger)_s = \beta^\dagger_s(x);$

- $[\![f(\vec{e})]\!]^u_{(\Sigma^\circ, X)}(M^\circ, \beta^\dagger)_s = \begin{cases} f^{M^\circ}(\vec{v}) & \text{if } \forall i \,.\, \vec{v}_i = [\![\vec{e}_i]\!]^u_{(\Sigma^\circ, X)}(M^\circ, \beta^\dagger)_{s_i} \neq \dagger \\ \dagger & \text{otherwise} \end{cases};$

- $[\![\mathbf{undef}]\!]^u_{(\Sigma^\circ, X)}(M^\circ, \beta^\dagger)_s = \dagger;$

- $[\![e.\mathtt{isUndef}()]\!]^u_{(\Sigma^\circ, X)}(M^\circ, \beta^\dagger)_{\mathtt{Bool}} = \begin{cases} \mathit{tt} & \text{if } [\![e]\!]^u_{(\Sigma^\circ, X)}(M^\circ, \beta^\dagger)_s = \dagger \\ \mathit{ff} & \text{otherwise} \end{cases};$

- $[\![\mathtt{if}\ e\ \mathtt{then}\ e_{tt}\ \mathtt{else}\ e_{\mathit{ff}}\ \mathtt{endif}]\!]^u_{(\Sigma^\circ, X)}(M^\circ, \beta^\dagger)_s =$
  $\begin{cases} [\![e_b]\!]^u_{(\Sigma^\circ, X)}(M^\circ, \beta^\dagger)_s & \text{if } [\![e]\!]^u_{(\Sigma^\circ, X)}(M^\circ, \beta^\dagger)_{\mathtt{Bool}} = b \in \{\mathit{ff}, \mathit{tt}\} \\ \dagger & \text{otherwise} \end{cases}.$

The corresponding properties $(\mathrm{R_u})$ and $(\mathrm{T_u})$, where $\mathcal{T}^u_\Sigma(\xi)$ and $\mathcal{T}^u_{\sigma, X'}$ now also preserve **undef**, isUndef(), and the conditional, can be proved by induction on term formation.

3   Term Charter Domains and Term Charters

We present an abstract framework capturing the basic properties of term evaluation over structures, where the terms are formed according to a grammar and the structures can consist of extended algebras. Signatures, values and variables, structures, and underlying values are comprised into a *term charter domain*; the grammar of term formation, variable renaming, variable embedding, and the evaluation proper is collected into a *term charter* over such a domain requiring conditions for variable embedding and invariance under renaming and translation. We use indexed categories [15, 17] (see Appendix A.1) as a foundation for the abstract framework, since they provide a close match with the algebraic signatures as indexes also used in institutions [14]. We show that *term structure constructors* induce term charters. Additionally, we discuss a different form for term translation and a notion of *substitutions* in term charters. Term charters have already been introduced in [6]. The presentation there, however, employed the technical means of Grothendieck categories throughout, thereby somewhat obscuring the relation of term charters with generalised evaluation.

3.1 Term Charter Domains

A *term charter domain* $(\mathbb{S}, Val, Str, U)$ is given by a category $\mathbb{S}$ of *signatures*, an indexed category $Val : \mathbb{S}^{\mathrm{op}} \to \mathbf{Cat}$ of *value variables*, an indexed category $Str : \mathbb{S}^{\mathrm{op}} \to \mathbf{Cat}$ of *structures*, and an *underlying* indexed functor $U : Str \stackrel{.}{\to} Val$.

We use the terminology of "value variables", since Val plays the rôle of both. In fact, variables in Val can only be assigned values in Val, not, e.g., sets of values or functions.

Example 3. (1) A term charter domain $(\mathbb{S}^{\mathrm{m}}, Val^{\mathrm{m}}, Str^{\mathrm{m}}, U^{\mathrm{m}})$ for many-sorted algebras can be obtained as follows (order-sorted or higher-order algebras can be handled similarly): The signature category $\mathbb{S}^{\mathrm{m}}$ comprises the many-sorted signatures $\Sigma = (S, F)$ and the signature morphisms $\sigma = (\sigma_{\mathrm{S}}, \sigma_{\mathrm{F}}) : \Sigma \to \Sigma'$. The category $Val^{\mathrm{m}}(\Sigma)$ of Σ-value variables comprises the set families $X = (X_s)_{s \in S}$ and the renamings $\xi = (\xi_s : X_{1,s} \to X_{2,s})_{s \in S} : X_1 \to X_2$; the reduct functor $Val^{\mathrm{m}}(\sigma) : Val^{\mathrm{m}}(\Sigma') \to Val^{\mathrm{m}}(\Sigma)$ yields $Val^{\mathrm{m}}(\sigma)(X') = (X'_{\sigma_{\mathrm{S}}(s)})_{s \in S}$ and $Val^{\mathrm{m}}(\sigma)(\xi') = (\xi'_{\sigma_{\mathrm{S}}(s)})_{s \in S}$. The category $Str^{\mathrm{m}}(\Sigma)$ of Σ-structures comprises the many-sorted structures $(S^M = (s^M)_{s \in S}, F^M = (F^M_{\bar{s}})_{\bar{s} \in S^+})$ and the homomorphisms $\mu = (\mu_s : s^{M_1} \to s^{M_2})_{s \in S} : M_1 \to M_2$ with $\mu(f^{M_1}(\vec{v})) = f^{M_2}(\mu(\vec{v}))$ for $f \in F$; the reduct functor $Str^{\mathrm{m}}(\sigma) : Str^{\mathrm{m}}(\Sigma') \to Str^{\mathrm{m}}(\Sigma)$ yields $Str^{\mathrm{m}}(\sigma)(M') = ((\sigma_{\mathrm{S}}(s)^{M'})_{s \in S}, (\sigma_{\mathrm{F}}(F_{\sigma_{\mathrm{S}}(\bar{s})})^{M'})_{\bar{s} \in S^+})$ and $Str^{\mathrm{m}}(\sigma)(\mu') = (\mu'_{\sigma_{\mathrm{S}}(s)})_{s \in S}$. Finally, define $U^{\mathrm{m}}_{\Sigma}(M) = (s^M)_{s \in S}$ and $U^{\mathrm{m}}_{\Sigma}(\mu : M_1 \to M_2) = (\mu_s)_{s \in S}$ for the underlying value variables and renamings, such that indeed $U^{\mathrm{m}}_{\Sigma} \circ Str^{\mathrm{m}}(\sigma) = Val^{\mathrm{m}}(\sigma) \circ U^{\mathrm{m}}_{\Sigma'}$.

(2) For `iterate` in Example 1, the term charter domain $(\mathbb{S}^{\circ}, Val^{\circ}, Str^{\circ}, U^{\circ})$ is obtained by restricting $(\mathbb{S}^{\mathrm{m}}, Val^{\mathrm{m}}, Str^{\mathrm{m}}, U^{\mathrm{m}})$: $\mathbb{S}^{\circ}$ shows all signatures with predefined sorts `Bool`, `Int`, `Seq`(s) and function symbols `0`, `+`, etc., as well as all signature morphisms preserving these predefined symbols; Val° is only defined on $\mathbb{S}^{\circ}$; the structures in Str° are those with standard interpretations of the predefined symbols; and the underlying functor U° operates only on Str°.

(3) For the undefinedness extension in Ex. 2, the term charter domain $(\mathbb{S}^{\circ}, Val^{\dagger}, Str^{\circ}, U^{\dagger})$ is defined using the indexed endo-functor $\dagger : Val^{\circ} \stackrel{.}{\to} Val^{\circ}$ with $\dagger_{\Sigma^{\circ}}(X) = (X_s \uplus \{\dagger\})_{s \in S}$ and $\dagger_{\Sigma^{\circ}}(\xi) = (\xi_s \{\dagger \mapsto \dagger\})_{s \in S}$ for a Kleisli construction [1]: The objects of $Val^{\dagger}(\Sigma^{\circ})$ and $Val^{\circ}(\Sigma^{\circ})$ coincide, but a morphism $\xi^{\dagger} : X_1 \to X_2$ of $Val^{\dagger}(\Sigma^{\circ})$ is given by the $Val^{\circ}(\Sigma^{\circ})$-morphism $\xi : X_1 \to \dagger_{\Sigma^{\circ}}(X_2)$; the $Val^{\dagger}(\Sigma^{\circ})$-identities $1_X : X \to X$ are the inclusions $\iota_X : X \to \dagger_{\Sigma^{\circ}}(X)$, the composition $\xi^{\dagger}_1 ; \xi^{\dagger}_2$ of $\xi^{\dagger}_1 : X_1 \to X_2$ and $\xi^{\dagger}_2 : X_2 \to X_3$ is $(\xi_1 ; \xi_2 \{\dagger \mapsto \dagger\})^{\dagger} : X_1 \to X_3$. The underlying functor $U^{\dagger} : Str^{\circ} \stackrel{.}{\to} Val^{\dagger}$ is chosen as $U^{\dagger}_{\Sigma^{\circ}}(M) = U^{\circ}_{\Sigma^{\circ}}(M)$ and $U^{\dagger}_{\Sigma^{\circ}}(\mu : M_1 \to M_2) = (U^{\circ}_{\Sigma^{\circ}}(\mu); \iota_{U^{\mathrm{m}}_{\Sigma^{\circ}}(M_2)})^{\dagger}$.

3.2 Term Charters

Let $(\mathbb{S}, Val, Str, U)$ be a term charter domain. Let $\mathscr{T} : Val \stackrel{..}{\to} Val$ be a lax indexed functor, where the functors $\mathscr{T}_{\Sigma} : Val(\Sigma) \to Val(\Sigma)$ for each $\Sigma \in |\mathbb{S}|$ *construct terms* and *rename terms* along value variable renamings, and the natural transformations $\mathscr{T}_{\sigma} : Val(\sigma); \mathscr{T}_{\Sigma} \stackrel{.}{\to} \mathscr{T}_{\Sigma'}; Val(\sigma)$ for each $\sigma \in \mathbb{S}(\Sigma, \Sigma')$ *translate terms* along signature morphisms. Let furthermore $\nu : 1_{Val} \overset{\cdot}{\to} \mathscr{T}$ be a lax indexed natural transformation, where the natural transformations $\nu_\Sigma : 1_{Val(\Sigma)} \overset{\cdot}{\to} \mathscr{T}_\Sigma$ for each $\Sigma \in |\mathbb{S}|$ *embed value variables into terms*. Finally, for each $\Sigma \in |\mathbb{S}|$, $X \in |Val(\Sigma)|$, and $M \in |Str(\Sigma)|$, let

$$(ext_\Sigma)_X^M : Val(\Sigma)(X, U_\Sigma(M)) \to Val(\Sigma)(\mathscr{T}_\Sigma(X), U_\Sigma(M))$$

be a function *extending* a value variable valuation β into a term valuation $(ext_\Sigma)_X^M(\beta)$. Then $(\mathscr{T}, \nu, ext)$ is a *term charter* over $(\mathbb{S}, Val, Str, U)$ if the following *variable condition* (V), *renaming condition* (R), and *translation condition* (T) are satisfied:

(V) $\nu_\Sigma(X); (ext_\Sigma)_X^M(\beta) = \beta$

for all $\Sigma \in |\mathbb{S}|$, $\beta \in Val(\Sigma)(X, U_\Sigma(M))$, i.e., the term valuation over a value variable valuation indeed extends the value variable valuation;

(R) $\mathscr{T}_\Sigma(\xi); (ext_\Sigma)_{X_2}^M(\beta) = (ext_\Sigma)_{X_1}^M(\xi; \beta)$

for all $\Sigma \in |\mathbb{S}|$, $\xi \in Val(\Sigma)(X_1, X_2)$, $\beta \in Val(\Sigma)(X_2, U_\Sigma(M))$, i.e., the "renaming lemma" holds; and

(T) $\mathscr{T}_\sigma(X'); Val(\sigma)((ext_{\Sigma'})_{X'}^{M'}(\beta')) = (ext_\Sigma)_{Val(\sigma)(X')}^{Str(\sigma)(M')}(Val(\sigma)(\beta'))$

for all $\sigma \in \mathbb{S}(\Sigma, \Sigma')$, $\beta' \in Val(\Sigma')(X', U_{\Sigma'}(M'))$, i.e., the "translation lemma" holds.

This notion of term charters in fact directly translates the properties of concrete evaluation as discussed in Sect. 2 into an abstract framework: Assume that for each $\Sigma \in |\mathbb{S}|$ there is a faithful functor $\mathcal{U}_\Sigma : Val(\Sigma) \to \text{Set}$, i.e., each $Val(\Sigma)$ is a concrete category. Writing X for $\mathcal{U}_\Sigma(X)$ when $X \in |Val(\Sigma)|$, ξ for $\mathcal{U}_\Sigma(\xi)$ when $\xi \in Val(\Sigma)(X_1, X_2)$, $-|\sigma$ for both $Str(\sigma)(-)$ and $Val(\sigma)(-)$, $[\![t]\!]_{(\Sigma,X)}(M, \beta)$ for $(ext_\Sigma)_X^M(\beta)(t)$, $\xi(t)$ for $\mathscr{T}_\Sigma(\xi)(t)$, and $\sigma(t)$ for $\mathscr{T}_\sigma(X')(t)$, the conditions become

(V) $[\![x]\!]_{(\Sigma,X)}(M, \beta) = \beta(x)$;
(R) $[\![\xi(t)]\!]_{(\Sigma,X_2)}(M, \beta) = [\![t]\!]_{(\Sigma,X_1)}(M, \beta \circ \xi)$;
(T) $([\![\sigma(t)]\!]_{(\Sigma',X')}(M', \beta'))|\sigma = [\![t]\!]_{(\Sigma,X'|\sigma)}(M'|\sigma, \beta'|\sigma)$.

Example 4. (1) For many-sorted algebras as described in Sect. 2, $(\mathscr{T}^m, \nu^m, ext^m)$ with $\nu_\Sigma^m(X) = 1_X : X \hookrightarrow \mathscr{T}_\Sigma^m(X)$ and $(ext_\Sigma^m)_X^M(\beta) = [\![-]\!]_{(\Sigma,X)}^m(M, \beta)$ forms a $(\mathbb{S}^m, Val^m, Str^m, U^m)$-term charter. Note that indeed $\mathscr{T}^m : Val^m \overset{\cdot}{\to} Val^m$.

(2) For the iteration extension in Example 1, $(\mathscr{T}^{it}, \nu^{it}, ext^{it})$ with

$$\mathscr{T}_\sigma^{it}(X')_{s'}(c\text{->iterate}(i : s; \, a : s' = e_0 \mid e)) =$$
$$\mathscr{T}_\sigma^{it}(X')_{\text{Seq}(s)}(c)\text{->iterate}(i : \sigma_S(s); \, a : \sigma_S(s') = \mathscr{T}_\sigma^{it}(X')_{s'}(e_0) \mid$$
$$\mathscr{T}_\sigma^{it}(X' \uplus \{i : \sigma_S(s), a : \sigma_S(s')\})_{s'}(e)) \, ,$$

$\nu^{it}_{\Sigma^\circ}(X) = 1_X : X \hookrightarrow \mathscr{T}^{it}_\Sigma(X)$, and $(ext^{it}_{\Sigma^\circ})^{M^\circ}_X(\beta) = \llbracket - \rrbracket^{it}_{(\Sigma^\circ, X)}(M^\circ, \beta)$ consti-
tutes an $(\mathbb{S}^\circ, Val^\circ, Str^\circ, U^\circ)$-term charter, as the instantiated properties (V_{it}), (R_{it}), and (T_{it}) hold by induction on term construction.

(3) Similarly, for the undefinedness extension in Example 2, $(\mathscr{T}^u, \nu^u, ext^u)$ with $\nu^u_{\Sigma^\circ}(X) = 1_X : X \hookrightarrow \mathscr{T}^u_\Sigma(X)$ and $(ext^u_{\Sigma^\circ})^{M^\circ}_X(\beta^\dagger) = \llbracket - \rrbracket^u_{(\Sigma^\circ, X)}(M^\circ, \beta^\dagger)$ consti-
tutes an $(\mathbb{S}^\circ, Val^\dagger, Str^\circ, U^\dagger)$-term charter.

Since $\mathscr{T}$ is a lax indexed functor, the renaming condition (R) and the translation condition (T) can be equivalently combined into a single *context condition*
on term charters for expressing that "evaluation is invariant under change of
notation":

(C) $\mathscr{T}_\sigma(\xi); Val(\sigma)((ext_{\Sigma'})^{M'}_{X'}(\beta')) = (ext_\Sigma)^{Str(\sigma)(M')}_X(\xi; Val(\sigma)(\beta'))$

for all $\sigma \in \mathbb{S}(\Sigma, \Sigma')$, $\xi \in Val(\Sigma)(X, Val(\sigma)(X'))$, and $\beta' \in Val(\Sigma')(X', U_{\Sigma'}(M'))$,
where $\mathscr{T}_\sigma(\xi) = \mathscr{T}_\Sigma(\xi); \mathscr{T}_\sigma(X')$.

3.3 Obtaining a Term Charter from a Term Structure Constructor

In the many-sorted case, the terms themselves form an algebra. In particular,
for each $\Sigma \in |\mathbb{S}^m|$, there is a functor $\mathscr{S}^m_\Sigma : Val^m(\Sigma) \to Str^m(\Sigma)$ that is left
adjoint to the underlying functor U^m_Σ with a unit natural transformation $\eta_\Sigma :$
$1_{Val^m(\Sigma)} \dot{\to} \mathscr{S}^m_\Sigma; U^m_\Sigma$ and a unique lifting $\beta^{\#^{m,M}_{\Sigma,X}} : \mathscr{S}^m_\Sigma(X) \to M$ in $Str^m(\Sigma)$
for each $\beta : X \to U^m_\Sigma(M)$ in $Val^m(\Sigma)$. This adjunction, where $\mathscr{S}^m$ is a *term
structure constructor*, can equivalently be used to obtain the many-sorted term
charter of Example 4.

Indeed, for a term charter domain $(\mathbb{S}, Val, Str, U)$, let $(\mathscr{S}, U, \eta, (-)^\#)$ be an
$|\mathbb{S}|$-wise adjunction for the family of functors $\mathscr{S} = (\mathscr{S}_\Sigma : Val(\Sigma) \to Str(\Sigma))_{\Sigma \in |\mathbb{S}|}$,
the family of natural transformations $\eta = (\eta_\Sigma : 1_{Val(\Sigma)} \dot{\to} \mathscr{S}_\Sigma; U_\Sigma)_{\Sigma \in |\mathbb{S}|}$, and
the liftings $(-_2)^{\#^M_{\Sigma,-1}} : Val(\Sigma)(-_1, U_\Sigma(M)) \dot{\to} Str(\Sigma)(\mathscr{S}_\Sigma(-_1), M)$ for each
$\Sigma \in |\mathbb{S}|$ and $M \in |Str(\Sigma)|$. Then, for each $\sigma \in \mathbb{S}(\Sigma, \Sigma')$, there is a natural transformation $\mathscr{S}_\sigma : Val(\sigma); \mathscr{S}_\Sigma \dot{\to} \mathscr{S}_{\Sigma'}; Str(\sigma)$ defined by $\mathscr{S}_\sigma(X') =$
$(Val(\sigma)(\eta_{\Sigma'}(X')))^{\#^{Str(\sigma)(\mathscr{S}_{\Sigma'}(X'))}_{\Sigma, Val(\sigma)(X')}}$ such that $\mathscr{S} : Val \dot{\to} Str$ becomes a lax indexed
functor, for which

(∗) $(\xi; Val(\sigma)(\beta'))^{\#^{Str(\sigma)(M')}_{\Sigma,X}} = \mathscr{S}_\Sigma(\xi); \mathscr{S}_\sigma(X'); Str(\sigma)(\beta'^{\#^{M'}_{\Sigma',X'}})$

is satisfied for $\xi \in Val(\Sigma)(X, Val(\sigma)(X'))$. In order to construct a term char-
ter $(\mathscr{T}, \eta, ext)$, define the term constructor $\mathscr{T} : Val \dot{\to} Val$ by $\mathscr{T}_\Sigma = \mathscr{S}_\Sigma; U_\Sigma$,
$\mathscr{T}_\sigma = \mathscr{S}_\sigma; U_\Sigma$ and the evaluation morphisms as $(ext_\Sigma)^M_X(\beta) = U_\Sigma(\beta^{\#^M_{\Sigma,X}}) :$
$\mathscr{T}_\Sigma(X) \to U_\Sigma(M)$. The embedding $\eta : 1_{Val} \dot{\to} \mathscr{T}$ forms a lax indexed natural transformation, since $\eta_\Sigma(Val(\sigma)(X')); U_\Sigma(\mathscr{S}_\sigma(X')) = Val(\sigma)(\eta_{\Sigma'}(X'))$. Term
charter requirements (V) and (C) hold by expanding the definitions and using (∗).

3.4   Term Translations and Substitutions in Term Charters

The term translation $\mathscr{T}_\sigma^m(X') : \mathscr{T}_\Sigma^m(Val^m(\sigma)(X')) \to Val^m(\sigma)(\mathscr{T}_{\Sigma'}^m(X'))$ along a signature translation $\sigma : \Sigma = (S, F) \to \Sigma' = (S', F')$ used by the many-sorted term charter operates on the terms over the σ-reduct of the value variables $X' \in |Val^m(\Sigma')|$. It may seem more natural (and is indeed assumed in context institutions, see Sect. 5.2) to have a term translation work on terms over an $X \in |Val^m(\Sigma)|$. This can be achieved via a map $\mathscr{T}^{m,\sigma}(X) : \mathscr{T}_\Sigma^m(X) \to Val^m(\sigma)(\mathscr{T}_{\Sigma'}^m(\sigma^{Val^m}(X)))$ when defining $\sigma^{Val^m}((X_s)_{s \in S}) = (\biguplus\{X_s \mid \sigma_S(s) = s'\})_{s' \in S'}$ and setting $\mathscr{T}^{m,\sigma}(X)_s(x) = \eta_\sigma^m(X)_s(x)$ for the canonical injection $\eta_\sigma^m(X) : X \hookrightarrow Val^m(\sigma)(\sigma^{Val^m}(X))$ with $\eta_\sigma^m(X)_s(x) = x$. In particular, the functor $\sigma^{Val^m} : Val^m(\Sigma) \to Val^m(\Sigma')$ with $\sigma^{Val^m}((\xi_s)_{s \in S} : X_1 \to X_2) = (\biguplus\{\xi_s \mid \sigma_S(s) = s'\})_{s' \in S'}$ is left adjoint to the reduct functor $Val^m(\sigma)$ (cf. [2, Prop. 2.1]). Hence, both translation approaches are equivalent.

For the general case of a term charter $(\mathscr{T}, \nu, ext)$ over a term charter domain $(\mathbb{S}, Val, Str, U)$ with adjunctions $(\eta_\sigma, \kappa_\sigma) : \sigma^{Val} \dashv Val(\sigma)$ for each signature morphism σ, we obtain natural transformations $\mathscr{T}^\sigma = (\eta_\sigma^*; \mathscr{T}_\Sigma); (\sigma^{Val*}; \mathscr{T}_\sigma) : \mathscr{T}_\Sigma \overset{\cdot}{\to} \sigma^{Val}; \mathscr{T}_{\Sigma'}; Val(\sigma)$ such that the translation condition (T) becomes

(T$\dashv$) $\mathscr{T}^\sigma(X'); Val(\sigma)((ext_{\Sigma'})^{M'}_{\sigma^{Val}(X)}(\beta')) = (ext_\Sigma)^{Str(\sigma)(M')}_X (Val(\sigma)(\beta'); \eta_\sigma(X))$.

Moreover, term construction for many-sorted algebras is idempotent up to isomorphism, i.e., it holds that $\mathscr{T}_\Sigma^m(\mathscr{T}_\Sigma^m(X)) \cong \mathscr{T}_\Sigma^m(X)$; this, in fact, applies to the iteration and the undefinedness extensions as well. In particular, for a term substitution $\theta : X \to \mathscr{T}_\Sigma^m(Y)$ assigning the value variables in $X \in |Val^m(\Sigma)|$ full terms over $Y \in |Val^m(\Sigma)|$ and not only value variables, the "substitution lemma"

$$[\![\theta_s(t)]\!]^m_{(\Sigma, Y)}(M, \beta)_s = [\![t]\!]^m_{(\Sigma, X)}(M, [\![-]\!]^m_{(\Sigma, Y)}(M, \beta) \circ \theta)_s$$

holds for all $t \in \mathscr{T}_\Sigma^m(X)_s$ and $\beta : Y \to U_\Sigma^m(M)$, where $\mathscr{T}_\Sigma^m(\theta)$ is abbreviated by θ.

The idempotency property may also be obtained for a general term charter $(\mathscr{T}, \nu, ext)$ when requiring that there is a lax natural transformation $\mu : \mathscr{T}; \mathscr{T} \overset{\cdot}{\to} \mathscr{T}$ for flattening nested term constructions such that $(\mathscr{T}, \nu, \mu)$ is an indexed monad [11]. A substitution condition on the term charter can then be expressed as

$$\mathscr{T}_\Sigma(\theta); \mu_\Sigma(Y); (ext_\Sigma)^M_Y(\beta) = (ext_\Sigma)^M_X(\theta; (ext_\Sigma)^M_Y(\beta))$$

for all $\theta \in Val(\Sigma)(X, \mathscr{T}_\Sigma(Y))$, $\beta \in Val(\Sigma)(Y, U_\Sigma(M))$.

4   Alternative Term Charter Definitions

As demonstrated in Sect. 3.3, the evaluation maps ext_Σ of a term charter $(\mathscr{T}, \nu, ext)$ resemble the liftings $(-)^{\sharp_\Sigma}$ of an adjunction $(\mathscr{S}, U, \eta, (-)^\sharp)$ with $\mathscr{S} : Val \overset{\cdot}{\to} Str$; the palpable difference is that, for $\beta \in Val(\Sigma)(X, U_\Sigma(M))$,

$(ext_\Sigma)_X^M(\beta) \in Val(\Sigma)(\mathscr{T}_\Sigma(X), U_\Sigma(M))$ whereas $\beta^{\natural M}_{\Sigma,X} \in Str(\Sigma)(\mathscr{S}_\Sigma(X), M)$. The situation of a term charter is thus asymmetric, and ext_Σ only affects the first parameter of the hom-functor $Val(\Sigma)(-,-)$. Lawvere [7] (see [8, Exc. IV.1.2]) observed that the symmetric constellation of an adjunction $(\eta, \kappa) : F \dashv G$ between the functors $F : C \to D$ and $G : D \to C$ can be equivalently expressed by an isomorphism $H : F \downarrow 1_D \to 1_C \downarrow G$ of comma categories such that the following diagram commutes, with π_i the projections:

$$
\begin{array}{ccc}
F \downarrow 1_D & \underset{H^{-1}}{\overset{H}{\rightleftarrows}} & 1_C \downarrow G \\
 & \searrow \pi_1 \times \pi_2 \qquad \pi_1 \times \pi_2 \swarrow & \\
 & C \times D &
\end{array}
$$

We transfer this observation to term charters in Sect. 4.1 where we capture the evaluation maps into a single indexed functor $ext : 1_{Val} \downarrow U \to \mathscr{T} \downarrow U$ and thus obtain a quite succinct characterisation using indexed comma categories (briefly summarised in Appendix A.2).

On the other hand, the interface of a term in a term charter is given by its signature Σ and its value variables X; see condition (C). It thus seems natural to combine these two into a single entity $\langle \Sigma, X \rangle$ and to consider terms to be constructed over the combined interface. This is afforded by an application of the Grothendieck construction (briefly recapitulated in Appendix A.3) turning the indexed category Val into a flat category $\mathcal{G}(Val)$ with objects $\langle \Sigma, X \rangle$. The structures M and the valuations β also belong together, and can be combined into $Str^\mathcal{G} = \mathcal{G}(1_{Val}) \downarrow U$ with objects (M, β). In Sect. 4.2 we thus again obtain a more compact equivalent presentation of term charters where the evaluation maps can be comprised into a single indexed functor $ext^\mathcal{G} : Str^\mathcal{G} \dot\to \mathcal{G}(\mathscr{T})^{\mathrm{op}}; Str^\mathcal{G}$.

4.1 Characterising Term Charters with Comma Categories

Let $(\mathbb{S}, Val, Str, U)$ be a term charter domain. Let $\mathscr{T} : Val \dot\to Val$ be a lax indexed functor, $\nu : 1_{Val} \dot\to \mathscr{T}$ a lax indexed natural transformation, and $ext : 1_{Val} \downarrow U \dot\to \mathscr{T} \downarrow U$ an $\mathbb{S}$-indexed functor. Then $(\mathscr{T}, \nu, ext)$ is a term charter over $(\mathbb{S}, Val, Str, U)$ if, and only if, the following diagram commutes:

$$
\begin{array}{ccc}
1_{Val} \downarrow U & \xrightarrow{ext} & \mathscr{T} \downarrow U \\
 & \searrow{\scriptstyle 1_{1_{Val} \downarrow U}} & \downarrow{\scriptstyle \nu \downarrow U} \\
 & & 1_{Val} \downarrow U
\end{array}
$$

where the $\mathbb{S}$-indexed functor $\nu \downarrow U : \mathscr{T} \downarrow U \dot\to 1_{Val} \downarrow U$ is given by $(\nu \downarrow U)_\Sigma(X, \beta^\natural, M) = (X, \nu_\Sigma(X); \beta^\natural, M)$ and $(\nu \downarrow U)_\Sigma(\xi, \mu) = (\xi, \mu)$.

Indeed, $ext; (\nu \downarrow U) = 1_{1_{Val} \downarrow U}$ yields that $\pi_1 \times \pi_2 = ext; (\pi_1 \times \pi_2)$ holds. Thus, ext induces the family of functions $(ext_\Sigma)_X^M : Val(\Sigma)(X, U_\Sigma(M)) \to Val(\Sigma)(\mathscr{T}_\Sigma(X), U_\Sigma(M))$ which, for each $\Sigma \in |\mathbb{S}|$ and $M \in |Str(\Sigma)|$, forms a natural transformation in $X \in |Val(\Sigma)|$, such that the renaming condition (R) holds. Furthermore, $(X, \beta, M) = (ext_\Sigma; (\nu \downarrow U)_\Sigma)(X, \beta, M) = (X, \nu_\Sigma(X); (ext_\Sigma)_X^M(\beta), M)$ yields the variable condition (V). Finally, by the indexedness of ext it holds that $ext_{\Sigma'}; (\mathscr{T} \downarrow U)(\sigma) = (1_{Val} \downarrow U)(\sigma); ext_\Sigma$, which is the translation condition (T), as

$$(\mathscr{T} \downarrow U)(\sigma)(ext_{\Sigma'}(X', \beta', M')) = (\mathscr{T} \downarrow U)(\sigma)(X', (ext_{\Sigma'})_{X'}^{M'}(\beta'), M') =$$

$$(Val(\sigma)(X'), \mathscr{T}_\sigma(X'); Val(\sigma)((ext_{\Sigma'})_{X'}^{M'}(\beta')), Str(\sigma)(M')) \quad \text{and}$$

$$ext_\Sigma((1_{Val} \downarrow U)(\sigma)(X', \beta', M')) = ext_\Sigma(Val(\sigma)(X'), Val(\sigma)(\beta'), Str(\sigma)(M')) =$$

$$(Val(\sigma)(X'), (ext_\Sigma)_{Val(\sigma)(X')}^{Str(\sigma)(M')}(Val(\sigma)(\beta')), Str(\sigma)(M')) \ .$$

4.2   Characterising Term Charters with Grothendieck Categories

Using the Grothendieck construction for a term charter domain $(\mathbb{S}, Val, Str, U)$ we obtain the $\mathcal{G}(Val)$-indexed category $Str^\mathcal{G} = \mathcal{G}(1_{Val}) \downarrow U$ such that $\mathcal{G}(\mathscr{T})^{\mathrm{op}}; Str^\mathcal{G} = \mathcal{G}(\mathscr{T}) \downarrow U$ and $\mathcal{G}(\nu)^{\mathrm{op}}; Str^\mathcal{G} = \mathcal{G}(\nu) \downarrow U$. A term charter $(\mathscr{T}, \nu, ext)$ over the term charter domain $(\mathbb{S}, Val, Str, U)$ then yields a $\mathcal{G}(Val)$-indexed functor $ext^\mathcal{G} : Str^\mathcal{G} \overset{\cdot}{\to} \mathcal{G}(\mathscr{T})^{\mathrm{op}}; Str^\mathcal{G}$ with $ext^\mathcal{G}_{\langle \Sigma, X \rangle}(M, \beta) = (M, (ext_\Sigma)_X^M(\beta)) \in |Str^\mathcal{G}(\langle \Sigma, \mathscr{T}_\Sigma(X) \rangle)|$ and $ext^\mathcal{G}_{\langle \Sigma, X \rangle}(\mu) = \mu$ such that indeed for $\langle \sigma, \xi \rangle : \langle \Sigma, X \rangle \to \langle \Sigma', X' \rangle$

$$Str^\mathcal{G}(\mathcal{G}(\mathscr{T})(\langle \sigma, \xi \rangle))(ext^\mathcal{G}_{\langle \Sigma', X' \rangle}(M', \beta')) =$$

$$(Str(\sigma)(M'), \mathscr{T}_\sigma(\xi); Val(\sigma)((ext_{\Sigma'})_{X'}^{M'}(\beta'))) \overset{(C)}{=}$$

$$(Str(\sigma)(M'), (ext_\Sigma)_X^{Str(\sigma)(M')}(\xi; Val(\sigma)(\beta'))) =$$

$$ext^\mathcal{G}_{\langle \Sigma, X \rangle}(Str^\mathcal{G}(\langle \sigma, \xi \rangle)(M', \beta')) \ .$$

Furthermore, it holds that $ext^\mathcal{G}; (\mathcal{G}(\nu)^{\mathrm{op}}; Str^\mathcal{G}) = 1_{Str^\mathcal{G}}$, since

$$(ext^\mathcal{G}; (\mathcal{G}(\nu)^{\mathrm{op}}; Str^\mathcal{G}))_{\langle \Sigma, X \rangle} = ext^\mathcal{G}_{\langle \Sigma, X \rangle}; (Str^\mathcal{G}(\mathcal{G}(\nu)(\langle \Sigma, X \rangle)) \overset{(V)}{=} 1_{Str^\mathcal{G}(\langle \Sigma, X \rangle)} \ .$$

Conversely, given an $\mathcal{G}(Val)$-indexed functor $ext^\mathcal{G} : Str^\mathcal{G} \overset{\cdot}{\to} \mathcal{G}(\mathscr{T})^{\mathrm{op}}; Str^\mathcal{G}$ (i.e., (C) holds), which satisfies $ext^\mathcal{G}; (\mathcal{G}(\nu)^{\mathrm{op}}; Str^\mathcal{G}) = 1_{Str^\mathcal{G}}$ (i.e., (V) holds), we can reconstruct the evaluation morphisms by setting $(ext_\Sigma)_X^M(\beta) = \beta^\natural$ for $ext^\mathcal{G}_{\langle \Sigma, X \rangle}(M, \beta) = (M^\natural, \beta^\natural)$. Indeed, we obtain $M = M^\natural$ since $(M, \beta) = Str^\mathcal{G}(\mathcal{G}(\nu)(\langle \Sigma, X \rangle))(M^\natural, \beta^\natural) = (M^\natural, \nu_\Sigma(X); \beta^\natural)$.

Summarising, a term charter is equivalently given by a lax indexed functor $\mathscr{T} : Val \overset{\cdot}{\to} Val$, a lax indexed natural transformation $\nu : 1_{Val} \overset{\cdot}{\to} \mathscr{T}$, and a

$\mathcal{G}(Val)$-indexed functor $ext^{\mathcal{G}} : Str^{\mathcal{G}} \to \mathcal{G}(\mathcal{T})^{\mathrm{op}}; Str^{\mathcal{G}}$ such that the following diagram commutes:

$$
\begin{array}{ccc}
Str^{\mathcal{G}} & \xrightarrow{\ ext^{\mathcal{G}}\ } & \mathcal{G}(\mathcal{T})^{\mathrm{op}}; Str^{\mathcal{G}} \\
& {\scriptstyle 1_{Str^{\mathcal{G}}}} \searrow & \downarrow {\scriptstyle \mathcal{G}(\nu)^{\mathrm{op}} * Str^{\mathcal{G}}} \\
& & Str^{\mathcal{G}}
\end{array}
$$

We write $|ext^{\mathcal{G}}_{\langle \Sigma, X \rangle}(M, \beta)|$ for $\beta^{\natural}$ when $ext^{\mathcal{G}}_{\langle \Sigma, X \rangle}(M, \beta) = (M^{\natural}, \beta^{\natural})$.

5 Constructing Institutions from a Term Charter

Institutions [3,5] provide an abstract framework for studying logical systems. Term charters concentrate on the evaluation of terms yielding values rather than the satisfaction of formulæ. Still, as shown in Sect. 5.1, if there is a notion of truth values in the structures of a term charter domain, an institution can be derived from a term charter, thus embedding term charters into the landscape of logical systems. This construction resembles the generation of an institution from a charter [4], which has been the original reason for the choice of the name "term charters" in [6]. It turns out that also a context institution can be obtained, as introduced by Pawłowski [12] for capturing open formulæ in the framework of institutions; after summarising the definition of context institutions, we demonstrate their relationship with term charters in Sect. 5.2.

5.1 Institutions

An *institution* $(\mathbb{S}, Str, Sen, \models)$ is given by a category $\mathbb{S}$ of *signatures*; an indexed category $Str : \mathbb{S}^{\mathrm{op}} \to \mathbf{Cat}$ of *structures*; a *sentence functor* $Sen : \mathbb{S} \to \mathbf{Set}$; and a family $\models = (\models_{\Sigma} \subseteq |Str(\Sigma)| \times Sen(\Sigma))_{\Sigma \in |\mathbb{S}|}$ of *satisfaction relations*, such that for all $\sigma \in \mathbb{S}(\Sigma, \Sigma')$, $M' \in |Str(\Sigma')|$, and $\varphi \in Sen(\Sigma)$ the *satisfaction condition* holds:

$$
Str(\sigma)(M') \models_{\Sigma} \varphi \iff M' \models_{\Sigma'} Sen(\sigma)(\varphi) .
$$

For constructing an institution from a term charter $\mathfrak{T} = (\mathcal{T}, \nu, ext)$ over a term charter domain $\mathbf{D} = (\mathbb{S}, Val, Str, U)$ we assume that $\mathbf{D}$ is *logical* via a family of functors $\mathcal{F}^* = (\mathcal{F}^*_{\Sigma} : Val(\Sigma) \to \mathbf{Set})_{\Sigma \in |\mathbb{S}|}$ yielding *formulæ* and being equipped with *truth values* $*^M_{\Sigma} \subseteq \mathcal{F}^*_{\Sigma}(U_{\Sigma}(M))$ for each $\Sigma \in |\mathbb{S}|$ and $M \in |Str(\Sigma)|$ such that $Val(\sigma); \mathcal{F}^*_{\Sigma} = \mathcal{F}^*_{\Sigma'}$ and $*^{Str(\sigma)(M')}_{\Sigma} = *^{M'}_{\Sigma'}$ for all $\sigma : \Sigma \to \Sigma'$ in $\mathbb{S}$ and $M' \in |Str(\Sigma')|$.

Example 5. (1) For the term charter domain $(\mathbb{S}^{\mathrm{m}}, Val^{\mathrm{m}}, Str^{\mathrm{m}}, U^{\mathrm{m}})$, we may base the formulæ on equations between value variables, representing $x_1 = x_2$ as the pair (x_1, x_2): $\mathcal{F}^{*\mathrm{m}}_{(S,F)}((X_s)_{s \in S}) = (X_s \times X_s)_{s \in S}$, $\mathcal{F}^{*\mathrm{m}}_{(S,F)}((\xi_s)_{s \in S}) = (\xi_s \times \xi_s)_{s \in S}$, and $*^{\mathrm{m}, M}_{(S,F)} = (\{(v, v) \mid (v, v) \in U^{\mathrm{m}}_{(S,F)}(M)_s\})_{s \in S}$. In fact, this construction can be applied to all term charters domains with a concrete category of value variables.

(2) For the term charter domain $(\mathbb{S}^{\circ}, Val^{\circ}, Str^{\circ}, U^{\circ})$, every signature $\Sigma^{\circ} \in |\mathbb{S}^{\circ}|$ shows the predefined sort $\texttt{Bool}$ that is interpreted by $\texttt{Bool}^{M^{\circ}} = \{\mathit{ff}, \mathit{tt}\}$ in every structure $M^{\circ} \in |Str^{\circ}(\Sigma^{\circ})|$. Thus we can choose $\mathcal{F}^{*\circ}_{\Sigma^{\circ}}(X) = X_{\texttt{Bool}}$ and $*^{\circ, M^{\circ}}_{\Sigma^{\circ}} = \{\mathit{tt}\}$.

(3) For the term charter domain $(\mathbb{S}^{\circ}, Val^{\dagger}, Str^{\circ}, U^{\dagger})$, we may again choose $\mathcal{F}^{*\dagger}_{\Sigma^{\circ}}(X) = X_{\texttt{Bool}}$, although now also the value $\dagger$ for undefinedness will be contained. We may also again set $*^{\dagger, M^{\circ}}_{\Sigma^{\circ}} = \{\mathit{tt}\}$ since $\mathcal{F}^{*\dagger}_{\Sigma^{\circ}}(U^{\dagger}_{\Sigma^{\circ}}(M^{\circ})) = \{\dagger, \mathit{ff}, \mathit{tt}\}$.

Based on Sect. 4.2 we obtain an institution $(\mathbb{S}^{\triangleright}, Str^{\triangleright}, Sen^{\triangleright}, \models^{\triangleright})$ over $\mathfrak{T}$ and $\mathcal{F}^{*}$ (where the superscript $\triangleright$ abbreviates $\mathfrak{T}, \mathcal{F}^{*}$) as follows: The category of signatures $\mathbb{S}^{\triangleright}$ is defined to be $\mathcal{G}(Val)$; the indexed category $Str^{\triangleright} : (\mathbb{S}^{\triangleright})^{\mathrm{op}} \to \mathrm{Cat}$ of structures is defined to be $Str^{\mathcal{G}}$; the sentence functor $Sen^{\triangleright} : \mathbb{S}^{\triangleright} \to \mathrm{Set}$ is defined as $Sen^{\triangleright}(\langle \Sigma, X \rangle) = \mathcal{F}^{*}_{\Sigma}(\mathcal{T}_{\Sigma}(X))$ and $Sen^{\triangleright}(\langle \sigma, \xi \rangle) = \mathcal{F}^{*}_{\Sigma}(\mathcal{T}_{\sigma}(\xi))$; the family of satisfaction relations $(\models^{\triangleright}_{\langle \Sigma, X \rangle} \subseteq |Str^{\triangleright}(\langle \Sigma, X \rangle)| \times |Sen^{\triangleright}(\langle \Sigma, X \rangle)|)_{\langle \Sigma, X \rangle \in |\mathbb{S}^{\triangleright}|}$ is defined by

$$(M, \beta) \models^{\triangleright}_{\langle \Sigma, X \rangle} \varphi \iff \mathcal{F}^{*}_{\Sigma}(|ext^{\mathcal{G}}_{\langle \Sigma, X \rangle}(M, \beta)|)(\varphi) \in *^{M}_{\Sigma} .$$

For the satisfaction condition it suffices to prove that

$$\mathcal{F}^{*}_{\Sigma}(|ext^{\mathcal{G}}_{\langle \Sigma, X \rangle}(Str^{\mathcal{G}}(\langle \sigma, \xi \rangle)(M', \beta'))|) = \mathcal{F}^{*}_{\Sigma}(\mathcal{T}_{\sigma}(\xi)); \mathcal{F}^{*}_{\Sigma'}(|ext^{\mathcal{G}}_{\langle \Sigma', X' \rangle}(M', \beta')|) ,$$

which follows from the term charter requirement (C).

5.2   Context Institutions

Context institutions [12] have been introduced to capture open formulæ in institutions. A context institution, like an ordinary institution, shows a category $\mathbb{S}$ of *signatures* and an indexed category of *structures* $Str : \mathbb{S}^{\mathrm{op}} \to \mathrm{Cat}$. Instead of the sentences, however, *formulæ* are built by a family of functors $(Frm_{\Sigma} : Ctxt_{\Sigma} \to \mathrm{Set})_{\Sigma \in |\mathbb{S}|}$ over a family of *context* categories $(Ctxt_{\Sigma})_{\Sigma \in |\mathbb{S}|}$ that allow to incorporate variables. Contexts are *translated*, i.e., variables are renamed, by a family of functors $(Ctxt_{\sigma} : Ctxt_{\Sigma} \to Ctxt_{\Sigma'})_{\sigma \in \mathbb{S}(\Sigma, \Sigma')}$, and formulæ are translated along a context translation by a family of natural transformations $(Frm_{\sigma} : Frm_{\Sigma} \overset{.}{\to} Ctxt_{\sigma}; Frm_{\Sigma'})_{\sigma \in \mathbb{S}(\Sigma, \Sigma')}$. *Valuations* are given by a family of functors $(Vlt_{\Sigma} : (Ctxt_{\Sigma})^{\mathrm{op}} \times Str(\Sigma) \to \mathrm{Set})_{\Sigma \in |\mathbb{S}|}$ together with a family of natural transformations $(\sigma^{Vlt} : Vlt_{\Sigma'}(Ctxt_{\sigma}(-1), -2) \overset{.}{\to} Vlt_{\Sigma}(-1, Str(\sigma)(-2)))_{\sigma \in \mathbb{S}(\Sigma, \Sigma')}$ constructing *adjoint* valuations along signature morphisms, and, for each $\Sigma \in |\mathbb{S}|$, families of natural transformations $(\gamma^{Vlt} : Vlt_{\Sigma}(\Delta, -) \overset{.}{\to} Vlt_{\Sigma}(\Gamma, -))_{\gamma \in Ctxt_{\Sigma}(\Gamma, \Delta)}$ *translating* valuations along context translations, such that the *coherence condition* for $\sigma \in \mathbb{S}(\Sigma, \Sigma')$, $\gamma \in Ctxt_{\Sigma}(\Gamma, \Delta)$, and $M' \in |Str(\Sigma')|$ is satisfied:

(1) $Ctxt_{\sigma}(\gamma)^{Vlt}(M'); \sigma^{Vlt}(\Gamma, M') = \sigma^{Vlt}(\Delta, M'); \gamma^{Vlt}(Str(\sigma)(M')) .$

Finally, context institutions show for all $\Sigma \in |\mathbb{S}|$, $M \in |Str(\Sigma)|$, and $\Gamma \in |Ctxt_\Sigma|$ *satisfaction relations* $M, -_1 \models_{\Sigma,\Gamma} -_2 \subseteq Vlt_\Sigma(\Gamma, M) \times Frm_\Sigma(\Gamma)$ for which the *substitution condition* (2) and the *satisfaction condition* (3) have to be satisfied:

$$(2) \quad M, v \models_{\Sigma,\Delta} Frm_\Sigma(\gamma)(\phi) \iff M, \gamma^{Vlt}(M)(v) \models_{\Sigma,\Gamma} \phi$$

for all $\Sigma \in |\mathbb{S}|$, $v \in Vlt_\Sigma(\Delta, M)$, $\gamma \in Ctxt_\Sigma(\Gamma, \Delta)$, $\phi \in Frm_\Sigma(\Gamma)$;

$$(3) \quad M', v' \models_{\Sigma', Ctxt_\sigma(\Gamma)} Frm_\sigma(\Gamma)(\phi) \iff Str(\sigma)(M'), \sigma^{Vlt}(\Gamma, M')(v') \models_{\Sigma,\Gamma} \phi$$

for all $\sigma \in \mathbb{S}(\Sigma, \Sigma')$, $v' \in Vlt_{\Sigma'}(Ctxt_\sigma(\Gamma), M')$, $\phi \in Frm_\Sigma(\Gamma)$.

Summarising, a context institution can be represented as the tuple $(\mathbb{S}, Str, Ctxt, Frm, Vlt, -^{Vlt}, \models)$. In fact, this account (besides calling the valuations Vlt instead of Val) omits some parts of the original definition in [12] that has been formulated somewhat more concretely: For contexts and formulæ categories with an inclusion system are used and it is required that an indexed set of *carriers* can be computed from a structure as well as a sorted set of *variables* from a context. Then, the valuations can be represented as a concrete hom-set and the adjoint valuations can be derived.

Let $\mathfrak{T} = (\mathscr{T}, \nu, ext)$ be a term charter over a logical term charter domain $(\mathbb{S}, Val, Str, U)$ with formulæ functor $\mathcal{F}^*$, as above. For obtaining a context institution $(\mathbb{S}^\triangleright, Str^\triangleright, Ctxt^\triangleright, Frm^\triangleright, Vlt^\triangleright, -^{Vlt^\triangleright}, \models^\triangleright)$ from $\mathfrak{T}, \mathcal{F}^*$ it is straightforward to choose $\mathbb{S}^\triangleright = \mathbb{S}$ and $Str^\triangleright = Str$, as well as $Ctxt_\Sigma^\triangleright = Val(\Sigma)$, $Frm_\Sigma^\triangleright = \mathscr{T}_\Sigma; \mathcal{F}_\Sigma^*$, and $Vlt_\Sigma^\triangleright = Val(\Sigma)(-_1, U_\Sigma(-_2))$ for each $\Sigma \in |\mathbb{S}|$, as the value variables correspond to the notion of context. However, the context translation functors $Ctxt_\sigma^\triangleright : Ctxt_\Sigma^\triangleright \to Ctxt_{\Sigma'}^\triangleright$ along $\sigma : \Sigma \to \Sigma'$ have to be defined as going in the opposite direction than $Val(\sigma) : Val(\Sigma') \to Val(\Sigma)$. We thus have to require that there is an adjunction $(\eta_\sigma, \kappa_\sigma) : \sigma^{Val} \dashv Val(\sigma)$, as discussed in Sect. 3.4, and then can define $Ctxt_\sigma^\triangleright = \sigma^{Val}$ and $Frm_\sigma^\triangleright = \mathscr{T}^\sigma; \mathcal{F}^*$ with $\mathscr{T}^\sigma = (\eta_\sigma; \mathscr{T}_\Sigma); (\sigma^{Val}; \mathscr{T}_\sigma) : \mathscr{T}_\Sigma \dot{\to} \sigma^{Val}; \mathscr{T}_{\Sigma'}; Val(\sigma)$; for each $\sigma : \Sigma \to \Sigma$ in $\mathbb{S}^\triangleright$ define $\sigma^{Vlt^\triangleright}(X, M')(\beta') = \eta_\sigma(X); Val(\sigma)(\beta')$, and for each $\xi : X_1 \to X_2$ in $Ctxt_\Sigma^\triangleright$ define $\xi^{Vlt^\triangleright}(M)(\beta) = \xi; \beta$. The coherence condition (1) then reads

$$\eta_\sigma(X_1); Val(\sigma)(\sigma^{Val}(\xi); \beta') = \xi; \eta_\sigma(X_2); Val(\sigma)(\beta') ,$$

which is evident by the naturality of η_σ. For the satisfaction relations we finally can define

$$M, \beta \models_{\Sigma,X}^\triangleright \phi \iff \mathcal{F}_\Sigma^*((ext_\Sigma)_X^M(\beta))(\phi) \in *_\Sigma^M ;$$

the substitution condition (2) and the satisfaction condition (3) then become

$$M, \beta \models_{\Sigma,X_2}^\triangleright \mathcal{F}_\Sigma^*(\mathscr{T}_\Sigma(\xi))(\phi) \iff M, \xi; \beta \models_{\Sigma,X_1}^\triangleright \phi \quad \text{and}$$

$$M', \beta' \models_{\Sigma',\sigma^{Val}(X)}^\triangleright \mathcal{F}_\Sigma^*(\mathscr{T}^\sigma(X))(\phi) \iff Str(\sigma)(M'), \eta_\sigma(X); Val(\sigma)(\beta') \models_{\Sigma,X}^\triangleright \phi ,$$

and follow from the conditions (R) and (T$_\dashv$) of term charters.

6   Morphisms for Term Charter Domains and Term Charters

For institutions there are four basic types of relationships, the institution (co-)morphisms and the institution forward (co-)morphisms [14]. For example, an *institution morphism* expresses a kind of projection from a "richer" source to a "poorer" target logic, or, conversely, how the "richer" logic is built over the "poorer" logic. Formally, an institution morphism $\mu = (\mu^{\mathbb{S}}, \mu^{Str}, \mu^{Sen})$: $(\mathbb{S}, Str, Sen, \models) \rightarrow (\mathbb{S}', Str', Sen', \models')$ consists of a functor $\mu^{\mathbb{S}} : \mathbb{S} \rightarrow \mathbb{S}'$, an indexed functor $\mu^{Str} : Str \xrightarrow{\cdot} (\mu^{\mathbb{S}})^{op}; Str'$, and a natural transformation μ^{Sen} : $\mu^{\mathbb{S}}; Sen' \xrightarrow{\cdot} Sen$, such that for all $\Sigma \in |\mathbb{S}|$, $M \in |Str(\Sigma)|$, and $\varphi' \in Sen'(\mu^{\mathbb{S}}(\Sigma))$ the following *satisfaction condition* holds:

$$M \models_{\Sigma} \mu^{Sen}(\Sigma)(\varphi') \iff \mu_{\Sigma}^{Str}(M) \models'_{\mu^{\mathbb{S}}(\Sigma)} \varphi' .$$

In fact, the sentence translation μ^{Sen} may be split off, yielding an *institution semi-morphism* $(\mu^{\mathbb{S}}, \mu^{Str})$; an *institution forward morphism* then just reverses the direction of the sentence translation. Similarly, an *institution semi-co-morphism* has components $\nu^{\mathbb{S}} : \mathbb{S} \rightarrow \mathbb{S}'$ and $\nu^{Str} : (\nu^{\mathbb{S}})^{op}; Str' \xrightarrow{\cdot} Str$; it can be extended into an *institution (forward) co-morphism* with a sentence translation going in the opposite (the same) direction as the structure translation.

For term charters and their term charter domains, a similar family of relationships arises, where the notions of semi-(co-)morphisms applies to term charter domains and the extension to (forward) (co-)morphisms to term charters. We concentrate on projecting from a more complex evaluation framework to a simpler one and show that its definition gives rise to an institution morphism on the institutions constructed in Sect. 5.1.

A *term charter domain morphism* $\mathsf{d} = (\mathsf{d}^{\mathbb{S}}, \mathsf{d}^{Val}, \mathsf{d}^{Str}) : (\mathbb{S}, Val, Str, U) \rightarrow (\mathbb{S}', Val', Str', U')$ is given by a functor $\mathsf{d}^{\mathbb{S}} : \mathbb{S} \rightarrow \mathbb{S}'$ and indexed functors $\mathsf{d}^{Val} : Val \xrightarrow{\cdot} (\mathsf{d}^{\mathbb{S}})^{op}; Val'$ and $\mathsf{d}^{Str} : Str \xrightarrow{\cdot} (\mathsf{d}^{\mathbb{S}})^{op}; Str'$ such that $U; \mathsf{d}^{Val} = \mathsf{d}^{Str}; ((\mathsf{d}^{\mathbb{S}})^{op} * U')$.

Example 6. There is a term charter domain morphism $\mathsf{d}° : (\mathbb{S}°, Val°, Str°, U°) \rightarrow (\mathbb{S}^m, Val^m, Str^m, U^m)$: $\mathsf{d}°^{\mathbb{S}}$ is the injection of $\mathbb{S}°$ into $\mathbb{S}^m$, and also $\mathsf{d}°^{Val}$ and $\mathsf{d}°^{Str}$ just inject the value variables and structures, respectively.

Let now $\mathfrak{T} = (\mathcal{T}, \nu, ext)$ and $\mathfrak{T}' = (\mathcal{T}', \nu', ext')$ be term charters over the term charter domains $\mathsf{D} = (\mathbb{S}, Val, Str, U)$ and $\mathsf{D}' = (\mathbb{S}', Val', Str', U')$, respectively, and let $\mathsf{d} : \mathsf{D} \rightarrow \mathsf{D}'$ be a term charter domain morphism. A d-*term charter morphism* $\mathfrak{m} : \mathfrak{T} \rightarrow \mathfrak{T}'$ is given by a lax natural transformation $\mathfrak{m} : \mathsf{d}^{Val}; ((\mathsf{d}^{\mathbb{S}})^{op} * \mathcal{T}') \xrightarrow{\cdot} \mathcal{T}; \mathsf{d}^{Val}$ such that for all $\Sigma \in |\mathbb{S}|$, $X \in |Val(\Sigma)|$, and $\beta \in Val(\Sigma)(X, U_{\Sigma}(M))$ it holds that

$(\mathfrak{m}_1)\quad \nu'_{\mathsf{d}^{\mathbb{S}}(\Sigma)}(\mathsf{d}_{\Sigma}^{Val}(X)); \mathfrak{m}_{\Sigma}(X) = \mathsf{d}_{\Sigma}^{Val}(\nu_{\Sigma}(X));$

$(\mathfrak{m}_2)\quad (ext'_{\mathsf{d}^{\mathbb{S}}(\Sigma)})_{\mathsf{d}_{\Sigma}^{Val}(X)}^{\mathsf{d}_{\Sigma}^{Str}(M)}(\mathsf{d}_{\Sigma}^{Val}(\beta)) = \mathfrak{m}_{\Sigma}(X); \mathsf{d}_{\Sigma}^{Val}((ext_{\Sigma})_X^M(\beta)).$

Example 7. There is a d°-term charter morphism $\mathfrak{m}^\circ$: $(\mathscr{T}^{it}, \nu^{it}, ext^{it})$ → $(\mathscr{T}^m, \nu^m, ext^m)$ where $\mathfrak{m}^\circ_\Sigma(X) : \mathscr{T}^m_{d^S(\Sigma)}(d^{\circ Val}_\Sigma(X)) \to d^{\circ Val}_\Sigma(\mathscr{T}^{it}_\Sigma(X))$ is the embedding of many-sorted terms into iteration terms. The relation guarantees that both evaluations coincide on many-sorted terms.

For the Grothendieck representation of term charters in Sect. 4.2, $d : D \to D'$ induces an indexed functor $d^{Str^\mathcal{G}} : Str^\mathcal{G} \xrightarrow{\cdot} \mathcal{G}(d^{Val})^{op}; Str'^\mathcal{G}$ with $d^{Str^\mathcal{G}}_{\langle \Sigma, X \rangle}(M, \beta) = (d^{Str}_\Sigma(M), d^{Val}_\Sigma(\beta))$. Condition $(\mathfrak{m}_1)$ for $\mathfrak{m} : \mathfrak{T} \to \mathfrak{T}'$ then is $(\mathcal{G}(d^{Val}); \mathcal{G}((d^S)^{op}; \nu'));$ $\mathcal{G}(\mathfrak{m}) = \mathcal{G}(\nu); \mathcal{G}(d^{Val})$ and condition $\mathfrak{m}_2$ is $d^{Str^\mathcal{G}}; ext'^\mathcal{G} = ext^\mathcal{G}; (\mathcal{G}(\mathfrak{m})^{op}; d^{Str^\mathcal{G}})$.

In order to compare this definition of a d-term charter morphism $\mathfrak{m} : \mathfrak{T} \to \mathfrak{T}'$ with institution morphisms, let the term charter domains D and D' be logical with formulæ functors $\mathcal{F}^*_\Sigma : Val(\Sigma) \to Set$ and $\mathcal{F}^{*\prime}_{\Sigma'} : Val'(\Sigma') \to Set$ such that $\mathcal{F}^*_\Sigma = d^{Val}; \mathcal{F}^{*\prime}_{d^S(\Sigma)}$ and $*^M_\Sigma = *^{\prime d^{Str}_\Sigma(M)}_{d^S(\Sigma)}$. We obtain an institution morphism $\mu^\triangleright : \mathfrak{I}^\triangleright \to \mathfrak{I}^{\triangleright\prime}$ for $\mathfrak{I}^\triangleright = (\mathbb{S}^\triangleright, Str^\triangleright, Sen^\triangleright, \models^\triangleright)$ and $\mathfrak{I}^{\triangleright\prime} = (\mathbb{S}^{\triangleright\prime}, Str^{\triangleright\prime}, Sen^{\triangleright\prime}, \models^{\triangleright\prime})$ constructed over $\triangleright = \mathfrak{T}, \mathcal{F}^*$ and $\triangleright\prime = \mathfrak{T}', \mathcal{F}^{*\prime}$ as in Sect. 5.1 with $\mu^{\triangleright S} = \mathcal{G}(d^{Val})$, $\mu^{\triangleright Str} = d^{Str^\mathcal{G}}$, and $\mu^{\triangleright Sen}(\langle \Sigma, X \rangle) = \mathcal{F}^{*\prime}_{d^S(\Sigma)}(\mathfrak{m}_\Sigma(X))$: Using the abbreviations $\Sigma' = d^S(\Sigma)$, $X' = d^{Val}_\Sigma(X)$, $M' = d^{Str}_\Sigma(M)$, and $\beta' = d^{Val}_\Sigma(\beta)$, the satisfaction condition

$$(M, \beta) \models^\triangleright_{\langle \Sigma, X \rangle} \mathcal{F}^{*\prime}_{\Sigma'}(\mathfrak{m}_\Sigma(X))(\varphi') \iff (M', \beta') \models^{\triangleright\prime}_{\langle \Sigma', X' \rangle} \varphi'$$

for $\varphi' \in \mathcal{F}^{*\prime}_{\Sigma'}(\mathscr{T}'_{\Sigma'}(X'))$ follows from the observation that

$$\mathcal{F}^{*\prime}_{\Sigma'}(\mathfrak{m}_\Sigma(X)); \mathcal{F}^*_\Sigma(|ext^\mathcal{G}_{\langle \Sigma, X \rangle}(M, \beta)|) =$$
$$\mathcal{F}^{*\prime}_{\Sigma'}(\mathfrak{m}_\Sigma(X)); \mathcal{F}^{*\prime}_{\Sigma'}(d^{Val}_\Sigma(|ext^\mathcal{G}_{\langle \Sigma, X \rangle}(M, \beta)|)) = \mathcal{F}^{*\prime}_{\Sigma'}(|ext'^\mathcal{G}_{\langle \Sigma', X' \rangle}(M', \beta')|) .$$

To achieve further accordance with institutions, a d-*term charter forward morphism* must reverse the direction of the term translation. A *term charter domain co-morphism* $\mathsf{p} : D \to D'$ must reverse the direction of the value variables and structures translation, and then can again be extended to a p-*term charter (forward) co-morphism* with term translation in the opposite (the same) direction as structure translation. As for institutions, these morphisms provide for embeddings, projections, and encodings of term charters.

7   Conclusions

We have presented term charter domains and term charters as a framework for general term evaluation such that evaluation is compatible with variable renamings and signature translations. This account simplifies our previous definition in [6] and puts term charters in a more general perspective. Term charter domains and term charters arrange values and variables, structures, term construction and term evaluation, all indexed over signatures, such that "evaluation is invariant under change of notation". Term structure constructors give rise to term charters and also substitutions can be captured in term charters. We have re-presented term charters using comma and Grothendieck categories to highlight the interface character of signatures and variables. We have demonstrated a tight connection with institutions in general and context institutions in particular; along the lines of institution (semi-)morphisms we have introduced term charter (domain) morphisms.

The use of indexed categories should be complemented by fibrations [1] which may lead to another compact presentation of term charters. From the viewpoint of institutions, on the one hand substitutions in term charters should be connected with the notion of generalised substitutions [3, 16] and generalised terms in 2-institutions [2]. On the other hand, an alignment with parchments [4], that focus on directly establishing the satisfaction relation rather than on term evaluations, could be based on the requirement of formulæ and truth values as above which are used for constructing an institution from a term charter. This also applies to Mayoh's galleries [9] (similar to generalized institutions [4]) and Poigné's foundations [13] which are based on the overall extension of functions or frames instead of values of terms.

Our original motivation for [6] has been to "institutionalise" OCL by combining small, well-understood expression language fragments, all captured as term charters, into a bigger whole using a sequencing operator and co-limits. For this purpose, the term charter (domain) morphisms now provide a basis for term charter combinations also over heterogeneous term charter domains. What is most notably missing for an OCL-institution is the possibility to handle pre-/post-condition specifications. For the evaluation of the OCL expression for the post-condition, a pre- and a post-state must be present, which necessitates a construction on term charters or a suitable extension such that two structures can be accessed simultaneously.

Acknowledgements. We have profited much from discussions with Till Mossakowski, Rolf Hennicker, and Daniel Calegari. We thank the anonymous referees for their insightful comments and suggestions.

A   Categorical Terminology

We briefly summarise the categorical terminology used in the main text; for indexed categories our account is based on [3, 14, 15, 17], for comma categories on [8], and for Grothendieck categories on [17]. We write $\stackrel{\ast}{,}$ for the horizontal composition of natural transformations when using diagrammatic notation.

A.1   Indexed Categories

An *indexed category* N over an index category I is a functor $N : I^{\text{op}} \to \text{Cat}$.

A *lax indexed functor* $F : M \stackrel{\cdot}{\to} N$ between the I-indexed categories M and N is given by families of functors $(F_i : M(i) \to N(i))_{i \in |I|}$ and natural transformations $(F_u : M(u); F_{i_1} \stackrel{\cdot}{\to} F_{i_2}; N(u))_{u \in I(i_1, i_2)}$ with $F_{1_i} = 1_{F_i}$ such that $F_{u_1; u_2} = (M(u_2) \stackrel{\ast}{,} F_{u_1}); (F_{u_2} \stackrel{\ast}{,} N(u_1))$ for all $u_1 \in I(i_1, i_2)$, $u_2 \in I(i_2, i_3)$.

The composition $F; G : L \dashrightarrow N$ of $F : L \dashrightarrow M$ and $G : M \dashrightarrow N$ for the I-indexed categories L, M, N is given by $(F; G)_i = F_i; G_i$ for $i \in |I|$ and $(F; G)_u = (F_u; G_{i_1}); (F_{i_2}; G_u)$ for $u \in I(i_1, i_2)$. An *indexed functor* $F : M \dashrightarrow N$ is a lax indexed functor $F : M \dashrightarrow N$ with $1_{M(u); F_{i_1}} = F_u = 1_{F_{i_2}; N(u)}$ for all $u \in I(i_1, i_2)$, i.e., a natural transformation from M to N.

For M, N I-indexed categories and $F, G : M \dashrightarrow N$ lax indexed functors, a *lax indexed natural transformation* $\eta : F \dashrightarrow G$ is given by a family of natural transformations $(\eta_i : F_i \dashrightarrow G_i)_{i \in |I|}$ such that $(M(u); \eta_{i_1}); G_u = F_u; (\eta_{i_2}; N(u))$ for $u \in I(i_1, i_2)$. If F and G are both indexed functors, $\eta : F \dashrightarrow G$ is also called an *indexed natural transformation*; it then has to hold that $M(u); \eta_{i_1} = \eta_{i_2}; N(u)$ for all $u \in I(i_1, i_2)$.

A.2   Comma Categories

Given two functors $F_1 : A_1 \to C$ and $F_2 : A_2 \to C$, the *comma category* $F_1 \downarrow F_2$ has as objects the triples (X_1, f, X_2) with $X_1 \in |A_1|$, $X_2 \in |A_2|$, and $f : F_1(X_1) \to F_2(X_2)$ in C; and as morphisms from (X_{11}, f_1, X_{21}) to (X_{12}, f_2, X_{22}) the pairs (x_1, x_2) with $x_1 : X_{11} \to X_{12}$ in A_1 and $x_2 : X_{21} \to X_{22}$ in A_2 such that $f_1; F_2(x_2) = F_1(x_1); f_2$. It is equipped with the *projection functors* $\pi_i : F_1 \downarrow F_2 \to A_i$ defined by $\pi_i(X_1, f, X_2) = X_i$ and $\pi_i(x_1, x_2) = x_i$ for $i \in \{1, 2\}$.

For the functors $F_1, G_1 : A_1 \to C$ and $F_2, G_2 : A_2 \to C$ consider the functor $H : F_1 \downarrow F_2 \to G_1 \downarrow G_2$ with $H(X_1, f, X_2) = (X_1, f^H, X_2)$ and $H(x_1, x_2) = (x_1, x_2)$. Then $(F_1(x_1); f_2)^H = G_1(x_1); f_2^H$ and $(f_1; F_2(x_2))^H = f_1^H; G_2(x_2)$ for all $X_i \in |A_i|$, $x_i \in A_i(X_{i1}, X_{i2})$, $f_1 : F_1(X_1) \to F_2(X_{21})$, and $f_2 : F_1(X_{12}) \to F_2(X_2)$. Thus, H induces natural transformations

$$H^{X_2} : C(F_1(-), F_2(X_2)) \dashrightarrow C(G_1(-), G_2(X_2)) \,,$$
$$H_{X_1} : C(F_1(X_1), F_2(-)) \dashrightarrow C(G_1(X_1), G_2(-)) \,.$$

Conversely, a bi-natural transformation $\eta : C(F_1(-_1), F_2(-_2)) \dashrightarrow C(G_1(-_1), G_2(-_2))$ induces the functor $\eta : F_1 \downarrow F_2 \to G_1 \downarrow G_2$ given by $\eta(X_1, f, X_2) = (X_1, \eta(X_1, X_2)(f), X_2)$ and $\eta(x_1, x_2) = (x_1, x_2)$.

The *indexed comma category* $F \downarrow G : I^{\text{op}} \to \text{Cat}$ for a lax indexed functor $F : M_1 \dashrightarrow N$ and an indexed functor $G : M_2 \dashrightarrow N$ over I-indexed categories M_1, M_2, and N is defined at $i \in |I|$ as the comma category $(F \downarrow G)(i) = F_i \downarrow G_i$, and at $u \in I(i_1, i_2)$ as the functor $(F \downarrow G)(u) : (F \downarrow G)(i_2) \to (F \downarrow G)(i_1)$ given by

$$(F \downarrow G)(u)(O_{21}, p_2, O_{22}) = (M_1(u)(O_{21}), F_u(O_{21}); N(u)(p_2), M_2(u)(O_{22})) \,,$$
$$(F \downarrow G)(u)(o_{21}, o_{22}) = (M_1(u)(o_{21}), M_2(u)(o_{22})) \,.$$

A.3   Grothendieck Categories

The (contravariant) *Grothendieck category* $\mathcal{G}(N)$ over an I-indexed category N has as objects the pairs $\langle i, O \rangle$ with $i \in |I|$ and $O \in |N(i)|$; and as morphisms from

$\langle i_1, O_1 \rangle$ to $\langle i_2, O_2 \rangle$ the pairs $\langle u, o \rangle$ with $u \in I(i_1, i_2)$ and $o \in N(i_1)(O_1, N(u)(O_2))$ where the composition of $\langle u_1, o_1 \rangle : \langle i_1, O_1 \rangle \to \langle i_2, O_2 \rangle$ and $\langle u_2, o_2 \rangle : \langle i_2, O_2 \rangle \to \langle i_3, O_3 \rangle$ is $\langle u_1, o_1 \rangle; \langle u_2, o_2 \rangle = \langle u_1; u_2, o_1; N(u_1)(o_2) \rangle$. The *projection functor* π_N from $\mathcal{G}(N)$ to I is defined by $\pi_N(\langle i, O \rangle) = i$ and $\pi_N(\langle u, o \rangle) = u$.

The *Grothendieck functor* $\mathcal{G}(F) : \mathcal{G}(M) \to \mathcal{G}(N)$ over a lax indexed functor $F : M \dashrightarrow N$ for I-indexed categories M and N is defined by $\mathcal{G}(F)(\langle i, O \rangle) = \langle i, F_i(O) \rangle$ for each $\langle i, O \rangle \in |\mathcal{G}(M)|$; and $\mathcal{G}(F)(\langle u, o \rangle) = \langle u, F_u(o) \rangle : \langle i_1, F_{i_1}(O_1) \rangle \to \langle i_2, F_{i_2}(O_2) \rangle$ with $F_u(o) = F_{i_1}(o); F_u(O_2) : F_{i_1}(O_1) \to N(u)(F_{i_2}(O_2))$ for each $\langle u, o \rangle : \langle i_1, O_1 \rangle \to \langle i_2, O_2 \rangle$ in $\mathcal{G}(M)$.

A lax indexed natural transformation $\eta : F \dashrightarrow G$ induces the *Grothendieck natural transformation* $\mathcal{G}(\eta) : \mathcal{G}(F) \dashrightarrow \mathcal{G}(G)$ defined by $\mathcal{G}(\eta)(\langle i, O \rangle) = \langle 1_i, \eta_i(O) \rangle$.

For a lax indexed functor $F : M_1 \dashrightarrow N$ and an indexed functor $G : M_2 \dashrightarrow N$ over I-indexed categories M_1, M_2, and N define the indexed category $\mathcal{G}(F) \downarrow G : \mathcal{G}(M_1)^{\mathrm{op}} \to \mathrm{Cat}$ on objects by $(\mathcal{G}(F) \downarrow G)(\langle i, O_1 \rangle) = F_i(O_1) \downarrow G_i$, where we abbreviate an object $(F_i(O_1), p, O_2)$ of this comma category to (O_2, p) and a morphism $(1_{F_i(O_1)}, o_2)$ to o_2, and on morphisms by $(\mathcal{G}(F) \downarrow G)(\langle u, o_1 \rangle : \langle i_1, O_{11} \rangle \to \langle i_2, O_{12} \rangle) : (\mathcal{G}(F) \downarrow G)(\langle i_2, O_{12} \rangle) \to (\mathcal{G}(F) \downarrow G)(\langle i_1, O_{11} \rangle)$ with $(\mathcal{G}(F) \downarrow G)(\langle u, o_1 \rangle)(O_{22}, p_2) = (M_2(u)(O_{22}), F_u(o_1); N(u)(p_2))$ and $(\mathcal{G}(F) \downarrow G)(\langle i, o_1 \rangle)(o_{22}) = M_2(u)(o_{22})$.

A lax indexed natural transformation $\eta : F_1 \dashrightarrow F_2$ then induces the indexed functor $\mathcal{G}(\eta) \downarrow G : \mathcal{G}(F_2) \downarrow G \dashrightarrow \mathcal{G}(F_1) \downarrow G$ defined by $(\mathcal{G}(\eta) \downarrow G)_{\langle i, O_1 \rangle}(O_2, p) = (O_2, \eta_i(O_1); p)$ and $(\mathcal{G}(\eta) \downarrow G)_{\langle i, O_1 \rangle}(o_2) = o_2$.

References

1. Borceux, F.: Handbook of Categorical Algebra: Vol. 2, Categories and Structures. Cambridge University Press, Cambridge (1994)
2. Climent Vidal, J., Soliveres Tur, J.: A 2-categorial generalization of the concept of institution. Stud. Logica **95**, 301–344 (2010)
3. Diaconescu, R.: Institution-independent Model Theory. SUL. Birkhäuser, Basel (2008). https://doi.org/10.1007/978-3-7643-8708-2
4. Goguen, J.A., Burstall, R.M.: A study in the foundations of programming methodology: specifications, institutions, charters and parchments. In: Pitt, D., Abramsky, S., Poigné, A., Rydeheard, D. (eds.) Category Theory and Computer Programming. LNCS, vol. 240, pp. 313–333. Springer, Heidelberg (1986). https://doi.org/10.1007/3-540-17162-2_131
5. Goguen, J.A., Burstall, R.M.: Institutions: abstract model theory for specification and programming. J. ACM **39**, 95–146 (1992)
6. Knapp, A., Cengarle, M.V.: Institutions for OCL-like expression languages. In: De Nicola, R., Hennicker, R. (eds.) Software, Services, and Systems. LNCS, vol. 8950, pp. 193–214. Springer, Cham (2015). https://doi.org/10.1007/978-3-319-15545-6_14
7. Lawvere, F.W.: Functorial semantics of algebraic theories. Ph.D. thesis, Columbia University (1963)
8. Mac Lane, S.: Categories for the Working Mathematician. GTM, vol. 5. Springer, New York (1978). https://doi.org/10.1007/978-1-4757-4721-8

9. Mayoh, B.H.: Galleries and institutions. Technical report DAIMI PB - 191, Aarhus University (1985)

10. Object management group: object constraint language. Standard formal/2014-02-03, OMG (2014). http://www.omg.org/spec/OCL/2.4

11. Paré, R., Schumacher, D.: Abstract families and the adjoint functor theorems. Indexed Categories and Their Applications. LNM, vol. 661, pp. 1–125. Springer, Heidelberg (1978). https://doi.org/10.1007/BFb0061361

12. Pawłowski, W.: Context institutions. In: Haveraaen, M., Owe, O., Dahl, O.-J. (eds.) ADT/COMPASS -1995. LNCS, vol. 1130, pp. 436–457. Springer, Heidelberg (1996). https://doi.org/10.1007/3-540-61629-2_57

13. Poigné, A.: Foundations are rich institutions, but institutions are poor foundations. In: Ehrig, H., Herrlich, H., Kreowski, H.-J., Preuß, G. (eds.) Categorical Methods in Computer Science with Aspects from Topology. LNCS, vol. 393, pp. 82–101. Springer, Heidelberg (1989). https://doi.org/10.1007/3-540-51722-7_6

14. Sannella, D., Tarlecki, A.: Foundations of Algebraic Specification and Formal Software Development. EATCS. Springer, Heidelberg (2012). https://doi.org/10.1007/978-3-642-17336-3

15. Tarlecki, A., Burstall, R.M., Goguen, J.A.: Some fundamental algebraic tools for the semantics of computation, Part 3: indexed categories. Theoret. Comput. Sci. **91**, 239–264 (1991)

16. Ţuţu, I., Fiadeiro, J.: From conventional to institution-independent logic programming. J. Log. Comput. **27**(6), 1679–1716 (2015)

17. Wolter, U., Martini, A.: Shedding new light in the world of logical systems. In: Moggi, E., Rosolini, G. (eds.) CTCS 1997. LNCS, vol. 1290, pp. 159–176. Springer, Heidelberg (1997). https://doi.org/10.1007/BFb0026987

Constructing Constraint-Preserving Interaction Schemes in Adhesive Categories

Jens Kosiol[1(✉)] [ID], Lars Fritsche[2] [ID], Nebras Nassar[1] [ID], Andy Schürr[2] [ID], and Gabriele Taentzer[1] [ID]

[1] Philipps-Universität Marburg, Marburg, Germany
{kosiolje,nassarn,taentzer}@mathematik.uni-marburg.de
[2] TU Darmstadt, Darmstadt, Germany
{lars.fritsche,andy.schuerr}@es.tu-darmstadt.de

Abstract. When using graph transformations to formalize model transformations, it is often desirable to design transformations that preserve consistency with respect to a given set of (model) integrity constraints. The standard approach is to equip transformations with suitable application conditions such that the introduction of constraint violations is prevented. This may lead to rules that are applicable seldom or even inapplicable at all, though. To supplement this approach, we present a new and systematic procedure to develop correct-by-construction transformations with respect to a special kind of constraints. Instead of controlling the applicability of a rule we complement its action in such a way that a given constraint holds after application: For every way in which the rule could introduce a violation of the constraint, we derive a supplementary action for the rule that remedies that violation. We formalize this construction in the setting of adhesive categories for monotonic rules and positive atomic constraints and present sufficient conditions for its correctness.

Keywords: Algebraic graph transformation · Interaction scheme · Graph constraints · Correctness-by-construction · Adhesive categories

1 Introduction

Algebraic graph transformation [4] has proved to be a suitable formal framework to reason about model transformations [3]. In application scenarios like model generation and editing or refactoring of models, it is desirable that transformations preserve consistency with respect to a set of integrity constraints. Nested constraints [7] allow to express first-order properties of graphs and a large subset of constraints formulated in OCL [17] – a widespread constraint language in modeling – may be translated into those [14,18]. In the context of algebraic graph transformation, the standard approach to ensure the validity of results

© IFIP International Federation for Information Processing 2019
Published by Springer Nature Switzerland AG 2019
J. L. Fiadeiro and I. Țuțu (Eds.): WADT 2018, LNCS 11563, pp. 139–153, 2019.
https://doi.org/10.1007/978-3-030-23220-7_8

of transformations with respect to a constraint is to equip transformation rules with suitable application conditions. This approach is elaborated for arbitrarily nested constraints in $\mathcal{M}$-adhesive categories [7] and has tool support for EMF model transformations [14]. It comes in two variants: Given a constraint c and a rule, one can construct a *c-guaranteeing* and a *c-preserving* application condition for the rule. The c-guaranteeing application condition ensures that the rules' application is possible if and only if the constraint c is fulfilled afterwards. The c-preserving one is logically weaker: The constraint c is only ensured to be fulfilled after a rule application if it already was before. Though sound from the formal point of view for every constraint, from the practical point of view the results are especially satisfactory in the case of *negative* constraints, which forbid a certain structure to exist. Then the new application conditions prohibit applications of the rule that would introduce this structure. However, for *positive* constraints requiring structures to exist, an application of a rule may be prohibited, e.g., because it creates a structure that necessitates another structure to exist that is not created likewise. In this way, frequently the application conditions stemming from positive constraints lead to rules which are applicable only rarely or are even inapplicable at all (see Sect. 2 for a concrete example).

To supplement the approach described above, we develop an alternative construction. Given a positive constraint c, instead of using application conditions, our idea is to *complement the action of a rule* in such a way that c holds after its application. Our construction works for *monotonic rules*, i.e., rules which only create structure, and *positive atomic constraints*. Some instance G satisfies a positive atomic constraint – which may be compactly notated as $\forall\,(P, \exists\,C)$ where P is a subobject of C – if for all subobjects of G that are isomorphic to P there exists a subobject isomorphic to C which includes the image of P. Positive atomic constraints are highly relevant in practice, e.g., they occur frequently when translating OCL into graph constraints and the application conditions arising from them in the standard approach are often far too restrictive. The crucial idea of our approach is to calculate all possible ways in which the application of a rule r may lead to a new match for the *premise* P of a constraint $c = \forall\,(P, \exists\,C)$. These are the different ways in which an application of r may introduce a new violation of c. They can significantly differ from each other and thus require diverging actions to resolve the would-be introduced violation. Hence, for each such situation we derive a rule that includes r as subrule but additionally creates structure that complements the new match for P to a new match for C. All these rules are collected into an *interaction scheme* [6] that is *constraint-preserving*: Applying an interaction scheme means to apply a common subrule – here r – once and every other rule from the interaction scheme as often as possible but with fixed partial match given by the match of the common subrule (the common actions are only performed once). In this way, every image of P that gets newly created by an application of r is complemented to an image of C by application of one of the rules of the interaction scheme and the validity of the constraint is preserved. Slightly extending this construction also gives a *constraint-guaranteeing interaction scheme*, i.e., an interaction scheme that additionally includes rules that "repair" already existing violations.

The original motivation for this research is to continue work from [13]. There, multi-rules for triple graph grammars (TGGs) [20] – a formalism for the declarative description of consistency relationships between two modeling languages with graph-like representations – have been developed. The exemplary multi-rules in [13] serve to preserve consistency with (informally described) constraints but were developed "by hand". This has the disadvantage that preservation of the constraint is not ensured by construction and has to be checked on a case-by-case basis. Our work paves the way to automate the design of those multi-rules in a way that guarantees correctness by construction. Our restriction to monotonic rules corresponds to that motivation since TGGs are composed of those.

The main contribution of this paper is the introduction and formalization of constraint-preserving and -guaranteeing interaction schemes in the setting of adhesive categories [12]. It is organized as follows. In Sect. 2 we illustrate our results with an example. Section 3 recalls relevant background. In Sect. 4 we present our construction of interaction schemes while Sect. 5 points out further possibilities to refine that construction. Section 6 compares to related work before we conclude in Sect. 7. An extended version of this paper [11] includes all proofs.

2 Introductory Example

We adapt the example from [13] since, in a way, we continue the work of constructing multi-amalgamated rules for triple-graph grammars (TGGs). There, a TGG for co-evolution of a class diagram and a documentation structure is given. We use a simplified version of this example, namely a plain graph grammar.

The meta-model in Fig. 1 is a blueprint for simple documentation structures. They consist of Docs owning Entries. Moreover, Docs reference Docs and Entries. Figure 2 presents a grammar allowing to create instances of the meta-model. Black elements have to exist for a rule to be applicable and green elements (additionally marked with ++) are newly created upon application. The rules allow for creation of a new Doc, creation of an Entry to an existing Doc, and insertion of the references, respectively.

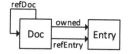

Fig. 1. Meta-model for documentation structures

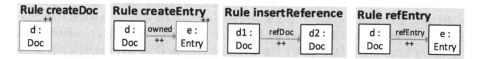

Fig. 2. Monotonic rules to create documentation structures (Color figure online)

If an instance of that meta-model is to be understood as documentation structure for a class-diagram, it is reasonable; e.g., to expect owned Entries of referenced Docs to be referenced, too. This constraint is expressible as a positive atomic constraint. Figure 3 depicts it in an intuitive graphical representation.

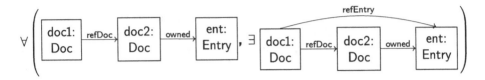

Fig. 3. Constraint *PropagationOfEntries*

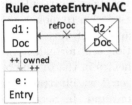

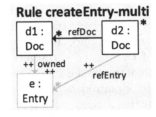

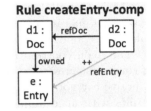

Rule createEntry-NAC

Rule createEntry-multi

Rule createEntry-comp

Fig. 4. Rule *createEntry* with *negative application condition* (the crossed-out red elements are forbidden to exist) (Color figure online)

Fig. 5. Multi-rule of *createEntry* (when seen as interaction scheme, the parts decorated with a Kleene star are applied as often as possible)

Fig. 6. Complement rule of *createEntry-multi* for *createEntry* as subrule

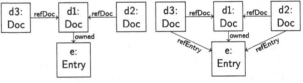

Fig. 7. Example for an instance graph

Fig. 8. After application of rule *createEntry* at d1

Fig. 9. After application of *createEntry-multi* at d1

The (simplified) constraint-preserving version of *createEntry* with respect to *PropagationOfEntries* is depicted in Fig. 4. Its application is prohibited at every Doc that is already referenced by another one. Thus, the creatable instances and the order of possible rule applications are severely restricted. As an alternative, we will automatically derive so-called multi-rules like *createEntry-multi* depicted in Fig. 5. Applying it as a so-called *interaction scheme* with kernel rule *createEntry* at a Doc still creates an Entry but additionally inserts a reference to this Entry from every Doc that references the chosen Doc. This is equivalent to applying its complement rule (Fig. 6) at every possible match with fixed partial match induced by a precedent application of *createEntry*. Applying, e.g., the rule *createEntry* at node d1 to the graph depicted in Fig. 7 leads to the graph in Fig. 8. This clearly violates the constraint *PropagationOfEntries*. While the rule *createEntry-NAC* is not applicable at that match, applying the rule *createEntry-multi* at it as interaction scheme leads to the valid instance depicted in Fig. 9.

3   Preliminaries

In this section, we present some technical preliminaries. We conduct our work in the framework of adhesive categories [12]. They have been introduced as a general setting for double pushout rewriting and can be understood as categories where pushouts along monomorphisms behave like pushouts along injective functions in the category of sets and functions. Here, we only recall rules and transformations in adhesive categories with a focus on multi-amalgamation after introducing positive atomic constraints.

To express properties of graphs in a way fitting to the algebraic approach to graph transformation, first graph predicates or graph conditions have been developed (being expressively equivalent to a first-order logic on graphs) and later been generalized to the setting of so-called $\mathcal{M}$-adhesive categories [7,19]. Our approach deals with a small but nonetheless in practice highly important fragment of that logic, namely *positive atomic constraints* [4].

Definition 1 (Positive atomic constraint). *In an adhesive category $\mathcal{C}$, a positive atomic constraint c is a monomorphism $p : P \hookrightarrow C$ between two objects. We will write $c = \forall (P, \exists p : P \hookrightarrow C)$ or $\forall (P, \exists C)$ for short for such a constraint. We call P the* premise *and C the* conclusion *of the constraint.*

An object G satisfies a positive atomic constraint c, denoted by $G \models c$, if for every monomorphism $g : P \hookrightarrow G$ there exists a monomorphism $q : C \hookrightarrow G$ such that $g = q \circ p$.

Positive atomic constraints are the only kind of constraints we consider, so we will just call them constraints when this is not apt to introduce misunderstanding.

Rules are a declarative way to define transformations of objects. They consist of a left-hand side L, a right-hand side R, and an interface K. Informally, in the category of graphs, the application of a rule to a graph G means to delete the elements of L and create those of R while preserving the elements stemming from the interface K. A match identifies the "location" in G where this is done. Formally and more generally in adhesive categories, a transformation can be defined using two pushout diagrams.

Definition 2 ((Monotonic) Rule. Transformation). *Given an adhesive category $\mathbf{C}$, a rule p consists of three objects $L, K,$ and R, called left-hand side (LHS), interface, and right-hand side (RHS), and two monomorphisms $l : K \hookrightarrow L, r : K \hookrightarrow R$. Its inverse rule is the rule $p^{-1} = (R \hookleftarrow K \hookrightarrow L)$. A rule $p = (L \hookleftarrow K \hookrightarrow R)$ is called monotonic (or non-deleting) if $l : K \hookrightarrow L$ is an isomorphism. In that case we just write $r : L \hookrightarrow R$. Given a rule $p = (L \hookleftarrow K \hookrightarrow R)$, an object G, and a monomorphism $m : L \hookrightarrow G$, called match, a (direct) transformation $G \Rightarrow_{p,m} H$ from G to H via p at match m is defined by the diagram to the right where both squares are pushouts.*

$$
\begin{array}{ccccc}
L & \xleftarrow{\;l\;} & K & \xrightarrow{\;r\;} & R \\
\scriptstyle m \downarrow & & \downarrow & & \downarrow \scriptstyle n \\
G & \longleftarrow & D & \longhookrightarrow & H
\end{array}
$$

A rule p is called applicable at match m if the first pushout square above exists, i.e., if $m \circ l$ has a pushout complement.

Since we exclusively consider monotonic rules in this paper, we will just call them rules and give the following definition for the monotonic case only. *Subrules* and their *multi-rules* have a twofold purpose. First, the application of a rule, then called a multi-rule, may be equivalently split into the application of a subrule followed by one of a *complement rule* with respect to that subrule. The construction of such a complement rule is not unique; a quite involved one can be found in [6]. For a simpler one for monotonic rules, also used in [13], we refer to the extended version of this paper [11]. An example is displayed in Fig. 6. This decomposition of a rule application allows for important extensions in two directions: coordinated parallelism and a for-each like syntax. A subrule may capture the common behavior of several multi-rules and thus serve as a kernel to amalgamate their respective actions into application of a single *multi-amalgamated* rule. Secondly, often a subrule is intended to be applied once followed by as many applications of the complement rule as possible. *Interaction schemes* unify both ideas into one concept: An interaction scheme consists of a bundle of multi-rules for the same *kernel rule*. Its application is defined by applying the kernel rule once and each of the complement rules of the multi-rules as often as possible with the fixed partial match given by application of the kernel rule.

Definition 3 (Subrule. Multi-rule. Interaction scheme. Application).
A subrule or kernel rule r_0 of a rule $r_1 : L_1 \hookrightarrow R_1$ is a rule $r_0 : L_0 \hookrightarrow R_0$ with kernel morphism $s_1 : r_0 \hookrightarrow r_1$ consisting of the monic components $s_{1,L} : L_0 \hookrightarrow L_1$ and $s_{1,R} : R_0 \hookrightarrow R_1$ such that the arising square in the diagram to the right is a pullback. The rule r_1 is then called a multi-rule *for r_0.*

$$
\begin{array}{ccc}
L_0 & \xrightarrow{r_0} & R_0 \\
\downarrow{\scriptstyle s_{1,L}} & & \uparrow{\scriptstyle s_{1,R}} \\
L_1 & \xrightarrow{r_1} & R_1
\end{array}
$$

An interaction scheme is a finite set $ias = \{s_1, \ldots, s_n\}$ of kernel morphism from a kernel rule r_0 to different multi-rules $r_1 : L_1 \hookrightarrow R_1, \ldots, r_n : L_n \hookrightarrow R_n$ of r_0. The application of the interaction scheme ias to an object G with kernel match $m_0 : L_0 \hookrightarrow G$ is defined as follows: A maximal matching J for ias is computed, i.e., a family of matches $(m_j : L_j \hookrightarrow G)_{j \in J}$ with $L_j \in \{L_1, \ldots, L_n\}$ for all $j \in J$ that is (i) consistent, i.e.,

$$m_0 = m_j \circ s_{j,L} \text{ for all } j \in J$$

and (ii) maximal, i.e., no further match for one of the LHSs $L_1, \ldots, L_n$ can be added to the family of matches such that it still is consistent.

Then, the (multi-)amalgamated rule $r_s : L_s \hookrightarrow R_s$, that is the rule arising by computing the colimits L_s of the family of morphisms $(s_{j,L})_{j \in J}$ and R_s of the family of morphisms $(s_{j,R})_{j \in J}$ with r_s being induced by the universal property of L_s, is applied.

Remark 1. In adhesive categories, for every finite family J of matches the colimits exist (as iterated pushouts along monomorphisms), the morphism r_s is a monomorphism, and all rules r_j are subrules of the resulting multi-amalgamated rule r_s [6]. In practical applications, e.g., when working with finite graph-like structures, this property is automatically fulfilled.

For formalizing our intended construction, we need a way to express the difference between objects in the setting of adhesive categories. The concept of initial pushouts [4] allows for this.

Definition 4 (Initial pushout). *Given a morphism $e : E \to P$, an initial pushout over e is a pushout (0) as in the left square below such that b_P is a monomorphism and the pushout (0) factors as a pushout (1) uniquely through every pushout (2) over e where b'_P is a monomorphism as in the right diagram below. Given an initial pushout (0) over e, B_P is called the* boundary object *and C_P the* context object *with respect to e.*

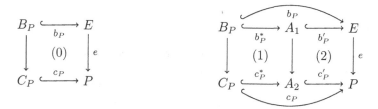

In the category of sets, if the morphism $e : E \to P$ is injective, the set B_P is empty and C_P is isomorphic to $P \backslash e(E)$. In the category of graphs, if e is injective, C_P is the graph arising by adding to $P \backslash e(E)$ those nodes from E necessary to complete it to a graph and B_P consists exactly of those *boundary nodes*. Thus, B_P consists of those nodes of E which get mapped to a node with an adjacent edge in P that has no preimage in E. Thus, we will often use $P \backslash E$ instead of C_P to denote the context object in an initial pushout over a monomorphism.

4   Constraint-Preserving Interaction Schemes

In this section, we develop our construction of constraint-preserving and -guaranteeing interaction schemes. We prove the construction to be well-defined, i.e., it results in a family of multi-rules, and present sufficient conditions for the desired preservation property of the arising interaction schemes.

The central idea of the construction of a constraint-preserving interaction scheme is to identify each way in which the application of a rule may introduce a violation of a given positive atomic constraint $c = \forall(P, \exists C)$. These are the different ways in which the rule can create a new occurrence of P. For each such situation we derive a multi-rule that additionally amends this new P to C. Applying the such arising interaction scheme instead of the original rule preserves the validity of the constraint (if the multi-rules themselves do not introduce new violations again). Slightly extending this strategy additionally provides rules that repair already existing violations of the constraint, i.e., enable to not only preserve but guarantee consistency.

We first introduce *compatible rule-constraint intersections* to classify the ways in which a rule $r : L \hookrightarrow R$ may introduce an image of the premise P

of a constraint $\forall\,(P, \exists C)$. Assuming a transformation $G \Rightarrow_{r,m} H$ to be given, the co-match is an embedding of R in H. If there is an image of P in H, it intersects with that image of R in H (maybe emptily). This intersection restricts to an intersection between the images of L and P in H as well. Thus, we introduce compatible intersections as monomorphisms $\iota : D \hookrightarrow E$ where E is a subobject of R and P and D is a subobject of L and P in a compatible way. The intuition is that D is that part of P already matched by the rule and $E \backslash D$ is the part the rule's application created anew. This suggests that if ι is an isomorphism, a situation is captured where the rule only matches some part of an image of P without creating a part of it (compare Lemma 2). We only need to consider those intersections that actually stem from applications of rules. Thus, calculating all such intersections gives all conceivable different ways in which an application of the rule might introduce a new subobject (isomorphic to) P.

Definition 5 (Compatible rule-constraint intersection). *Let $\mathcal{C}$ be an adhesive category, $r : L \hookrightarrow R$ a monotonic rule, and $c = \forall\,(P, \exists C)$ a positive atomic constraint in $\mathcal{C}$. A compatible rule-constraint intersection for r and c is a pair of spans of monomorphisms $d : L \xleftarrow{d_L} D \xrightarrow{d_P} P$ and $e : R \xleftarrow{e_R} E \xrightarrow{e_P} P$ with monomorphism $\iota : D \hookrightarrow E$ such that (compare Fig. 10)*

1. *$d_P = e_P \circ \iota$,*
2. *the square (1) is a pullback, i.e., $\iota : D \hookrightarrow E$ is a subrule of r, and*
3. *there exists an object H and monomorphisms $n_1 : R \hookrightarrow H$ and $m_2 : P \hookrightarrow H$ such that the arising square (2) is a pullback and a pushout complement G for $n_1 \circ r$ exists (i.e., the rule r^{-1} is applicable at H with match n_1).*

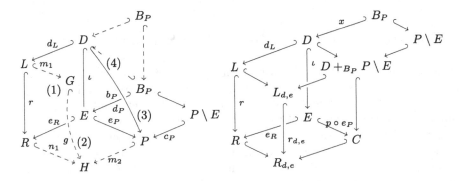

Fig. 10. Compatible intersections   **Fig. 11.** Construction of the multi-rule $r_{d,e}$

Example 1. The diagram in Fig. 12 depicts a compatible rule-constraint intersection for rule *createEntry* and the constraint *PropagationOfEntries*. It is the only compatible intersection for them where ι is not an isomorphism. Only intersecting the node of type Entry from the rule's RHS with the one from the constraint's premise (inducing an empty intersection between the LHS and the premise) leads to a pair of intersections that satisfy the first two properties of Definition 5 but not the third one: It is not possible that an application of *createEntry* only creates the node of type Entry of an occurrence of the premise but not its corresponding incoming edge of type ownedEntry as this would imply that the edge existed without a target node before the application of the rule *createEntry* which is not allowed in a graph.

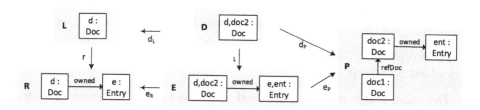

Fig. 12. Compatible rule-constraint intersection for rule *createEntry* and constraint *PropagationOfEntries* (node names indicate the morphisms)

In the example above, the node doc2 is a (in fact the only) boundary element: When deleting E from P, this node needs to be added to the result again for it to become a graph (so that the edge of type refDoc is not dangling). This signifies that this node must have existed before application of the rule and is one of the places (here even *the place*) at which E and $P\backslash E$ are glued to receive a complete copy of P. Hence, this node needs to be matched by the rule application to create P and, thus, is already part of D, the intersection of L and P. The next lemma states that this generalizes, i.e., the boundary object B_P is always a subobject of D and the existence of this inclusion morphism is vital for our construction.

Lemma 1 (Covering of boundary elements). *Let $\mathcal{C}$ be an adhesive category with initial pushouts, $r : L \hookrightarrow R$ a rule, $c = \forall\,(P, \exists p : P \hookrightarrow C)$ a constraint in $\mathcal{C}$, and $(d : L \hookleftarrow D \hookrightarrow P, e : R \hookleftarrow E \hookrightarrow P)$ with monomorphism $\iota : D \hookrightarrow E$ a compatible rule-constraint intersection. Let B_P be the boundary object of the initial pushout over $e_P : E \hookrightarrow P$. Then there exists a monomorphism $x : B_P \hookrightarrow D$ such that $\iota \circ x = b_P$. In particular, B_P is a pullback object for the monomorphisms $\iota : D \hookrightarrow E$ and $b_P : B_P \hookrightarrow E$ (compare Fig. 10).*

Given a compatible rule-constraint intersection (d, e), we use it to compute a multi-rule $r_{d,e}$. Its RHS is just the join of R and C along E, thus completing a newly created P to C. The multi-rule $r_{d,e}$ should match exactly in those cases where r creates a new P by adding $E\backslash D$ to some already existing structure. Thus, P has to exist except for the part $E\backslash D$ before rule application and the multi-rule needs to match that structure. This is achieved by joining L with the join of $P\backslash E$ and D along the boundary object B_P.

Construction 1 (Constraint-guaranteeing and constraint-preserving interaction scheme). *Let $\mathcal{C}$ be an adhesive category with initial pushouts,*

$r : L \hookrightarrow R$ a monotonic rule, and $c = \forall\,(P, \exists\, p : P \hookrightarrow C)$ a positive atomic constraint in $\mathcal{C}$. For each (up to isomorphism) compatible rule-constraint inter-section $(d : L \xleftarrow{d_L} D \xrightarrow{d_P} P, e : R \xleftarrow{e_R} E \xrightarrow{e_P} P)$ with monomorphism $\iota : D \to E$ for r and c, compute the multi-rule $r_{d,e} : L_{d,e} \hookrightarrow R_{d,e}$ in the following way (compare Fig. 11):

1. Compute the LHS $L_{d,e}$ of $r_{d,e}$ as pushout of the morphisms $d_L \circ x : B_P \hookrightarrow L$ and $B_P \hookrightarrow P \backslash E$.
2. Compute the RHS $R_{d,e}$ of $r_{d,e}$ as pushout of the morphisms $e_R : E \hookrightarrow R$ and $p \circ e_P : E \hookrightarrow C$.
3. The morphism $r_{d,e} : L_{d,e} \hookrightarrow R_{d,e}$ is induced by the universal property of the pushout computing $L_{d,e}$.

The constraint-guaranteeing interaction scheme for r with respect to c con-sists of the arising multi-rules and is denoted with $ias_{r,c}$. Its restriction $ias_{r,c}^p$ consists of those multi-rules stemming from pairs of intersections (d, e) where $\iota : D \hookrightarrow E$ is not an isomorphism and is called constraint-preserving interac-tion scheme.

Example 2. Given the rule *createEntry* and the constraint *PropagationOfEn-tries*, the constraint-preserving interaction scheme consists only of the kernel morphism that embeds *createEntry* into the multi-rule *createEntry-multi* as depicted in Fig. 5. That is because the only possible choice for a compatible rule-constraint intersection that is not an isomorphism is the one presented in Example 1.

The constraint-guaranteeing interaction scheme additionally contains the multi-rules depicted in Fig. 13. The intersections from which they are arising are given by the two isomorphisms from the empty graph to itself and from one node of type Doc to itself, respectively. The node of type Doc then might by identified with each of the two nodes of type Doc occurring in the constraint.

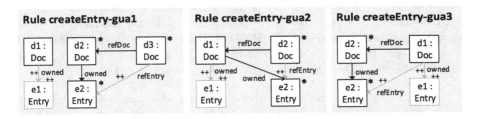

Fig. 13. Additional multi-rules contained in the constraint-guaranteeing interaction scheme of rule *createEntry* and constraint *PropagationOfEntries*

Remark 2. We introduced interaction schemes, as usual, as *finite sets* in Defini-tion 3. For the construction of the amalgamated rule (Definition 3 and Remark 1) it is important that the set J is finite – otherwise the colimits might not exist. The most natural setting to guarantee that both the interaction schemes arising by the above construction and the number of matches in their maximal matchings are finite is that of finitary categories, i.e., categories where every object has only finitely many subobjects. Moreover, in finitary adhesive categories initial pushouts always exist [5, Fact 3.12] – thus they do not need to be required as additional precondition. But since, for the above construction, the number of compatible rule-constraint intersections is not relevant and the number of matches in a maximal matching might be finite even if the considered interaction scheme is not, we did not restrict ourselves to finitary categories.

Showing that this construction actually leads to multi-rules of the original rule exploits the van Kampen property of the cube in Fig. 11; in this way the right front face is a pullback.

Theorem 1 (Well-definedness of construction). *Let C be an adhesive category with initial pushouts, $r : L \hookrightarrow R$ a monotonic rule, and $c = \forall \, (P, \exists \, p : P \hookrightarrow C)$ a positive atomic constraint in C. Then for every compatible rule-constraint intersection (d, e) the rule $r_{d,e} : L_{d,e} \hookrightarrow R_{d,e}$ as introduced in Construction 1 is a multi-rule of r and the morphism $r_{d,e}$ is a monomorphism.*

The next lemma states that compatible rule-constraint intersections are capable of distinguishing if an application of a rule r first enabled a matching of P in H or if this match already restricts to a match in G where $G \Rightarrow_r H$.

Lemma 2 (Classification of compatible rule-constraint intersections). *Let C be an adhesive category with initial pushouts, $r : L \hookrightarrow R$ a monotonic rule, $c = \forall \, (P, \exists \, p : P \hookrightarrow C)$ a positive atomic constraint, and $(d : L \xleftarrow{d_L} D \xrightarrow{d_P} P, e : R \xleftarrow{e_R} E \xrightarrow{e_P} P)$ with morphism $\iota : D \hookrightarrow E$ a compatible rule-constraint intersection for the rule r and the premise P of the constraint c. Let H be an object with monomorphisms $n_1 : R \hookrightarrow H$ and $m_2 : P \hookrightarrow H$ such that the induced square is a pullback and a pushout complement G for $n_1 \circ r$ exists. Then P already embeds into G in a way compatible to its embedding in H if and only if $\iota : D \hookrightarrow E$ is an isomorphism.*

Intuitively, applying the original rule r and the complement rules of the constructed interactions scheme afterwards, these complement rules supplement each currently existing image of the premise P of the constraint with an image of its conclusion C. But it may happen that the application of such complement rules introduces new occurrences of P which, by nature of our construction, are not supplemented. Consequently, it may happen that after applying the interaction scheme the constraint is violated, nonetheless. The next definition serves to be able to exclude situations like that rigorously and assumes familiarity with the concept of parallel independence [4]. The subsequent theorem states that this condition of independence is a sufficient (not necessary) condition for the constructed interaction schemes to preserve (guarantee) consistency with respect to a constraint. Its proof uses this independence to show that occurrences of P must stem from application of r or have already existed before. Then one needs to check that each such situation is covered by a multi-rule which is done by showing the arising intersections to be compatible (see Definition 5).

Definition 6 (Complementable). *Given a monotonic rule* $r : L \hookrightarrow R$ *and a positive atomic constraint* $c = \forall\,(P, \exists\,C)$, r *is called* (strongly) *complementable with respect to* c *if for every multi-rule* $r_{d,e} : L_{d,e} \hookrightarrow R_{d,e}$ *from the interaction scheme* $ias_{r,c}^p$ *($ias_{r,c}$) the inverse of its complement rule and the constant rule* $P \hookrightarrow P$ *are parallel independent.*

Theorem 2 (Guarantee and preservation). *Let an adhesive category* $\mathcal{C}$ *with initial pushouts be given. Let* $r : L \hookrightarrow R$ *be a monotonic rule,* $c = \forall\,(P, \exists\,p : P \hookrightarrow C)$ *a positive atomic constraint, and* $ias_{r,c}$ *and* $ias_{r,c}^p$ *the constraint-guaranteeing and constraint-preserving interaction schemes from Construction 1, respectively. Let* m_1 *be a match for* r *at an arbitrary object* G *with maximal matchings* J *and* J^p *for* $ias_{r,c}$ *and* $ias_{r,c}^p$ *extending* m_1.

1. *If* r *is strongly complementable with respect to* c *and* J *is finite, then the object* H *arising by application of* $ias_{r,c}$ *with that matching satisfies the constraint* c.
2. *If* r *is complementable with respect to* c *and* J^p *is finite then the object* H *arising by application of* $ias_{r,c}$ *with that matching satisfies the constraint* c.

5   Prospects and Future Work

This paper focuses on presenting the general idea behind the construction of constraint-preserving interaction schemes and proving their fundamental property. However, there are a lot of possible refinements and interesting future work:

In adhesive categories with strict initial object $\emptyset$, a constraint of the form $\exists\,C$, which requires C to be a subobject of G to be valid for an object G, is semantically equivalent to $\forall\,(\emptyset, \exists\emptyset \hookrightarrow C)$, i.e., preservation or guarantee of those constraints is dealt with in our framework as well.

The general idea presented in this paper may be used for deleting rules $r = (L \hookleftarrow K \hookrightarrow R)$ as long as it is not possible that an application of that rule deletes an occurrence C of the relevant constraint $\forall\,(P, \exists\,C)$, e.g., always when $L \backslash K$ and C intersect emptily. The construction stays the same, in principle, with K playing the role of L. The difference is that every arising multi-rule gets equipped with left-hand side $L_{d,e}$ arising as pushout of $K \hookrightarrow L$ and $K \hookrightarrow K_{d,e}$.

The precondition of complementability that comes with Theorem 2 is a severe restriction. There are examples, where this precondition is not met, but where recursively repeating our construction for the computed multi-rules again terminates (with no new multi-rules arising anymore) and where these multi-rules of multi-rules can be equivalently expressed as simple multi-rules of the original rule and the constraint is preserved by that extended interaction scheme. We give an example for this, namely a constraint requiring transitive closure over edges of a certain type, in the extended version of this paper [11]. Investigating this possibility in more detail is future work.

We plan to further integrate application conditions into our approach. Another topic for future research is to support preservation or guarantee of more than one constraint simultaneously. It would be especially interesting to combine support for positive atomic constraints and negative ones of the form

$\neg \exists C$, forbidding C to be an subobject of G to be valid for G. Our vision is to characterize those combinations of rules and constraints such that it is possible to preserve consistency with the whole set of constraints by incorporating the negative ones as application conditions into the rules and then constructing the preserving interaction schemes to support the positive atomic ones.

6 Related Work

As already discussed in Sects. 1 and 2, our work can be seen as a continuation of [13] and a supplement to [7]. To the best of our knowledge, we are the first to suggest an automatable construction to alter a rule into an interaction scheme to preserve consistency with respect to a given constraint.

We are aware of two works, both with tool support, allowing for automatic construction of interaction schemes in the context of EMF model transformation, but none of them explicitly aims at preservation of constraints. In [1], Alshanqiti et al. derive visual contracts from Java programs. They monitor the execution of programs and generate transformation rules describing the behavior of the program. The process supports the generation of interaction schemes. In contrast to our work aiming at preservation of constraints, their derived rules provide an abstract and visual representation of observed behavior.

Kehrer et al. [9] allow a user to specify examples of how a transformation should (or should not) act and from that infer a rule subsuming the provided examples. Their tool is also able to derive interaction schemes. As above, the aim is not to preserve correctness of an explicitly given constraint, and a generated interaction scheme may or may not happen to do so (depending on the quality of the input of the user) or serve a completely different purpose.

There are two works, [15, 16] and [8], that derive repair programs from (graph) constraints. In both works, given a set of constraints, a set of rules and some control structure are derived such that applying the resulting program to an instance results in an instance satisfying those constraints. In neither case interaction schemes are derived, but by passing of parameters or marking and applying rules as often as possible, the same effects are achieved. The second work is done in the context of (labeled) graphs and supports quite a large class of graph constraints, though support for sets of constraints is limited. The first one is done in the context of EMF models and repairs violations of multiplicities while respecting the in-built constraints of EMF. Moreover, it is implemented [16].

In [2], Becker et al. propose a method to design consistency-preserving rule-based refactorings. Given such a refactoring and a constraint, an invariant checker provides the user with minimal counterexamples for situations in which the refactoring does not preserve consistency with respect to the constraint. The user may use this information to redesign the refactoring and iterate over this process. The class of supported constraints is slightly larger than ours (supporting also negative constraint). Refactorings are specified via graph transformation rules and though there is no explicit support for interaction schemes, it is possible to use marking and iterate the application of rules as often as possible, which can have the same effect. If a constraint-preserving specification of a refactoring is achieved, of course, depends on the user.

In [10], Kehrer et al. automatically derive edit rules from meta-models. Starting with atomic operations, they revise rules such that elementary consistency constraints, necessary to be met for a model to be opened in a typical editor, are preserved on application of those roles. When viewing lower bounds of multiplicities of containment edges as positive atomic constraints and applying our construction to these constraints and their elementary rules for node creation, we receive exactly the rules they are using, too. In this case, however, the resulting rules actually not are multi-rules since the LHSs of the resulting multi-rules are the LHSs of the original rules again.

7 Conclusion

In the setting of adhesive categories, given a positive atomic constraint and a monotonic rule, we presented a construction of a constraint-preserving (or -guaranteeing) interaction scheme. We showed that our construction is well-defined and gave (sufficient) conditions under which the constraint is preserved (or guaranteed) when applying the resulting interaction schemes. With this approach, we are aiming at being able to replace the computation of constraint-preserving (or -guaranteeing) application conditions for rules in a situation where this has the often undesired effect of severely restricting the applicability of the rule. With our approach we are already able to automate the construction of multi-rules that had to be developed by hand before in [13]. We pointed at promising directions of research to be able to generalize our construction, to overcome the precondition of complementability that was necessary for our main theorem to hold, and to increase the effectiveness of our method in practice.

Acknowledgments. This work was partially funded by the German Research Foundation (DFG), projects "Triple Graph Grammars (TGG) 2.0" and "Generating Development Environments for Modeling Languages". We thank Erhan Leblebici for many helpful remarks.

References

1. Alshanqiti, A., Heckel, R., Kehrer, T.: Inferring visual contracts from Java programs. Autom. Softw. Eng. **25**(4), 745–784 (2018)
2. Becker, B., Lambers, L., Dyck, J., Birth, S., Giese, H.: Iterative development of consistency-preserving rule-based refactorings. In: Cabot, J., Visser, E. (eds.) ICMT 2011. LNCS, vol. 6707, pp. 123–137. Springer, Heidelberg (2011). https://doi.org/10.1007/978-3-642-21732-6_9
3. Biermann, E., Ermel, C., Taentzer, G.: Formal foundation of consistent EMF model transformations by algebraic graph transformation. Softw. Syst. Model. **11**(2), 227–250 (2012)
4. Ehrig, H., Ehrig, K., Prange, U., Taentzer, G.: Fundamentals of Algebraic Graph Transformation. MTCSAES. Springer, Heidelberg (2006). https://doi.org/10.1007/3-540-31188-2

5. Gabriel, K., Braatz, B., Ehrig, H., Golas, U.: Finitary $\mathcal{M}$-adhesive categories. Math. Struct. Comput. Sci. **24**(4), 240403 (2014)
6. Golas, U., Habel, A., Ehrig, H.: Multi-amalgamation of rules with application conditions in $\mathcal{M}$-adhesive categories. Math. Struct. Comput. Sci. **24**(4), 240405 (2014)
7. Habel, A., Pennemann, K.H.: Correctness of high-level transformation systems relative to nested conditions. Math. Struct. Comput. Sci. **19**, 245–296 (2009)
8. Habel, A., Sandmann, C.: Graph Repair by Graph Programs. In: Mazzara, M., Ober, I., Salaün, G. (eds.) STAF 2018. LNCS, vol. 11176, pp. 431–446. Springer, Cham (2018). https://doi.org/10.1007/978-3-030-04771-9_31
9. Kehrer, T., Alshanqiti, A., Heckel, R.: Automatic inference of rule-based specifications of complex in-place model transformations. In: Guerra, E., van den Brand, M. (eds.) ICMT 2017. LNCS, vol. 10374, pp. 92–107. Springer, Cham (2017). https://doi.org/10.1007/978-3-319-61473-1_7
10. Kehrer, T., Taentzer, G., Rindt, M., Kelter, U.: Automatically deriving the specification of model editing operations from meta-models. In: Van Van Gorp, P., Engels, G. (eds.) ICMT 2016. LNCS, vol. 9765, pp. 173–188. Springer, Cham (2016). https://doi.org/10.1007/978-3-319-42064-6_12
11. Kosiol, J., Fritsche, L., Nassar, N., Schürr, A., Taentzer, G.: Constructing constraint-preserving interaction schemes in adhesive categories: extended version. Technical report, Philipps-Universität Marburg (2019). https://www.uni-marburg.de/fb12/arbeitsgruppen/swt/forschung/publikationen/2019/KFNST19-TR.pdf
12. Lack, S., Sobociński, P.: Adhesive and quasiadhesive categories. Theor. Inf. Appl. **39**(3), 511–545 (2005)
13. Leblebici, E., Anjorin, A., Schürr, A., Taentzer, G.: Multi-amalgamated triple graph grammars: formal foundation and application to visual language translation. J. Vis. Lang. Comput. **42**, 99–121 (2017)
14. Nassar, N., Kosiol, J., Arendt, T., Taentzer, G.: OCL2AC: automatic translation of OCL constraints to graph constraints and application conditions for transformation rules. In: Lambers, L., Weber, J. (eds.) ICGT 2018. LNCS, vol. 10887, pp. 171–177. Springer, Cham (2018). https://doi.org/10.1007/978-3-319-92991-0_11
15. Nassar, N., Kosiol, J., Radke, H.: Rule-based Repair of EMF Models: formalization and Correctness Proof. In: Corradini, A. (ed.) Graph Computation Models (GCM 2017), Electronic Pre-Proceedings (2017). http://pages.di.unipi.it/corradini/Workshops/GCM2017/papers/Nassar-Kosiol-Radke-GCM2017.pdf
16. Nassar, N., Radke, H., Arendt, T.: Rule-based repair of EMF Models: an automated interactive approach. In: Guerra, E., van den Brand, M. (eds.) ICMT 2017. LNCS, vol. 10374, pp. 171–181. Springer, Cham (2017). https://doi.org/10.1007/978-3-319-61473-1_12
17. OMG: Object Constraint Language. http://www.omg.org/spec/OCL/
18. Radke, H., Arendt, T., Becker, J.S., Habel, A., Taentzer, G.: Translating essential OCL invariants to nested graph constraints for generating instances of meta-models. Sci. Comput. Program. **152**, 38–62 (2018)
19. Rensink, A.: Representing first-order logic using graphs. In: Ehrig, H., Engels, G., Parisi-Presicce, F., Rozenberg, G. (eds.) ICGT 2004. LNCS, vol. 3256, pp. 319–335. Springer, Heidelberg (2004). https://doi.org/10.1007/978-3-540-30203-2_23
20. Schürr, A.: Specification of graph translators with triple graph grammars. In: Mayr, E.W., Schmidt, G., Tinhofer, G. (eds.) WG 1994. LNCS, vol. 903, pp. 151–163. Springer, Heidelberg (1995). https://doi.org/10.1007/3-540-59071-4_45

Structuring Theories with Implicit Morphisms

Florian Rabe[1,2]([✉]) and Dennis Müller[2]([✉])

[1] LRI, Paris, France
florian.rabe@gmail.com
[2] FAU, Erlangen-Nuremberg, Germany
d.mueller@kwarc.info

Abstract. We introduce *implicit* morphisms as a concept in formal systems based on theories and theory morphisms. The idea is that there may be at most one implicit morphism from a theory S to a theory T, and if S-expressions are used in T their semantics is obtained by automatically inserting the implicit morphism. The practical appeal of implicit morphisms is that they hit the sweet-spot of being extremely simple to understand and implement while significantly helping with structuring large collections of theories.

Concrete applications include elegantly identifying isomorphic theories and extending theories with definitions and theorems as well as efficiently building and maintaining large, fine-granular, and heterogeneous hierarchies of theories. Our results are formulated and implemented in the MMT language and system, and we expect they can be transferred to other morphism-based formalisms relatively easily.

1 Introduction

Motivation. Theory morphisms have proved an essential tool for managing collections of theories in logics and related formal systems. They can be used to structure theories and build large theories modularly from small components or to relate different theories to each other [SW83, AHMS99, FGT92]. Areas in which tools based on theories and theory morphisms have been developed include specification [GWM+93, MML07], rewriting [CELM96], theorem proving [FGT93, KWP99], and knowledge representation [RK13]. Closely related concepts are used in both object-oriented (*classes*) and functional (*type classes*) programming languages.

These systems usually use a logic L for the low-level formalization of domain knowledge, and a diagram D in the category of L-theories and L-morphisms for the high-level structure of large bodies of knowledge.

F. Rabe—The author was supported by DFG grant RA-18723-1 OAF and EU grant Horizon 2020 ERI 676541 OpenDreamKit.

© IFIP International Federation for Information Processing 2019
Published by Springer Nature Switzerland AG 2019
J. L. Fiadeiro and I. Ţuţu (Eds.): WADT 2018, LNCS 11563, pp. 154–173, 2019.
https://doi.org/10.1007/978-3-030-23220-7_9

For example, a document might reference an existing theory `Monoid`, define a new theory `Group` that extends `Monoid`, define a theory `DivGroup` (providing an alternative formulation of groups based on the division operation), and then define two theory morphisms G2DG : `Group` ↔ `DivGroup` : DG2G that witness an isomorphism between these theories. This would result in the diagram below.[1]

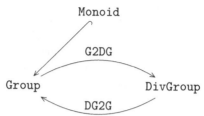

The key idea behind implicit morphisms is very simple: We maintain an additional diagram I, which is a commutative subdiagram of D and whose morphisms we call *implicit*. The condition of commutativity guarantees that I has at most one morphism i from theory S to theory T, in which case we write $S \xhookrightarrow{i} T$. Commutativity makes the following language extension well-defined: if $S \xhookrightarrow{i} T$, then any identifier c that is visible to S may also be used in T-expressions, with the semantics being that c abbreviates $i(c)$. For example, in the diagram above, we may choose to label DG2G implicit. Immediately, every abbreviation or theorem that we have formulated in the theory `DivGroup` becomes available for use in `Group` without any syntactic overhead. We can even label G2DG implicit as well if we prove the isomorphism property to ensure that I remains commutative, thus capturing the mathematical intuition that `Group` and `DivGroup` are just different formalizations of the same concept. While these morphisms must be labeled manually, any inclusion morphism like the one from `Monoid` to `Group` can be made implicit automatically.

Contribution. At the highest level, our contribution is the observation that implicit morphisms form a sweet spot of a very simple language feature that has substantial practical uses. We recommend using implicit morphisms in all theory morphism–based formalisms. More concretely, we present a formal system for developing structured theories with implicit morphisms based on the MMT language [RK13]. We choose MMT because it provides a simple framework for working with theories and morphisms while remaining logic-independent: MMT allows embedding a large variety of declarative languages L (logics, type-theories, etc.) so that our results immediately yield an implementation of implicit morphisms for any such L. We also expect but do not describe here that other morphism-based systems can be easily extended to allow for implicit morphisms.

We describe several example applications of implicit morphisms in detail: the identification of isomorphic theories, definitional extensions of theories, building large hierarchies of theories with many rarely used intermediate theories,

---

[1] Note that we use the syntactic direction for the arrows, e.g., an arrow $m : S \to T$ states that any S-expression E (e.g., a sort, term, formula, or proof) can be translated to a T-expression $m(E)$. Models are translated in the opposite direction.

seamlessly moving theories across logic morphisms, and transparently refactoring theory hierarchies.

Previous Work. Implicit morphism were first conceived by Rabe in 2010 and implemented as part of the Twelf system [PS99] (which implements the dependent type theory LF). The theory behind this implementation was never written up and not published. But the implementation already scaled well, and implicit morphisms were used in the LATIN logic atlas [CHK+11] built by Rabe and others in 2009–2012. The LATIN atlas already has around a 1000 theories and atomic morphisms, and about 50 of the latter are marked as implicit. It also has a few hundred inclusions, each of which induces another implicit morphism.

Since then, MMT has been developed, and

- implicit morphisms were generalized from LF to the logic-independent level of MMT,
- their theory was worked out,
- they were reimplemented from scratch as a part of MMT.

MMT is backwards-compatible with Twelf, and the LATIN atlas including its implicit morphisms can be used from within MMT. The present paper introduces these results in their final, most elegant form.

Overview. In Sect. 2, we present the syntax and semantics of MMT. Even though the MMT language is not new, our presentation is an entirely novel contribution in itself: it is much simpler and more elegant than the original one in [RK13]. Crucially, this increase in simplicity allows spelling out the syntax and semantics of implicit morphisms, which we do in Sect. 3, within a few pages. In Sect. 4, we present applications. Finally we discuss related and future work in Sect. 5.

2   Theories and Theory Morphisms

2.1   Overview

Flat Modules. **Flat theories** are lists of constant declarations $c : E[= e]$ where E and e are expressions, and the latter is optional. We write $\mathrm{dom}(T)$ for the set of constant identifiers c in T. Every theory induces the set $\mathrm{Obj}(T)$ for the set of closed **expressions** using only the symbols $c \in \mathrm{dom}(T)$. Constant declarations subsume virtually all basic declarations common in formal systems such as type-/function/predicate symbols, axioms, theorems, inference rules, etc. In particular, theorems can be represented via the propositions-as-types correspondence as declarations $c : F = P$, which establish theorem F via proof P. Similarly, MMT expressions subsume virtually all objects common in formal systems such as terms, types, formulas, proofs.

Flat morphisms from a theory S to a theory T are lists of assignments $c := e$ where $c \in \mathrm{dom}(S)$ and $e \in \mathrm{Obj}(T)$. Every morphism M induces a **homomorphic extension** $M(-) : \mathrm{Obj}(S) \to \mathrm{Obj}(T)$, which replaces every $c \in \mathrm{dom}(S)$ in an S-expression with the T-expression e such that $c := e$ in M.

A **diagram** consists of a set of theory and morphism declarations. For a given diagram, we write Thy for the set of declared **theories**. For theories $S, T \in$ Thy, we write $\mathrm{Mor}(S, T)$ for the set of **morphisms** defined by

- for every declaration $m : S \to T = \{\cdot\}$, we have $m \in \mathrm{Mor}(S, T)$,
- for every $T \in$ Thy, we have $id_T \in \mathrm{Mor}(T, T)$,
- for every $M \in \mathrm{Mor}(R, S)$ and $N \in \mathrm{Mor}(S, T)$, we have $M; N \in \mathrm{Mor}(R, T)$ (where $M; N$ corresponds to the usual function composition).

Thy and $\mathrm{Mor}(S, T)$ form the category of theories and morphisms.

The theories and morphisms in a diagram may be structured (e.g., by using *include* declarations), and MMT defines their semantics via **flattening**, which defines for each $T \in$ Thy the flat theory $T^\flat$, and for each $M \in \mathrm{Mor}(S, T)$ the flat morphism $M^\flat$ from $S^\flat$ to $T^\flat$.

Logics and Well-Formed Expressions. The logic and the definition of well-formed expressions are not a primary interest of this paper, and we only recap the essential structure needed in the sequel. We refer to [Rab17] for details.

MMT is independent of the base logic and provides a theory and theory morphism layer on top of an arbitrary declarative language. Individual logics L arise as fragments of MMT: they single out the well-formed expressions by defining the **judgment** $\vdash_T e = e' : E$ for typing and equality. (We treat the plain typing judgment $\vdash_T e : E$ as the special case $\vdash_T e = e : E$.) The logic L is itself represented as an MMT theory, which we call the **meta-theory** of T. L provides, in particular, the primitive operators and typing rules that are used to form the well-formed expressions of T. L may and often has a meta-theory as well, usually a logical framework used to define the logic. Unless mentioned otherwise, all results in this paper apply for a fixed arbitrary meta-theory, which we will occasionally omit from the notation.

The declarations in theories and assignments in morphisms are subject to typing conditions, and the main theorem about MMT is that under reasonable assumptions on L, the well-typed morphisms $M : S \to T$ preserve all judgments, i.e., if $\vdash_S e = e' : E$, then $\vdash_T M(e) = M(e') : M(E)$. This includes the preservation of truth via the propositions-as-types principle if E is a proposition and e its proof.

We do not give all rules for these judgments. The only rule that is relevant to our purposes here is the one for constants:

$$\frac{c : E[= e] \text{ in } T^\flat}{\vdash_T c[= e] : E}$$

(Here, we merge the two cases where c has a/no definiens e into one rule for convenience.) Correspondingly, the definition of the homomorphic extension of a morphism with domain S includes the following case for constants:

$$M(c) = \begin{cases} e & \text{if } (c : E) \in S^\flat, (c := e) \in M^\flat \\ M(e) & \text{if } (c : E = e) \in S^\flat \end{cases}$$

Here if c has a definiens in S, we expand it before applying M.[2]

These base cases introduce a mutual recursion between well-formedness and flattening: the well-formedness of a declaration in a theory depends on the flattening of all preceding declarations; correspondingly, the well-formedness of an assignment in a morphism depends on the homomorphic extension of the morphism obtained by flattening of all preceding assignments. Vice versa, well-formedness is a precondition for defining the flattening—the definition of flattening may become nonsensical if applied to ill-formed modules. It might be desirable to define well-formedness independently of flattening. But our definition captures the typical behavior of practical systems, which first parse, check, and flatten one declaration entirely before moving on to the next one.

Therefore, we will make flattening a partial function, i.e., $X^\flat$ is undefined if the module X is not well-formed.

2.2   Syntax

We start with the syntax for theories (which arises as a special case of the one given in [RK13]):

Definition 1 (Theory). *The grammar for theories and expressions is*

$TDec$	$::=$	$T[: T] = \{Dec, \dots, Dec\}$	*theory declaration*
Dec	$::=$	$n : E[= E]$	*constant declaration*
c	$::=$	$T?n$	*qualified constant identifiers*
E	$::=$	$c \mid \dots$	*expressions built from constants*

*In a theory declaration $T : L = \{\vec{D}\}$, the **meta-theory** L (if present) must be a previously declared theory, each symbol **name** n may be declared only once, and its **type** and **definiens** (if present) must be closed expressions over the previously introduced constants (including those of L). We omit the productions and typing rules for the remaining expressions, which include application, binding, variables, literals, etc.*

Example 1. For the purposes of our running examples, we assume a fixed meta-theory Log that provides a simple type system: type is the universe of types, $A \to B$ is the type of functions, and lambda abstraction is written $[x{:}A]\ t\ x$. We also use MMT notations, which are attached to constant declarations as # <notation>; these are omitted from the formal grammar above because we only use them in the examples.

Then the (flat) theories Group and DivGroup from the introduction are:

```
Group:  Log =
   U        : type
```

---

[2] The MMT tool accepts $(c := e) \in M^\flat$ even if $(c : E = e') \in S^\flat$. In that case, MMT checks $\vdash_T M(e') = e : M(E)$ and puts $M(c) = e$. This is important for efficiency but not essential for our purposes here.

```
op         : U → U → U    # 1 ∘ 2
unit       : U
inverse : U → U # 1 ⁻¹
// axioms omitted
```

```
DivGroup: Log =
  U    : type
  div : U → U → U # 1 / 2
  unit: U
  // axioms omitted
```

We proceed accordingly for flat morphisms:

Definition 2 (Morphism). *The grammar for **morphisms** is*

$MDec$	$::=$	$m : T \to T =^{[M]} \{Ass, \dots, Ass\}$	*flat morphism declaration*
Ass	$::=$	$c := E$	*assignment to symbol*
M	$::=$	$m \mid id_T \mid M; M$	*morphism expressions*

A morphism $m : S \to T =^M \{\vec{A}\}$ must contain exactly one assignment $c := e$ for each $(c : E) \in S^\flat$, all of which must satisfy $\vdash_T e : m(E)$. Moreover, if S has a meta-theory L, then M must be present and must be a morphism from L to T.

Example 2 (Morphisms). We give the morphism DG2G between the theories from Example 3:

```
DG2G : DivGroup -> Group =^{id_Log}
  U       := U
  div   := [a,b] a ∘ (b⁻¹)
  unit  := unit
  // assignments to axioms omitted
```

Here id_{Log} maps the meta-theory to itself. Then universe and unit of a division group are mapped to the corresponding notions of a group. And we have $DG2G(a/b) = a \circ b^{-1}$. Additionally, the morphism maps every axiom of DivGroup to a proof in Group of the translated statement, but we omit those assignments.

Finally, we define diagrams as collections of modules:

Definition 3 (Diagram). *A **diagram** is a list of theory and morphism declarations:*

$$Dia \quad ::= \quad (TDec \mid MDec)^* \quad diagrams$$

Each theory/morphism declaration must have a unique name and be well-formed relative to the diagram preceding it.

At this point, the grammar only allows forming flat theories and morphisms. Structuring features can be added to the language incrementally and individually.

Example 3 (Includes). We extend the grammar with

Dec	$::=$	**include** T	include a theory into a theory
Ass	$::=$	**include** M	include a morphism into a morphism

This allows writing the theory `Group` from Example 1 by extending a theory of monoids. Again omitting all axioms, this looks as follows:

```
Monoid: Log =
  U      : type
  op     : U → U → U      # 1 ∘ 2
  unit   : U
Group: Log =
  include Monoid
  inverse : U → U  # 1⁻¹
```

2.3   Semantics

Flattening. The definition of flattening is **compositional** in the sense that new modularity principles can be added independently of each other.

Definition 4 (Flattening). *For the base case, of a theory $t : L = \{\Sigma\}$, we define $t^\flat$ by induction on the declarations in Σ:*

$$t^\flat = \Sigma^\flat \quad \text{where} \quad \cdot^\flat = L^\flat \quad \text{and} \quad (\Sigma, D)^\flat = \Sigma^\flat \cup D^\flat,$$

where $\cdot$ denotes the empty sequence. If L is not present, we can assume it to be the empty theory.

Here $D^\flat$ is the flattening of declaration D relative to $\Sigma^\flat$. At this point, we only have one case for declarations D, namely constant declarations. Their flattening is trivial:

$$(n : E[= e])^\flat = \{t?n : E[= e]\}$$

where t is the name of the containing theory.

Correspondingly, for a declared morphism $m : S \to T =^{[M]} \{\sigma\}$, $m^\flat$ is defined by induction on the assignments in σ:

$$m^\flat = \sigma^\flat \quad \text{where} \quad \cdot^\flat = M^\flat \quad \text{and} \quad (\sigma, A)^\flat = \sigma^\flat \cup A^\flat$$

with the trivial base case

$$(c := e)^\flat = \{c := e\}$$

If M is not present, we can assume it to be empty morphism.

Moreover, for $T \in \mathsf{Thy}$ we define $id_T^\flat = \{c := c \mid (c : E) \in T^\flat\}$ And for $M; N \in \mathsf{Mor}(R, T)$, we define $(M; N)^\flat = \{c := N^\flat(M^\flat(c)) \mid (c : E) \in R^\flat\}$. Note that in both cases, we only have to consider constants without definiens.

Example 4 (Includes (continued from Example 3*)).* The **include** operator adds new declarations D to a theory, so we have to add cases to the definition of $D^\flat$. We do this as follows

$$(\textbf{include } S)^\flat = S^\flat$$

This has the effect of copying over all declarations from the included into the including theory.

There is some flexibility as to when the including and the included theory have different meta-theories L resp. L'. We define that such an include is only allowed if L' is also included into L. That way, an include declaration never changes the meta-theory of the including theory.

Note that, because $S^\flat$ is a *set* of declarations, the include relation is transitive: if t includes s via two different paths, $t^\flat$ only contains one copy of the declarations of $s^\flat$.

Because we use qualified identifiers $t?n$, includes can never lead to name clashes. The situation is slightly more complicated for morphisms: if a morphism σ out of t includes two different morphisms out of s, these have to agree. Therefore, flattening is not always defined:

$$(\textbf{include } M)^\flat = M^\flat$$

if $\sigma,$ **include** M is well-formed and $M^\flat$ agrees with $\sigma^\flat$ on any constant that is in the domain of both.

Example 5 (Continuing Example 3*).* `Group`$^\flat$ is obtained by copying all included symbols (from `Monoid`) over to `Group`, resulting in the theory as given in Example 1 except that the identifiers are now, e.g., `Monoid?U` instead of `Group?U`.

Remark 1 (Qualified Identifiers). According to the grammar, any occurrence of a constant c in an expression is of the form $t?n$, i.e., qualified by its theory name. In the definition all declarations in $t^\flat$ are qualified accordingly. This precludes any name clashes when constants of the same local name are declared in multiple theories that become part of $t^\flat$, e.g., via the meta-theory or includes.

The form $t?n$ is *abstract* system-facing syntax. In *concrete* user-facing syntax (as used in our examples), it is usually sufficient to write n and let the MMT parser infer which constant is meant.

3 Implicit Morphisms

3.1 Overview

Our key idea is to use a commutative subdiagram of the MMT diagram, which we call the *implicit diagram*. It contains all theories but only some of the morphisms—the ones designated as *implicit*. Because the implicit-diagram commutes, there can be at most one implicit morphism from S to T—if this morphism is i, we write $S \overset{i}{\hookrightarrow} T$. The implicit-diagram generalizes the inclusion relation: All identity and inclusion morphisms are implicit, and we recover the inclusion relation $S \hookrightarrow T$ as the special case $S \overset{id_S}{\hookrightarrow} T$. And just like inclusion, the relation "exists i such that $S \overset{i}{\hookrightarrow} T$" is a preorder.

Consequently, many of the advantages of inclusions carry over to implicit morphisms:

- It is very easy to maintain the implicit-diagram, e.g., as a partial map that assigns to a pair of theories the implicit morphism between them (if any).
- We can generalize the visibility of identifiers: If $S \overset{i}{\hookrightarrow} T$, we can use all S-identifiers in T as if S were included into T. Any $c \in \mathsf{dom}(S)$ is treated as a valid T-identifiers with definiens $M(c)$.
- We can use canonical identifiers $S?n$ without worrying about ambiguity.

  Because there can be at most one implicit morphism $S \overset{i}{\hookrightarrow} T$, using $S?n$ as an identifier in T is unambiguous.

In practice, the MMT system searches for an implicit morphism $S \overset{i}{\hookrightarrow} T$ whenever needed to make an expression well-formed, e.g.,

- An S-constant c is used in T: treat c as an abbreviation for $i(c)$.
- A model M of T is used even though a model of S is expected: reduce M via i.
- A morphism $M : R \to S$ is composed with a morphism $M' : T \to U$: treat $M; M'$ like $M; i; M'$.

3.2   Syntax

We introduce the family of sets $\mathsf{Mor}^i(S, T)$ as a subset of $\mathsf{Mor}(S, T)$, holding the *implicit* morphisms. The intuition is that Thy and $\mathsf{Mor}^i(S, T)$ (up to equality of morphisms) form a thin broad subcategory of Thy and $\mathsf{Mor}(S, T)$.

It remains to define which morphisms are implicit. For that purpose, we allow MMT declarations to carry *attributes*:

Definition 5 (Attributes for Implicitness). *We add the following productions*

$MDec$	$::=$	$Att\ MDec$	*attributed morphism*
Dec	$::=$	$Att\ Dec$	*attributed declaration*
Att	$::=$	**implicit** $\mid$ ...	*attributes*

The set of attributes is itself extensible, and the above grammar only lists the one that we use to get started. Additional attributes can be added when adding modularity principles.

Example 6. We can now change the declaration of the morphism DG2G from Example 2 by adding the attribute **implicit**.

3.3   Semantics

We only have to make two minor changes to the semantics to accommodate implicit morphisms. The first change governs how we obtain implicit morphisms, the second one how we use them.

Definition 6 (Obtaining Implicit Morphisms). *We define the set* $\mathrm{Mor}^i(S, T) \subseteq \mathrm{Mor}(S, T)$ *of **implicit** morphisms to contain the following elements:*

- *all declared morphisms* $m : S \to T = \{\sigma\}$ *whose declaration carries the attribute **implicit**,*
- *if t has meta-theory L, the identity map as an implicit morphism $L \to t$,*
- *all identity morphisms id_T,*
- *all compositions $M; N$ of implicit morphisms M and N,*
- *all morphisms that additional language features designate as implicit based on the use of additional attributes.*

*Adding an **implicit** attribute to a declaration is well-formed only if there is (up to equality of morphisms) at most one implicit morphism for any pair of theories.*

Example 7 (Includes (continued from Example 4)). For include morphisms, we add the following definition: if a theory T contains the declaration **include** S, then the induced morphism from S to T is implicit.

Combined with composition morphisms, we see that all transitive includes between theories are implicit. That corresponds to the intuition that anything that is included is available by its original (i.e. qualified) name.

Example 8. For our morphism `DG2G` from Example 6, this means that all symbols declared in the theory `DivGroup` (see Example 1) are now visible in the theory `Group` with the definitions provided by `DG2G`. For example, we can write a/b in `Group`, where / refers to the identifier `DivGroup?div`.

(Note that notations are carried over by implicit morphisms as well)

The intuition behind implicit morphisms is that all S-constants $c : E$ that can be mapped into the current theory via an implicit morphism $M : S \to T$ are directly available in T. We can practically realize this by adding new defined constants $c : M(E) = M(c)$ to T. However, physically adding definitions can be inefficient. It is more elegant to modify the typing rules such that $\vdash_T c : M(c) = M(E)$ holds without any changes to T.

To do that, we only have to make a small modification to the original rules of MMT as presented in Sect. 2. To illustrate how simple the modification is, the following definition repeat the original rule first for comparison:

Definition 7 (Using Implicit Morphisms). *We replace the rule*

$$\frac{c : E[= e] \text{ in } T^\flat}{\vdash_T c[= e] : E} \qquad \text{with} \qquad \frac{c : E[= e] \text{ in } S^\flat \qquad S \overset{M}{\hookrightarrow} T}{\vdash_T c = M(c) : M(E)}$$

Note that the modified rule gives every constant a definiens. This is a technical trick to subsume the original rule: if c is already declared in T, we use $M = id_T$ and obtain $\vdash_T c = c : E$.

The following theorem is our central theoretical result. It shows that the modification made in Definition 7 has the intended properties:

Theorem 1 (Conservativity of Implicit Morphisms). *For well-formed diagrams and $S, T \in$ Thy and $M \in \mathrm{Mor}^i(S, T)$:*

1. *Whenever the original system proves $\vdash_T e = e' : E$, so does the modified one.*
2. *Whenever the modified system proves $\vdash_T e = e' : E$, then the original system proves $\vdash_T \overline{e} = \overline{e'} : \overline{E}$.*

Here $\overline{E}$ is the expression that arises from E by recursively replacing every constant with its definiens.

Proof. For the first claim, we proceed by induction on derivations. We only need to consider the case where the original rule was applied. So assume it yields $\vdash_T c[= e] : E$, i.e., $(c : E[= e])$ in $T^\flat$. We apply the modified rule for the special case $T \overset{id_T}{\hookrightarrow} T$. The conclusion reduces to

- if e is absent: $\vdash_T c = c : E$, which is equivalent to $\vdash_T c : E$,
- if e is present: $\vdash_T c = e : E$ because $M(c) = M(e)$ according to the definition of $M(-)$.

For the second claim, we proceed by induction on derivations. We only need to consider the case where the modified rule was applied. So assume it yields $\vdash_T c = M(c) : M(E)$ for $(c : E[= e])$ in $S^\flat$ and $S \overset{M}{\hookrightarrow} T$. We distinguish two cases:

- $M(c) = c$, i.e., e is absent, and $\overline{c} = c$. According to the definition of $S^\flat$, this is only possible if $S \hookrightarrow T$ (including the special case $S = T$). In that case, $S^\flat \subseteq T^\flat$ and M is the include/identity morphism that maps all S-constants to themselves. Now applying the induction hypothesis to the well-formedness derivation of E yields $\vdash_T c : \overline{E}$ as needed.
- $M(c) \neq c$, i.e., e is present or M assigns a non-trivial value to c. Definition expansion eliminates c in favor of $M(c)$, and thus $\overline{c} = \overline{M(c)}$. We only have to show that $\vdash_T \overline{M(c)} : \overline{M(E)}$. That follows from the judgment preservation of morphisms.

With implicit morphisms, we can also relax the semantics of many structuring features:

Example 9 (Includes and Meta-Theories (continued from Example 4)). Consider $t : L = \{\ldots, \mathbf{include}\ S, \ldots\}$ where S has meta-theory L'. Instead of requiring $L' \hookrightarrow L$ as in Example 4, we require only $L' \overset{i}{\hookrightarrow} L$.

In that case, we treat **include** S as an abbreviation for **include** $i(S)$, where $i(S)$ is the pushout of S along i (see [Rab17] for details on MMT pushouts). If $L' \hookrightarrow L$, this reduces to the original semantics.

4   Applications

4.1   Identifying Theories via Implicit Isomorphisms

A common need in developing large libraries (both in formal and informal developments) is to identify two theories S and T via a canonical choice of isomorphisms. In these cases, it is often desirable to use S-syntax and T-syntax interchangeably. But one of the major short-comings of formal theories over traditional informal developments is that formal systems usually need to spell out these isomorphisms everywhere. In this section, we show that implicit morphisms elegantly allow exactly that kind of intuitive identification: we mark the canonical isomorphisms as implicit.

In the sequel, we present several ways to obtain implicit isomorphisms conveniently. In general, note that because identity morphisms are implicit, our uniqueness requirement for implicit morphisms implies that two theories S and T must be isomorphic if there are implicit morphisms in both directions. Moreover, making a pair of isomorphisms implicit is only allowed if there are no other implicit morphisms between S and T yet.

Renamings. We say that a named morphism $r : S \to T = \{\ldots\}$ is a **renaming** if

- all assignments in its body are of the form $c := c'$ for T-constants c' without definiens
- every T-constant c' without definiens occurs in exactly one assignment.

Clearly, every renaming is an isomorphism. The inverse morphisms contains the flipped assignments $c' := c$.

We make the following extension to syntax and semantics:

- A morphism declaration $r : s \to t = \{\ldots\}$ may carry the attribute **renaming**.
- This is allowed if there are no implicit morphisms between s and t yet.
- In that case, we define $r \in \mathtt{Mor}^i(s,t)$ and $r^{-1} \in \mathtt{Mor}(t,s)$.

Example 10 (Renaming). Consider a variation of the theory `Monoid` from Example 3 in a different library:

```
Monoid2: Log =
  M            : type
  connective : M → M → M # 1 ∘ 2
  neutral     : M
```

This theory is isomorphic to the previously introduced theory `Monoid` under the trivial renaming

```
renaming MonoidRen : Monoid2 -> Monoid =idLog
  M            := U
  connective := op
  neutral     := unit
```

Definitional Extensions. We say that the named theory T is a **definitional extension** of S if $T = S$ or the body of T contains only

- constant declarations with definiens, and
- include declarations of theories that are definitional extensions of S.

If T is a definitional extension of S, it is easy to prove that T and S are isomorphic: both isomorphisms map all constants without definiens to themselves. In particular, the isomorphism $T \to S$ maps S-constants to themselves and expands the definiens of all other constants.

We make the following extension to syntax and semantics:

- An include declaration **include** S of a named theory S inside a theory T may carry the attribute **definitional**.
- In that case, we define $id_S \in \text{Mor}^{\text{i}}(T, S)$ (in addition to the implicit morphism $id_T \in \text{Mor}^{\text{i}}(S, T)$ that is induced by the inclusion).

Example 11 (Extension with a Theorem). We extend the theory `Group` from Example 3 with a theorem

```
InverseInvolution: Log =
  definitional include Group
  inverse_invol : ∀[x] (x⁻¹)⁻¹≐ x = (proof omitted)
```

Remark 2 (Conservative Extensions). A definitional extension is a special case of a conservative extension. More generally, all retractable extensions are conservative, i.e., all extensions $S \hookrightarrow T$ such that there is a morphism $r : T \to S$ that is the identity on S. But we cannot make the retractions implicit morphisms in general because they are not necessarily isomorphisms.

Canonical Isomorphisms. If we have isomorphisms $m : S \to T$ and $n : T \to S$, we simply spell them out in morphism declarations and add the keyword **implicit** to both. This requires no language extensions.

Example 12. Having declared the morphism `DG2G` (as in Example 2) implicit, we do the same with the reverse morphism `G2DG`:

```
implicit G2DG : Group -> DivGroup =idₗₒg
  U       := U
  op      := [a,b] a/(unit/b)
  unit    := unit
  inverse := [a] unit/a
```

While making one of these isomorphisms implicit is straightforward, doing it for both requires checking that m and n are actually isomorphisms. Otherwise, the uniqueness condition would be violated. Thus, we have to check $m; n = id_s$ and $n; m = id_t$. In general, the equality of two morphisms $f, g : A \to B$ is equivalent to $\vdash_B f(c) = g(c)$ for all $(c : E) \in A^\flat$. Thus, if equality of expressions is decidable in the logic that MMT is instantiated with, then MMT can check this directly.

However, this does not work in practice. Already elementary examples require stronger, undecidable equality relations:

Example 13. Consider the isomorphism from Example 12. The result of mapping $x \circ y$ from `Group` to `DivGroup` and back is $x \circ (\mathtt{unit} \circ y^{-1})^{-1}$. Clearly, the group axioms imply that this is equal to $x \circ y$. But formally, that requires working with the undecidable equality of first-order logic.

Therefore, in our running example, we can only make one of the two isomorphisms implicit at this point.

In the sequel, we design a general solution to this problem. It allows systematically proving the equality of two morphisms and using that to make both isomorphisms implicit. This is novel work that requires significant prerequisites and is only peripherally related to implicit morphisms. Therefore, we only sketch the idea and leave the details to future work.

We add a language feature to MMT to prove equalities between morphisms: We add the productions

$$
\begin{array}{lll}
Dia & ::= & (TDec \mid MDec \mid MEq)^* \\
MEq & ::= & \mathbf{equal}\, M = M : T \to T \,\mathbf{by}\{Ass^*\}
\end{array}
$$

We define the declaration $\mathbf{equal}\, M = N : S \to T \,\mathbf{by}\{\sigma\}$ to be well-formed iff

- $M : S \to T$ and $N : S \to T$ are well-formed morphisms
- σ contains exactly one assignment $c := p$ for every $(c : E) \in S^\flat$
- for each of these assignments $c := p$, the term p is a proof of $\vdash_T M(c) = N(c)$.

Example 14 (Isomorphisms). With the above extension in place, we can make both isomorphisms m and n from above implicit:

$$\mathbf{implicit} : \mathtt{DG2G} : \mathtt{DivGroup} \to \mathtt{Group} = (\text{as above})$$

$$\mathbf{implicit} : \mathtt{G2DG} : \mathtt{Group} \to \mathtt{DivGroup} = (\text{as above})$$

$$\mathbf{equal}\, \mathtt{G2DG}; \mathtt{DG2G} = id_{\mathtt{Group}} : \mathtt{Group} \to \mathtt{Group} = (\text{omitted})$$

$$\mathbf{equal}\, \mathtt{DG2D}; \mathtt{G2DG} = id_{\mathtt{DivGroup}} : \mathtt{DivGroup} \to \mathtt{DivGroup} = (\text{omitted})$$

where the isomorphisms are as above and we omit all the equality proofs.

There is a subtle difficulty in marking `G2DG` as **implicit**: the implicit-diagram only commutes after proving the equalities, which are only declared later. One option is to delay the commutativity check until the equalities have been checked. In that case, care must be taken to avoid using the implicitness of `G2DG` while proving the equalities. But we obtain a more elegant solution from the observation that it is always sound and harmless to automatically make the inverse of an implicit isomorphism implicit as well. Thus, we can omit the attribute **implicit** on `G2DG` altogether and use an implementation that infers that `G2DG` is the inverse of an implicit isomorphism.

4.2   Fine-Granular and Flexible Theory Hierarchies

A common problem when defining modular theory hierarchies is that the most natural include-hierarchy for the most important theories is not necessarily the same as the most comprehensive hierarchy. For example, Example 3 defines Group with an include from Monoid. Instead, we could have used an intermediate theory and includes Monoid $\hookrightarrow$ CancellationMonoid $\hookrightarrow$ Group.

It is very common to have increasingly strong theories R, S, T, where a design with two includes $R \hookrightarrow S \hookrightarrow T$ is not desirable:

- Often $R \hookrightarrow T$ has been defined first and S only later. This is very common because people usually formalize the most important theories (e.g., Monoid and Group) first. But inserting S is not easy in retrospect—changing the theory hierarchy (which is one of the most fundamental structures of a library) usually presents a very expensive refactoring problem. And even if we systematically use includes for every known intermediate theory like S (as done in [CFO11]), we might later discover a new intermediate theory that should have been added.
- Often the most natural axioms to use in T are the same independent of whether T includes R or S (e.g., users might prefer the usual inverse-element axioms in Group even if they have included CancellationMonoid). In that case, the axioms of S become provable in T if we use $R \hookrightarrow S \hookrightarrow T$. This either causes T to have redundant axioms or requires a more complex include mechanism that allows T to include S in a way that turns some of S-axioms into theorems.

Therefore, it is common to use a commuting triangle consisting of two includes $R \hookrightarrow T$ and $R \hookrightarrow S$ and one morphism $m : S \to T$. But this is awkward because the relation "every T is an S" is now mediated by m rather than being canonical. Implicit morphisms provide a simple solution to this problem: we keep the triangle but make the morphism m implicit. This captures exactly the canonical conversion from S to T.

Already the elementary algebraic hierarchy provides countless examples of such situations. For a small fragment of the hierarchy of magmas, Fig. 1 shows one possible design using numerous implicit morphisms. In particular, it uses some of the examples and features from this paper, e.g., an implicit isomorphism to identify the order-theoretic and the algebraic development of semilattices.

It also uses multiple implicit morphisms to introduce the various intermediate theories between Band $\hookrightarrow$ SemiLattice. All of these are of the form $t = \{\textbf{include } \text{Band}, a : F\}$, e.g., LeftRegularBand uses $F = \forall x, z.z \circ x \circ z \doteq z \circ x$. The implicit morphisms map the constants from Band to themselves and the axiom a to a proof. It is straightforward to prove that this part of the diagram commutes: any two morphisms are identical except for the assignment to the axiom a, and these are equal due to proof irrelevance.[3]

---

[3] Our formalization of bands can be found at https://gl.mathhub.info/MMT/examples/blob/devel/source/bands.mmt.

4.3   Logic Morphisms

So far, we have assumed all theories use the same fixed meta-theory, e.g., Log in the running examples. But in practice, we usually develop theories heterogeneously by using the weakest possible meta-theory for each module. A strength of MMT is that meta-theories are normal theories so that the same structuring formalism can be used for them, e.g., morphisms, includes, pushouts, and implicit morphisms are directly available for meta-theories.

For example, consider the example from Fig. 1. We could use first-order logic FOL as the common meta-theory of all theories. But actually the much weaker logic Horn (which uses restricted logical connectives that only allow creating Horn formulas) is sufficient for most of them.

We do not want to declare a direct include Horn → FOL for the same reasons as discussed in Sect. 4.2. Instead, we want to give a morphism EmbedHorn : Horn → FOL, which maps all Horn formula constructors to their FOL

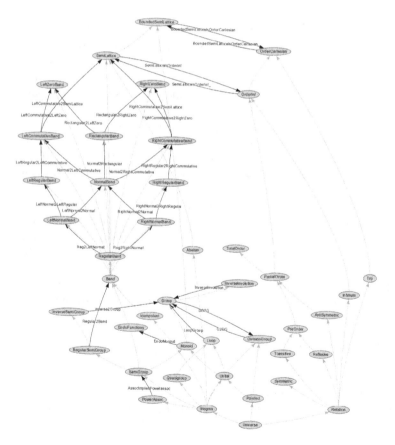

Fig. 1. Magma hierarchy with includes (gray) and implicit morphisms (black)

counterparts. We can now make `EmbedHorn` implicit, thus capturing the fact that Horn logic is a fragment of `FOL`.

Moreover, assume we have built the diagram in Fig. 1 using the meta-theory `Horn` where possible and `FOL` where necessary. An example for the latter is `TotalOrder`, which also uses $\vee$. Without implicit morphisms, we would have to write

$$\texttt{TotalOrder} : \texttt{FOL} = \{\texttt{include EmbedHorn(PartialOrder)}, \ldots\}$$

Here the `Horn`-theory `PartialOrder` must be explicitly translated to `FOL` before including it, which is awkward for users both when writing and reading. But using implicit morphisms and the semantics of Example 9, we can simply write **include** `PartialOrder`—the logic translation remains transparent to the user.

In practice, many logic morphisms are naturally implicit, either because they are includes to begin with or because they represent a canonical logic embedding.

4.4   Transparent Refactoring

A major drawback of using modular theories is that it can preclude transparent refactoring (to insert intermediate theories as mentioned in Sect. 4.2). As an example, we consider a theory $t = \{\textbf{include } r, \textbf{include } s\}$, and assume we want to move a constant declaration D for the name n from s to r. This change should be straightforward as it does not change the semantics of t.

However, this is not a local change. It also requires updating every qualified reference from $s?n$ to $r?n$. Even if the source files always use the unqualified reference n (because the checker is smart enough to dynamically disambiguate them), this still requires a global rebuild to reach a consistent state again. But such references can occur anywhere where t is used, and that may include files that the person who does the refactoring does not know about or does not have access to. One option in this case is to use an extra-logical refactoring tool that propagates such changes. But when managing releases of big libraries, it is often desirable to deprecate the original theories but still ensure backwards compatibility. Then after a transition period the original theories are removed from the library and users are expected to propagate the refactoring.

With implicit morphisms, we can solve this problem by making only the following local changes:

1. We keep r and s as they are.
2. We create a new theory $r' = \{\textbf{include } r, D\}$.
3. We create a new theory s' that is like s except for deleting the declaration D.
4. We change t to $t = \{\textbf{include } r', \textbf{include } s'\}$.
5. We add implicit morphisms $s' \rightarrow s$ (mapping $s'?x$ to $s?x$ for all x) and $s \rightarrow t$ (mapping $s?n$ to $r'?n$ and $s?x$ to $s'?x$ for all $x \neq n$).

The situation before (left) and after (right) refactoring is given below. Note that the right diagram commutes.

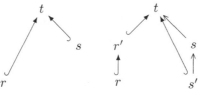

Afterwards, t has the desired new structure. But all old references to r and s stay well-formed so that no global changes are needed. Now r and s can be deprecated and eventually removed in favor of r' and s'.

5 Conclusion and Related Work

Implicit Conversions. The need for implicit conversions has been recognized in many formal systems. In all cases, similar uniqueness constraints are employed as in ours.

Type-level conversions are functions between types such as the conversion from natural numbers to integers. **Theory-level** conversions are morphisms between theories, like in this paper, or similar constructs. The latter can be seen as a special case of the former: if every theory is seen as the type of its models (as in [MRK18]), then reduction along an implicit morphism $S \to T$ induces a conversion from T-models to S-models. Type-level conversions are present in many systems, e.g., the Coq proof assistant [Coq15] or the Scala programming language. The novelty in our approach is to restrict conversions two-fold: firstly to the theory level, secondly to those conversion functions that can be expressed as theory morphisms. This significantly reduces the complexity and permits an elegant logic-independent semantics, while still being practically useful.

Some formal systems support theory-level conversions without explicitly using theory morphisms. This is common in systems that use type classes as an analogue to theories. For example, the `sublocale` declarations of the proof assistant Isabelle [KWP99] or the `deriving` declarations of the programming language Haskell can be seen as implicit morphisms even though no primitive concept of morphism objects is employed. Our implicit morphisms yield a simpler and more expressive theory-level conversion system at the price of having an additional primitive concept.

Structuring Theories. In systems that maintain large diagrams of theories, the problems solved by our approach have been recognized for some time. For example, the IMPS system [FGT93] allowed using theory morphisms to retroactively add defined constants to a previously declared theory. This corresponds to a definitional extension with an implicit retraction morphism as in Sect. 4.1.

In [CFK14], the idea of *realms* was introduced as a way to bundle a set of isomorphic theories and their definitional extensions into a single interface. The paper called for an implementation of realms as a new primitive concept in addition to theories and morphisms. In contrast, the much simpler feature of implicit morphisms achieves very similar goals: realms can be recovered by marking all isomorphisms as *implicit* and all extensions as *definitional*.

It remains future to investigate the relationship between implicit morphisms and other generalizations of the set-theoretic notion of inclusion such as factorization or inclusion systems.

Scalability and Scoping. Future work will focus on utilizing and evaluating implicit morphisms in large libraries, i.e., diagrams with thousands of theories and as many implicit morphisms as possible.

In doing so, we will pay particular attention to some problems that implicit conversions can cause at large scale. Users can be confused when implicit conversions are applied that they are not aware of, and different users may also have different preferences for which conversions should be implicit. Moreover, critically, different developments may be incompatible if they introduce different implicit morphisms between the same theories. For those reasons, Scala, for example, only applies implicit conversions that are imported into the current namespace.

We anticipate that these problems will lead to an evolution of our solution that allows more localized control over which morphisms are implicit. Thus, instead of a single global diagram of implicit morphisms, every context may carry its own local one. But we defer this until the current implementation has been used to conduct very large case studies.

References

[AHMS99] Autexier, S., Hutter, D., Mantel, H., Schairer, A.: Towards an evolutionary formal software-development using CASL. In: Bert, D., Choppy, C., Mosses, P.D. (eds.) WADT 1999. LNCS, vol. 1827, pp. 73–88. Springer, Heidelberg (2000). https://doi.org/10.1007/978-3-540-44616-3_5

[CELM96] Clavel, M., Eker, S., Lincoln, P., Meseguer, J.: Principles of Maude. In: Meseguer, J. (ed.) Proceedings of the First International Workshop on Rewriting Logic, vol. 4, pp. 65–89 (1996)

[CFK14] Carette, J., Farmer, W.M., Kohlhase, M.: Realms: a structure for consolidating knowledge about mathematical theories. In: Watt, S.M., Davenport, J.H., Sexton, A.P., Sojka, P., Urban, J. (eds.) CICM 2014. LNCS (LNAI), vol. 8543, pp. 252–266. Springer, Cham (2014). https://doi.org/10.1007/978-3-319-08434-3_19

[CFO11] Carette, J., Farmer, W.M., O'Connor, R.: MathScheme: project description. In: Davenport, J.H., Farmer, W.M., Urban, J., Rabe, F. (eds.) CICM 2011. LNCS (LNAI), vol. 6824, pp. 287–288. Springer, Heidelberg (2011). https://doi.org/10.1007/978-3-642-22673-1_23

[CHK+11] Codescu, M., Horozal, F., Kohlhase, M., Mossakowski, T., Rabe, F.: Project abstract: logic atlas and integrator (LATIN). In: Davenport, J.H., Farmer, W.M., Urban, J., Rabe, F. (eds.) CICM 2011. LNCS (LNAI), vol. 6824, pp. 289–291. Springer, Heidelberg (2011). https://doi.org/10.1007/978-3-642-22673-1_24

[Coq15] Coq Development Team: The Coq Proof Assistant: Reference Manual. Technical report, INRIA (2015)

[FGT92] Farmer, W., Guttman, J., Thayer, F.: Little theories. In: Kapur, D. (ed.) Conference on Automated Deduction, pp. 467–581 (1992)

[FGT93] Farmer, W., Guttman, J., Thayer, F.: IMPS: an interactive mathematical proof system. J. Autom. Reason. **11**(2), 213–248 (1993)

[GWM+93] Goguen, J., Winkler, T., Meseguer, J., Futatsugi, K., Jouannaud, J.: Introducing OBJ. In: Goguen, J., Coleman, D., Gallimore, R. (eds.) Applications of Algebraic Specification using OBJ. Cambridge University Press, Cambridge (1993)

[KWP99] Kammüller, F., Wenzel, M., Paulson, L.C.: Locales – a sectioning concept for Isabelle. In: Bertot, Y., Dowek, G., Théry, L., Hirschowitz, A., Paulin, C. (eds.) TPHOLs 1999. LNCS, vol. 1690, pp. 149–165. Springer, Heidelberg (1999). https://doi.org/10.1007/3-540-48256-3_11

[MML07] Mossakowski, T., Maeder, C., Lüttich, K.: The heterogeneous tool set, HETS. In: Grumberg, O., Huth, M. (eds.) TACAS 2007. LNCS, vol. 4424, pp. 519–522. Springer, Heidelberg (2007). https://doi.org/10.1007/978-3-540-71209-1_40

[MRK18] Müller, D., Rabe, F., Kohlhase, M.: Theories as types. In: Galmiche, D., Schulz, S., Sebastiani, R. (eds.) IJCAR 2018. LNCS (LNAI), vol. 10900, pp. 575–590. Springer, Cham (2018). https://doi.org/10.1007/978-3-319-94205-6_38

[PS99] Pfenning, F., Schürmann, C.: System description: Twelf — a meta-logical framework for deductive systems. CADE 1999. LNCS (LNAI), vol. 1632, pp. 202–206. Springer, Heidelberg (1999). https://doi.org/10.1007/3-540-48660-7_14

[Rab17] Rabe, F.: How to identify, translate, and combine logics? J. Logic Comput. **27**(6), 1753–1798 (2017)

[RK13] Rabe, F., Kohlhase, M.: A scalable module system. Inf. Comput. **230**(1), 1–54 (2013)

[SW83] Sannella, D., Wirsing, M.: A kernel language for algebraic specification and implementation extended abstract. In: Karpinski, M. (ed.) FCT 1983. LNCS, vol. 158, pp. 413–427. Springer, Heidelberg (1983). https://doi.org/10.1007/3-540-12689-9_122

Author Index

Printed in the United States
By Bookmasters